JOHN BUCHAN

A MEMOIR

BY THE SAME AUTHOR

The Exclusives
Personal Poems
Kumari
Helen All Alone
The Blue Pavilion

JOHN BUCHAN

A MEMOIR

William Buchan

BUCHAN & ENRIGHT, PUBLISHERS
LONDON

First published in 1982 by
Buchan & Enright, Publishers, Limited
21 Oakley Street, London SW3 5NT

ISBN 0 907675 03 4

Text designed by Sarah Jackson

Set in Great Britain by
Rowland Phototypesetting Limited
in 11/12pt Bembo
Printed and bound in Great Britain by
The Pitman Press, Bath

To
Alice and Johnnie
and the memory of Alastair

CONTENTS

ILLUSTRATIONS

Following page 84

John Buchan's grandfather
His Uncle Willie
JB aged four
'We is the Buchans'
John Buchan at Brasenose College
Three Oxford friends
Lord Milner
'I have ridden many miles'
In the veldt
Susan Grosvenor
On honeymoon on the Lido
JB skating with Susan
Walking, one of JB's passions
John Buchan with his first child, Alice
Lt-Col. John Buchan during the Great War
The manor-house of Elsfield
JB's library at Elsfield

Following page 180

'Fishing' with JB
John Buchan and his mother at Elsfield
With his children
Familiars
As Lord High Commissioner to the Church of Scotland, visiting a
    children's hospital
The Lord High Commissioner and his entourage
Leaving the Palace of Holyroodhouse
Preparing for a pageant
Their Excellencies the Governor-General of Canada and Lady
    Tweedsmuir
John Buchan with Mackenzie King and President Roosevelt
Outside Rideau Hall, February 1939
The C-in-C of the Armed Forces of the Dominion of Canada and
    his sons
'Teller of Tales'

tree of John Buchan

Grosvenor, 1ˢᵗ Lord Ebury (1801~93)
Hon. Charlotte Wellesley

James Stuart-Wortley, PC, QC, MP
m. Hon. Jane Lawley

| 1 | 2 | 3 | 5 | | 1 | 2 | 4 | 5 |

Caroline Stuart-Wortley   Hon. Norman de l'Aigle
(1856~1940)   Grosvenor (1845-98)

Margaret (1886~1981)
m. Jeremy Peyton-Jones

Susan Charlotte GROSVENOR (1882-1977)

Alice Caroline Helen
(b.1908) m. Sir Brian
Fairfax~Lucy, Bt.
(1899~1974)

John Norman Stuart,
2ⁿᵈ Ld. Tweedsmuir
(b.1911)

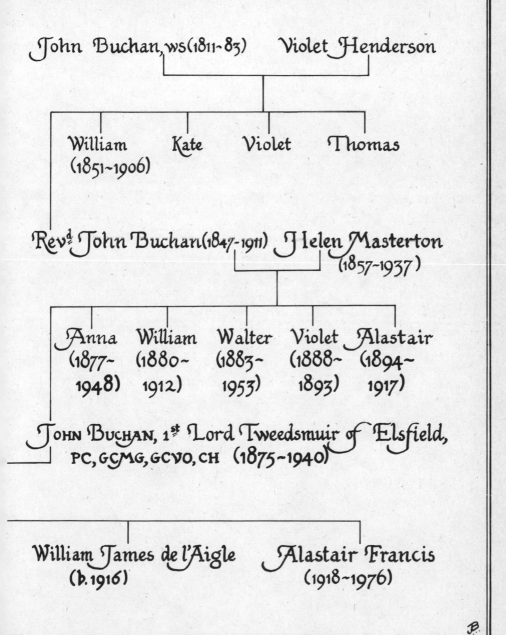

John Buchan, ws (1811~83)   Violet Henderson

William (1851~1906)   Kate   Violet   Thomas

Revd John Buchan (1847~1911)   Helen Masterton (1857~1937)

Anna (1877~1948)   William (1880~1912)   Walter (1883~1953)   Violet (1888~1893)   Alastair (1894~1917)

John Buchan, 1st Lord Tweedsmuir of Elsfield, PC, GCMG, GCVO, CH (1875~1940)

William James de l'Aigle (b. 1916)   Alastair Francis (1918~1976)

INTRODUCTION

This book is intended as a memoir, a personal recollection of a truly extraordinary man. It is in no sense a proper biography, and indeed any attempt at such a thing would be otiose, since an unsurpassable example already exists. In 1965 Janet Adam Smith's *John Buchan: A Biography* was published by Rupert Hart-Davis, a work which drew wide critical acclaim on both sides of the Atlantic, yet which, mystifyingly, has been allowed to go out of print. Before I write another word I must pay the warmest possible tribute to Dr Adam Smith's work, without which I should have floundered miserably in the uncertain seas of memory. It is not merely the most scrupulously professional source book for dates and occasions, but contains a just and accurate commentary upon events and characters, including the character of my father, and upon JB's writing itself. Many of the human sources used for it have gone from us since 1965, and I can only be glad that its author was able, at every stage of her researches, to call on my mother's astonishing memory, now, alas, denied to me.

Much of what I have written goes farther back into history than the time of my birth; I have therefore thought it necessary to sketch my father's Scottish background and to describe those early events of his life which seem to me the most significant.

When JB wrote his autobiography, *Memory Hold-the-Door*, he was sixty-four years old, and living in Canada, and there were some who thought it an excellent book about a number of other people, but not especially revealing about himself. I partly agree with that judgement but, nevertheless, have used the book as a secondary source, principally for the excellence of the writing, and have quoted from it quite extensively; all quotations from John Buchan for which I have not cited the source are from *Memory Hold-the-Door.*★

John Buchan died in 1940, after five and a half years as Governor-General of Canada. When a popular writer dies it very often happens that his reputation dies with him, at least until such time as some agency of revival, a film perhaps, or a new critical assessment, brings it back to life. JB's popularity, as gauged by the continuing demand for his books, never suffered a serious slump, and much credit for this must be given to my mother who, throughout thirty-seven years of widowhood, worked tirelessly to keep her husband's name alive. She published a set of memorials in *John Buchan by his Wife and Friends* and anthologies of his literary work and of his speeches. She herself broadcast, and personally handled negotiations for radio performances and television plays.

As I have said, this book is to be a memoir, a handful of domestic recollections, reinforced by some history and designed to complement the public idea of my father which developed in his lifetime, and which the very legend of his successes has somewhat distorted.

It would undoubtedly be easier for a son to write about a father whom he detested or feared, than about one who, in his day, was nearly universally loved and admired. Samuel Butler, Edmund Gosse, Osbert Sitwell have all made masterpieces about fathers who were dotty or ogreish or both. Like most other people I knew John Buchan only as a lovable, fascinating, mysterious man. To write with unqualified admiration about such a person might turn out to be a fairly nauseous exercise in filial piety. Our relationship, however, was not all roses. I frequently disappointed my father; our tastes and interests diverged. As a child of the post-1914 world I was open to influences, beguiled by ideas, which surely seemed to him unworthy or deleterious, if not positively bad. Nevertheless, and whatever our disagreements, he had always my sometimes exasperated admiration, affection and gratitude. That my gratitude, in youth, was less than commensurate with the benefits I had from my father I have later come to see. Very often, trying to find my way in a society more volatile, more incoherent than even he could

---

★The title has puzzled many people. Certainly an exhortation to the memory that holds the door to reminiscences, its form suggests Bunyan—in *The Pilgrim's Progress*, there is an unsavoury character called Mr Hold-the-World—while the idea perhaps harks back to *Hamlet* (I v):

> Remember thee!
> Ay, thou poor ghost, while memory holds a seat
> In this distracted globe.

appreciate, I would view John Buchan's generation with a mixture of irritation and wistfulness—irritation because the very lofty nature of their ideals seemed, in the light of my own time, unreal to the point of danger; wistfulness because those shattered certainties, those frustrated hopes, seemed, in their essence, so much part of a lost and better world.

When, in 1956, I was commissioned to write the foreword to the Penguin edition of John Buchan's works (ten titles, which sold just under a million copies in eight years) I wrote: 'John Buchan's life followed the interior logic of a good novel.' And so, on the worldly side of things it did. But by those who have only read, say, the Richard Hannay novels, or *Huntingtower* or *John Macnab*, and do not know *Witch Wood* or the short stories in *The Moon Endureth* and *The Watcher by the Threshold*, the less straightforwardly romantic, more mystical side, of John Buchan's nature may not be appreciated.

Left to myself I might have wished to call this book *The Stranger* or even *The Changeling*, something at any rate which would have conveyed a little of my sense that my father, in this world, was, more than most of us, a visitor: a charming, courteous and accomplished visitor, at pains to learn the customs and study the preferences of his hosts, but remaining always a little outside, while still enthusiastically sharing the blinkered preoccupations of his fellow-men. Such titles, with that of *Outsider*, have been used too often to be of much help. That great scholar Helen Waddell, presenting a copy of her book, *The Desert Fathers*, wrote on the flyleaf: 'John Buchan, who has read it all long ago.' A most graceful compliment was no doubt intended, but I like to think that Miss Waddell's penetrating intelligence had seen farther than mere compliments; that she had divined exactly how nearly the travail of St Jerome, of St Antony of Egypt, touched a deep nerve in my father's spirit. John Buchan's love of high and remote places, of solitary expeditions, of the brave struggles of lonely men, his frequent references to men 'making their souls', give a clue to the true direction of his thought. 'Alone to the alone . . .' said the Desert Fathers. Even as a child I could catch, sometimes, this hint of an 'otherness' in my father, and that is why I have written of him as mysterious.

It is a fact that people who have led apparently highly successful lives and who, in their time, have been the objects of much admiration, are likely to suffer unkindness at the hands of later generations. This pendulum certainly swung for my father, and much that has been written about him has been both obtuse and dismissive, where not actually malicious. Nevertheless, and although he was born more than a hundred years ago, he remains very much in mind. His books continue to be read, and even made into films; and it was perhaps from a feeling that he had begun to seem, in certain ways, two-dimensional—that his humanity had been lost sight of—that I thought of attempting to present him as I remembered him, within the framework of his most unusual career.

It has sometimes seemed to me that my father's talents, qualities, tastes, aspirations and temperament, so uniquely assembled in his sole person, were fragmented and, to some extent, divided among his four children.

Dying in 1940, when the Second World War was beginning in earnest, and all his children's plans and intentions were subordinated to it, John Buchan was never to see what they would make of their lives. Some brief notes on each of them might be of interest.

To my sister Alice (Lady Fairfax-Lucy) went a strong historical sense, a gift for witty writing, a passion for literature, and that devotion to the theatre which was common to John Buchan's family. She has written several books, one of them, *Charlecote and the Lucy*, a history of her husband's family. Her historical novel, *The Tapestry Men*, came out at the worst moment of wartime deprivation, and so never reached the sort of public which, in my view, it truly deserved. Her latest book, *A Scrap Screen*, from which I shall quote, is based on my mother's family papers. She is a Fellow of the Royal Society of Literature.

Johnnie (Lord Tweedsmuir, CBE, CD, FRSE) embodies perfectly one side of John Buchan's interests. He has been an explorer, a Colonial servant, a soldier, and a politician. He has his place in the history of the Second World War, where the Canadian regiment which he commanded, the Hastings and Prince Edward, captured the hill of Asoro at a crucial moment in the Allies' Sicilian campaign, (later, in Italy, he was severely wounded). When young, he was, to the life, the boy described in *The Island of Sheep*. He shared with his father a love of wild nature—the wilder the better—and a romantic devotion to those who performed, against all odds, courageous and difficult deeds. While the rest of us were discussing, perhaps with preciosity, our literary ambitions, Johnnie played the role of simple man of action. When he did come to write, he showed himself to be possibly the best stylist of us all. Furthermore, his books—*Hudson's Bay Trader, Always a Countryman* and *One Man's Happiness* are, unlike my own three novels, still in print.

Alastair, my younger brother (Professor Alastair Buchan, CBE) died tragically too early, at the age of fifty-seven. To him went much of his father's concentrated ambition together with his gift for journalism, for exposition and the making plain of complex subjects. He, too, served with the Canadian Army in Europe where, in spite of being one of the few survivors of Red Beach at Dieppe, he remained enthralled by military matters. John Buchan, too, had this fascination, and indeed he and Alastair are the only writers who have ever made me understand a battle, their descriptions are so lucid and their grasp of tactics so firm. After the war Alastair began a career in journalism, first with *The Economist* and later, for many years, with the *Observer*. It was his work for that paper, notably his articles on defence and diplomacy, which won him an Atlantic Award and led him to found the International Institute for Strategic Studies, now so highly regarded throughout the world. Alastair was an excellent writer, especially on the subjects which most interested him. He published a biography of Walter Bagehot, the Victorian economist, and I have always regretted that he never attempted a novel. At the time of his death he was Professor of International Relations at Oxford University.

I do not know what quality or characteristic of John Buchan's I can ascribe to myself, beyond a love of poetry and French literature and a tendency to train fever. Blessed with a rather large family of children, and having found my brand of literature an inadequate provider, I have passed most of my working life in industry and commerce. But I do share with my father a love of secret places, houses, gardens and 'all things counter, original, spare, strange'.

My thanks are due, first of all, to my friend Janet Adam Smith who discussed the book with me and lent me the notes for her own work, and certain letters which have been invaluable. I would thank my sister and brother, and all the members of my own family for their help, their continued interest and encouragement. I would thank Paul Willert for following Walter de la Mare's suggestion and finding me a 'piece of time' in which to do a large part of the writing. I am grateful to Michael Felgate Catt, formerly of Cassell, for urging me to write; to Lord and Lady Moyne for the photograph of Tommy Nelson; and to Michael Horniman of A. P. Watt Ltd for permission to quote from John Buchan's published works. And finally, profounder thanks than I know how to express must go to Sauré, my wife, who not only typed hundreds of thousands of words but, by her critical attention saved me from going, quite frequently, off my chosen path.

Broughton, Peeblesshire
Kennington, London, SE11
Hornton, Oxfordshire
1980–82

The sunflower and initials on the dedication page and throughout is from John Buchan's book-plate—that on the dedication page is reproduced actual size.

I

'A HOST OF MEMORIES'

The eldest son of a Scottish minister of the Free Church, who was born at Perth on 26 August 1875, died at the Montreal Neurological Institute on 11 February 1940, in his sixty-fifth year. By then his varied and unusual career had brought him, by way of literature and politics, to a high office of state. He died the first Lord Tweedsmuir of Elsfield, PC, GCMG, GCVO, CH, Governor-General and Commander-in-Chief of the Dominion of Canada. During his term of office a tribe of Canadian Indians had made him an honorary chief with the title of 'Teller of Tales', and it was in that role and under his familiar name of John Buchan, that he was to be best remembered by countless people throughout the world.

John Buchan had four children of which I was the third. By the time of his death my family had suffered some disruption, first by the removal to Canada, in 1935, of my parents and my younger brother; later, by the outbreak of war. Communication had become difficult. Letters from Canada were sent by sea to the Dominions Office for onward transmission: cables were often delayed. So it happened that the first news I had of my father's fatal illness came to me from newspaper posters in the London streets, as also did the announcement of his death. I mention this to show to what an extent my father had become, so to speak, public property, a figure of international significance. Some time after JB's death the editor of *The Times* told my mother that his paper had never received, in the memory of its oldest employee, so many tributes to a single commoner. Looking at the stack of press-cuttings books compiled at that time, it seems to me that a really vast number of people—not simply old friends, or close acquaintances, or the kind of public figures normally asked for a few words on the death of someone famous, but even total strangers—were moved by the need to have their say.

7

Of my father's importance in the world I was early to become aware. When I was about three years old somebody gave me a small attaché case and what was then called a 'stylographic pen'. The latter, an ancestor of the ball-point, had a sharp metal needle at its tip. Filled with ink it would write scratchily for a long time, if it would agree to write at all. Thus equipped, I invented a game which I would play by myself for hours, something I was obliged to do since Alastair, my younger brother, not yet a year old, was useless as a playmate, while Alice, aged eleven, and Johnnie, nearly eight, were too grown-up to play with me. The attaché case contained an assortment of papers, donated by grown-ups anxious to keep me quiet. My game was to rummage about in my case, pull out a sheaf of papers, shuffle them, and annotate them with squiggles from the stylographic pen. My expression, I think, was serious, preoccupied, statesmanlike. I did a good deal of frowning and muttering. When asked what I was doing I would reply: 'I am being important.'

I must have heard John Buchan called this, not once but many times. I must have sensed it in people's approach to him, a certain pleased deference in both servants and friends. At some time I must have complained of his absence—a visit to the nursery missed, or something of that sort—and have been told: 'Your father's much too busy. He is a very important man.' And so, by the time of my birth, he was.

My sister, my two brothers and I were all born in the West End of London—Alice in Hyde Park Square, Johnnie in Bryanston Street, Alastair in Portland Place and I, on 10 January 1916, at my grandmother's house in Upper Grosvenor Street. Early in 1920, just before my fourth birthday, we moved from Portland Place to Elsfield in Oxfordshire. As Janet Adam Smith, a true Scot herself, wrote in *John Buchan: A Biography*:

Like many Scots, Buchan had always appreciated the English-ness of England, greatly preferring the softer, greener South to the Lakes or the Pennines, which, till he knows better, often strike the Scot as a second-rate version of the hills and moors of his own country. Part of John Buchan's devotion to *The Compleat Angler* and *The Pilgrim's Progress* was that in the one he found 'a transcript of old English country life', and in the other 'an idyll of an older English world'.

8

My father loved Scotland, knew its land, its rhymes and legends and history as well as anyone living: but he loved South Africa too, and England, and Wales and, in the end, Canada. His roots may have been elastic, but they were as strong as nylon gut. As he makes clear in *Memory Hold-the-Door*, however, they were most strongly embedded in Scotland and in Oxfordshire.

> I have a host of memories of places which have strongly captured my fancy, and sometimes my affection—in Europe, in the Virginian and New England hills, above all, in South Africa and Canada. But I have never 'taken sasine' of them as I did of the Tweedside glens and in a lesser degree of the Oxfordshire valleys. For with the first I had the intimacy of childhood and with the second of youth.

On a snatched, short holiday with my mother in 1917, JB had explored and been captivated by the Cotswold country of the Oxfordshire–Gloucestershire border. Doing this, he renewed an acquaintance with that countryside made during day-long walking, riding and canoeing trips in his Oxford days; in a way he was finding his way back to a golden age of youth unsullied by war. By 1919, the year he published *Mr Standfast*, he had seen much of the world and of men; he was less than well and more than overworked; he was badly shaken by the war, saddened by the loss of many friends, and deeply apprehensive about the precarious peace which had just begun. He now longed for a place a little out of the London world which had pressed him so hard: somewhere not too far away, so that he could continue his work for Nelson's the publishers, which had been interrupted by the war, and keep an eye on the political scene; yet escape when he wished to different ploys and places, and save himself from ruthless and persistent raids on his time and strength.

> The war left me with an intense craving for a country life. It was partly that I wanted quiet after turmoil, the instinct that in the Middle Ages took men into monasteries. But it was also a new-found delight in the rhythm of nature, and in small homely things after so many alien immensities. In all times of public strife there has been this longing for rural peace: Chaucer had it, and Dunbar, and Izaak Walton. . . . So I sold my house and purchased the little manor house of Elsfield, four miles from the city of Oxford.

In 1920 Oxfordshire was still largely untouched by the twentieth century. The war over, most people had returned to their homes anxious to preserve or rebuild what they remembered of a peaceful world. Most of the larger houses in the county were still in the hands of families which had held them for generations. Those people knew their world and its duties. Appreciating them with intense sympathy, willingly according them their place in the history of the land, JB had not the slightest wish to 'play in their league'. Elsfield suited him almost ideally well precisely because it did not oblige him to assume responsibilities and attitudes which were as foreign to his nature as a Scotsman as they were to his spirit as a man.

There is a clue, I think, to my father's true feelings in the early pages of his last Richard Hannay book, *The Island of Sheep*. Here he has made Hannay (also, in a sense, a foreigner, being a Rhodesian of Scottish origin) into a full-blown Gloucestershire country gentleman, a practical landowner and farmer, a Justice of the Peace and so on. In order to get Hannay out of his rut, which Hannay himself declares is too comfortable—'I feel I'm getting old and soft and slack. I don't deserve this place and I'm not earning it'—he provides him with a final adventure which will handsomely disprove any such self-denigration.

Hannay speaks of a presentiment 'that an event was about to happen which would jog me out of my rut into something much less comfortable'. This idea that life is, and is intended to be, a series of challenges is central to John Buchan's view. Although, in the country, he looked and played the part of a countryman well settled as such, he must always have been awaiting a summons to action, or the chance to accept, or even to create, some special challenge. He who had every right to take it easy, quieten down, fight and perhaps overcome almost continual illness in peace, was temperamentally quite incapable of doing anything of the sort. In London he was, in dress, habits and knowledge of the town, as experienced a Londoner as any. He needed London, the chances it gave to meet people who might, elsewhere, never have come his way, to participate in affairs which appealed to his imagination. He needed Elsfield to keep touch with the land and its history, to read and write and reflect, to supervise his property, to ride and walk over many miles. I think that his friendship with T. E. Lawrence, his delight in Lawrence's rare visits, the opportunities he had to offer him help, illustrate better than anything else my father's undimmed enthusiasm for adventure, and perhaps the hope, never quite buried in an acceptance of domesticity, that life would one day provide him with a challenge which would indeed 'jog him out of his rut'.

When I first remember our Oxfordshire village, 'foreigners' were people from the other side of the county: few other foreigners came our way. Nevertheless I think that the people of Elsfield village took to the new owner of their manor house from the very start. Nothing could have been more foreign to them than a Scotsman: JB benefited, I think, from their lack of a preconceived idea. Being shrewd people in the main, and appreciative of a good thing, whether pig or person, when they saw it, I believe that they took to my father at once. They had had the habit of deference bred into them over centuries, but I doubt if ever before had they known their reserved and, obviously, at the beginning, rather cagey courtesies met with so vivid a response. There are several words or phrases fashionable at present which could be used to describe my father— 'outgoing', 'life-enhancing', possessed of a memorable 'charis-ma'—but it all boiled down in the end to a positive and abiding interest in people, combined with a delicate sense of what was due to their humanity. Charisma as a word he might have scouted—I certainly never heard him use it. He might have said (although equally certainly he never would have) that such a quality was simply part of being Christian.

If I linger upon the story of Elsfield, it is because it represented in so many ways the fulfilment of a dream, became as much a creation of JB's imagination and an illustration of his power to discover romance in ordinary life, as any of his books. Every writer is a magician: not all writers purvey a beneficent magic. JB was a beneficent magician, not only in what he wrote, but in his ability to create a safe and often magical world for his family and friends. I think that it was his reverence for ancient Rome and Roman thought that kept his ambitions within bounds, trimming their wilder edges, and enabled him first to conceive and then to execute plans which were Roman in their reasonableness, their propriety to time and place, their discipline by what was practicable.

With the opening of that year, 1920, a dream began to take shape, and to become absorbing. Plumbing and decoration once accomplished, attention could be turned to the surroundings of the house. The gardens must have suffered much the same kind of wartime neglect as they did in the last war; they had to be put back into shape, and then re-planned.

A not uncommon feature of the small manor houses of Oxford-shire and Gloucestershire is to front directly on the village street which is—or at any rate was—only a section of some more or less important highway. The metalled road which ran through Elsfield led directly from the Oxford–London road where it branched at the foot of Headington Hill. From there it wandered through the Marstons, New and Old, and took its way, dusty in summer, lightly muddy in winter, up a short, sharp hill, overhung by elm trees and topped by the first building in the long, strung-out village, which had more unbuilt spaces, almost, than houses.

I do not know quite how the house struck my parents when they first saw it. All my mother could ever tell me about her first visit was that the library seemed to be full of stuffed birds and piles of newspapers. Quite early on the birds in their glass cases must somehow have been got rid of, or found a new home. It was an abiding regret to me that this should have been so, since I could not for many years imagine anything more agreeable than a house full of stuffed birds. Newspapers, on the other hand, I could at any time easily do without.

Whatever my parents may have thought of the interior—and they could not have failed to be enchanted by the hall, the delicate staircase, the panelled drawing-room with its windows looking out to the west, and the morning-room, also panelled, with its deep window-seats—they fell immediately and finally in love with the view: a view which was to become famous, much talked- and written-about, a sure conversation-starter with shy guests.

It must have needed some imagination to be certain of the view's possibilities. Below the house on that western side lay a wide grassy terrace, at that time cut up into parterres, probably the worse for war. Beyond that a long lawn sloped down to an iron fence, a shallow ha-ha, and a hayfield. To the left of the lawn stood a handsome ilex tree, huge and rounded and glossy green; and right in the middle of the prospect towered an enormous Wellingtonia. This gloomiest of conifers—a relation, I believe of the Californian redwood but happily, in our climate, never so large—was, and often still is, a feature of gardens laid out in the middle of last century. Imagination was needed—enough at least mentally to abolish the Wellingtonia—and imagination both my parents had in plenty. As part of the process of re-planning the garden the Wellingtonia was felled and lay like a stricken ogre on the grass, its severed trunk and the chips around it red as blood. At the moment of its fall the view was unfolded as it is today.

The great ilex was spared. It did not interfere with the view and its massive dark-jade bulk would make, with a yew hedge on the other side of the lawn, an admirable sombre frame for the ever-varying picture of fields and woods and changeable Midland sky. Sad to say, it was blown over, clean uprooted by an enormous gale in 1929; the house itself was sold in 1954.

For most people there are houses, seen once perhaps or merely dreamed, which are the image of their ideal. In October 1918, John Buchan had gone on a second trip to the Cotswolds, this time with Hugh Macmillan.★ Writing to my mother on 14 October, JB mentions several houses, more or less desirable, that he has seen and then comes to Weald Manor, near Bampton:

> But Oh my darling! Weald!!! . . . It is a perfect jewel, most exquisitely *soignée* in every detail. . . . Such gardens as you must see to believe, and cottages of honey-coloured Cotswold stone. This is one of my Dreams and Hugh and I went daft about it. It belongs to delightful people who are hard-hit by the war. It has a little farm and a tiny lake. It is furnished with exquisite taste. I feel inclined to go a bust on it, dear as it is, for it is a unique jewel. . . .

This is the house so lovingly described in JB's short story 'Full-circle'. I do not know for exactly what reason my parents did not buy Weald Manor but most probably because it was too expensive.

With such a house in mind, however, my father and mother must have had to make a radical revision of their ideas on seeing Elsfield for the first time. They must have had to weigh the advantages—proximity to London, lack of encumbrances, the enchanting garden, the magnificent view—against any ideas of an architectural gem that they might have been cherishing.

There had been a house on this spot for at least three hundred years, possibly for longer still, although the late Sir George Clark, in his monograph *The Manor of Elsfield*, thought it probable that the original manor house stood on the other side of the road, near the church, where a fine sixteenth-century dovecote still stands.

In 1726 the Reverend Thomas Wise, scholar and antiquarian,

★An Edinburgh KC, later Lord Advocate in the first Labour Government in 1924.

13

who had been tutor to Lord Guilford, was given the living of Elsfield and lived at the manor house for a number of years. I cannot say whether it was he who remodelled the much older house, giving it the elegant eighteenth-century features it still possesses, and one at least which has gone: the storey above the present drawing-room, crowned with an imposing stone pediment, which shows in an engraving of his time. Our banker predecessor, Herbert Parsons, evidently did a good deal of remodelling himself, in the eighteen-eighties. He must have pulled down the long low wing, also probably seventeenth-century, which adjoined the Jacobean part, and in its place constructed a tall edifice with twin gables, more or less in the Cotswold style, rising to three floors above, of all things, a deep basement. It was the greatest good fortune, given the terms of his time, that he built his 'improvements' in grey stone with grey-brown Cotswold tiles. Even so, it cannot be denied that the Victorian side of the house is decidedly ugly.

The interior of the house, however, was completely belied by its rather forbidding appearance from the village street. Someone in the last century had clapped a wooden porch, mildly gothic in character, on to the front door. But once through that heavy oak, the house began to exert its charm on all who entered it. A long, panelled hall had a floor of stone flags and, at its far end, a broad staircase with prettily turned balusters, lit by a tall window facing west. The morning-room on the left and the drawing-room straight ahead, both panelled in white, with the cellars beneath, completed—with my parents' bedroom and dressing-room on the first floor and the three attic bedrooms above—what remained of the old house. On the left as you entered the hall a glazed door led into the garden; on the right there was an arch leading to the Victorian addition.

If the Georgians thought much of elegance, and even of luxury, and the Victorians of propriety and a certain solid comfort, neither gave much attention to convenience: certainly not to the convenience of servants and children. Considering how much lip-service was paid in Victorian times to progress, efficiency, neatness, economy and so on, one is continually struck by an apparently wilful disregard of the principles of these things, at least as we now understand them. Much had to do, of course, with the apparently inexhaustible supply of domestics: their almost total disappearance has made us all think hard about trouble-saving.

The basement contained the kitchen, large, warm and welcoming, and the cavernous scullery where cold water had still to be brought up from a well by a creaking iron pump, and the ever-troublesome, coke-consuming hot-water boiler was installed. Nearby were the servants' hall, a store-room and a larder with long slate shelves, cool in the hottest weather. Steep stairs ran up directly to the dining-room and pantry, and here is one of the oddities of other people's architectural thinking which one meets so often when looking over strange houses. As you turned right from the front door, leaving the older house, you came to a lobby hung with various weapons: a musket, a mother-of-pearl-decorated jezail, and a sword or two. Immediately to the left was the library door and then—and here is my point—a long passage which went, past the door of the cloakroom–lavatory, straight on to the butler's pantry, the back stairs and the dining-room door. This meant that, after being welcomed in the library, guests for meals had to troop down this narrow gangway to get to their food, in grave danger of colliding with someone rushing up from the kitchen with a dish or a tray. That this arrangement irked my mother I always knew, although it suited me rather well. I could sneak down the back stairs during dinner on a summer evening and beg a water-ice (black-currant, home-made) from among the uneaten extras being brought away from the dining-room.

I do not suppose that my father gave that passage arrangement much thought. He never in all his life wasted time or regret on states of affairs that he could not alter. Also, the passage gave him scope for one of his favourite occupations, hanging pictures. The passage became the repository of a number of smallish pictures, either insignificant in themselves, or unplaceable elsewhere, but each with a particular association. Association, not only in pictures but in objects as well, meant a great deal to my father. So the guest, as he went towards the dining-room, could glance, if he wished, at two coloured plates of the second Lord Astor, one with his horse Buchan (named after my father), and another with Buchan's offspring Saucy Sue, winner of the Oaks. There was a savage, beefy colour print (I think by Gillray) of a crowd of red-faced academics, in cap and gown, grinning and carousing, entitled *The Bacon-faced Fellows of Brasenose Broke Loose*. There was a photograph of the House of Auchmacoy, a coloured drawing by Basil Blackwood, and much besides.

The pictures at Elsfield were a highly eclectic mixture, their provenance generally governed by accident—wedding presents, bequests, for instance—or, as I have said, association. One in particular belonged to the house, and had been there since the

eighteenth-century panelling was put in. It was set into the panelling, above the fireplace in the hall, and never failed to give me
pleasure in spite, or perhaps because, of the fact that time and smoke
had darkened it. This picture represented either a hunting scene, or
a picnic. It showed a cavalcade proceeding through rough mountain
country, Italian-looking, which suggested hunting; while the
fact of a pointed scarlet parasol, the one sharp note of colour
in the whole composition, implied an especially upper-class
kind of picnic.

The drawing-room, that light and lovely place, with three
windows facing the westward view, and one looking south across a
rose garden, did not need many pictures, having crystal wall-lights
and baroque cabinets for decoration. A big Hondekoeter of flowers
and fruit and cocks and hens hung over the fireplace, a work in that
artist's familiar genre once described by someone as 'Poultry at
Play'. The staircase had two of those useful but rarely identifiable
Italian landscapes of the seventeen-hundreds, full of improbable
palaces, trees, water and neatly disposed small groups of people.
There was a large engraving of my great-grandmother, Jane Stuart-
Wortley, with her parents, of the kind done to be given away in the
days before photography became general. There was a framed
Confederate flag which had much important association for my
father, since it had been given to him at the time of his visit to
America in 1924 by an admirer who knew him for a passionate
student of American history.

Many small pictures, college groups and the like, decorated my
father's dressing-room, and scattered through other bedrooms and
spare rooms were such things as a water-colour of fairies in a Celtic
twilight by the Irish poet George Russell ('A.E.'), a Romney
pen-and-wash, *The Infant Shakespeare Nursed by Comedy and
Tragedy*, and a coloured print of the ice-bridge between Quebec and
Point Levis, a view which JB would one day see during his term as
Governor-General of Canada.

If my father was given, or had been interested enough to acquire,
a picture of any kind, then a place had to be found for it. Thus, when
I came to have a room of my own at the top of the house, I was given
a large photograph, in an oak frame, of Cecil Rhodes. My father
had greatly admired Rhodes, without particularly liking him, and
his picture had to have a home. As he looked a little like Jack Allam,
our gamekeeper, I thought for a long time that they must be related;
but he lacked Jack's kindly air, and I never really took to him.

However, a day came when Rhodes was displaced. My father,

16

who preferred stalking to any other kind of shooting, chiefly, I think, because it involved a particularly taxing kind of physical exercise, had killed a couple of stags one summer, and—thinking I would be pleased—had given me a head to hang in Rhodes's place. The head had not sufficient 'points' to justify full-scale taxidermy, with glassy eyes and a mournful muzzle. As mounted it was simply the beast's frontal bone with the horns springing from it, on a wooden shield with an ivory label saying 'Glen Etive' and the date.

I was pleased to begin with, pleased and flattered. But it was summertime and, as the slow dusk fell, the white bone began to glimmer, and the antlers to loom, and the upshot was that the thing gave me nightmares. I even had the sense (rare in children) to come straight out with what was upsetting me. The antlers were removed. Rhodes was not replaced. Shortly afterwards my mother gave me a coloured print of Holbein's *Ambassadors*, and even though this too contained a skull, curiously elongated in a rare trick of perspective, it held no terrors for me.

It was for the morning-room that my father reserved his best effort in the picture line. This tall room, although designed to match, and communicate with, the drawing-room, had windows looking east and south, the former into the high, grey wall on the road side, and so was a stiller, more sober, more antique-feeling place than its neighbour. Where the drawing-room had been given a new floor of golden hardwood, surrounded by parquet, the morning-room still had its broad, beautiful elm boards.

This room seemed, in my father's view, to demand some dark old pictures and so, to reinforce a pleasant Claudesque landscape of trees and people and ruins which hung over a carved wood and marble chimney-piece, he set about collecting portraits.

In those days it was neither difficult nor expensive to pick up late seventeeth-century portraits of unknown people by forgotten hands, and of these my father acquired four: three red-faced gentlemen in heavy wigs, and a clergyman with a long nose. These pictures, which looked well enough when hung, and certainly achieved the effect required of them (my father used to speak of such things as 'furniture pictures'), were the subject of one of his thought-out and entirely typical jokes. He announced that he knew perfectly well who the people were: they were members of the Stumpson family. He then proceeded to invent a pedigree and a family history for them. The other day I came across a coat-of-arms which he had drawn up for the Stumpsons: 'A stump proper argent on field azure with helm and mantling'. He was not much good at

17

drawing, but there it is, the stump, roots and all, last relic of a faded but endearing joke.

Three other pictures directly attributable to JB's particular interests are worth mentioning, if only because they illustrate his inability, which I shall return to later, to sustain a prejudice. My father did not care for the Irish—few Scotsmen do—and was particularly angry with them for (as he saw it) stabbing Britain in the back in 1916. Nevertheless he had employed an impecunious Irishman to paint him three pictures, one a copy of a Raeburn, another of a Zucchero, and a portrait of my sister Alice in the dress and pose of Velasquez' little Infanta. These were done, I should think, in about 1912. The Irishman then became a rebel, and I wish very much that I knew what happened to him. JB never ceased to like the man whose work he had commissioned. The artist was known to the family simply as 'Papa's Sinn Feiner'.

Next door to my parents' bedroom was my father's dressing-room. This was directly over the front porch, and its single window looked out into the ancient elm tree which served as the village notice-board. The walls, as much as you could see of them, were papered in dark red, which gave the room its cosy, masculine feeling. Where they were not obscured by a huge mahogany tallboy or other furniture they made space for a number of small pictures all of which, in different ways, interested me greatly. I liked the groups of serious young athletes, staring so straight into the camera's eye. I liked the cartoons illustrating jokes and situations long passed away, but amusing to guess at. What a reproduction of Bocklin's *Island of the Dead* was doing there I never had the sense to ask. Instead, I allowed it to haunt and fascinate me and give me scope for imagining what could be meant by those tall funereal cypresses, those sheeted figures in the boat, that incomprehensible German legend beneath.

The dressing-room had a door into my parents' room and a bed in one corner. For various reasons, when I was very young, I was often put to sleep in the dressing-room. As far as I was concerned this arrangement was pure pleasure. I do not suppose that I was always awake when JB came to bed, but as he usually retired early, at about half-past ten, and however stealthily he moved about the room, I often woke to watch, while pretending to sleep, the regular, unvarying routine of his preparations for the night. His dressing-table had a glass top, and I can still hear the sound of keys and money being dropped on to it. I can still see the pattern of my father's movements, neat and economical, as he stepped between chair and wardrobe and wash basin. Like all young children I was awed and intrigued by a grown-up in a state of nudity: sometimes my father would stand still for a while, quite naked, lost in thought under the hanging light, before briskly getting into his blue-and-white striped pyjamas.

At some point in his long and painful experience of the medical profession, some distinguished doctor must have decreed the removal of all JB's teeth, as a means of improving his duodenal condition. This was once a fashionable idea but, if not futile in all cases, was certainly so in his. I do not think that his teeth were bad: I never heard them referred to until it was announced that he was going to lose them all. For months he had a most uncomfortable time with his false set, which temporarily altered his diction, giving him an odd lisp, and made eating even more difficult and fraught with prohibitions than ever before. It also altered the routine of going to bed and getting up, since the wretched new teeth had to be taken out at night and put in again in the morning with a huge, gaping grimace which still had something of rueful humour about it.

The dressing-room, as I have said, had great interest for me, not only when it was being used for its proper purpose of containing JB dressing and undressing, but even when I could explore it by myself. For example there were a number of those solid accoutrements without which a gentleman's life, in those days, would have been incomplete. There were ivory-backed hair-brushes and an ebony hand-glass, all monogrammed; ivory-handled steel hooks for pulling on riding boots, and a heavy wooden bootjack for pulling them off. There were the boots themselves, with their wooden trees, and other boots for shooting or walking, all appropriately treed and polished. There was a leather collar-box and a heavy, much battered leather hat-box containing a top hat.

A jewel-case in faded green morocco held JB's few items of jewellery: some cuff-links, a solitaire stud in turquoise and diamonds which I never saw him wear, four or five stick-pins, including the pearl which he generally favoured. There was also (most fascinating to me) a slim tube of morphia tablets, given to him for emergencies in the war and never either used or thrown away. Then there were his cut-throat razors in a leather case, and their long leather strop which hung from a hook on the wall. Next to the sound of keys dropping on to glass I remember most clearly the sounds of the razor being stropped, the slop and slap of draughts, and to give an exciting sense of surprise as one came round it to survey the room. Directly ahead was a long oak table, loaded with books and magazines, and pots and baskets of flowers brought in from the greenhouse. Wide windows, glazed with plate-glass—still a relatively new material when this part of the house was built—let in the western light and let out one's vision to the view. Being well above ground level, these windows looked down on to the terrace, so that the eye could enjoy a foreground as well.

Between the windows stood the solid partners' desk which my parents shared. Between it and the fireplace were a comfortable big sofa and armchairs. Over the fireplace hung the copy of Zucchero's *Sir Walter Raleigh*, which my father's Sinn Feiner had done for him. That piece of wall was papered a darkish blue. The rest of the room, from floor to ceiling, was walled and coloured by books.

Describing Haraldsen's library in *The Island of Sheep*, JB wrote: 'That library was the pleasantest room in the house, for it had the air of a place cherished and lived in . . . it was lined everywhere with books, books which had the look of being used, and which consequently made that soft tapestry which no collection of august bindings can provide.'

The Victorians could not have thought very highly of the famous view which, possibly, they considered bleak. At all events the Wellingtonia's black exclamation-mark must have held attention to the foreground and, in addition, one of the library windows had once been made of stained glass. I think that the room had been used more as a business room and home for stuffed birds than a library as we were to know the term. It was a big room with a high, deeply coffered ceiling, well proportioned, but if the plate-glass windows let in light they also induced cold, and it was difficult to heat satisfactorily.

John Buchan needed a library, wanted a library, and set about creating one of the most delightful that I have ever known. The stained-glass window was removed. Almost every inch of wall-space became shelves and cupboards. There was even a slim rebate of shelving between the windows, adjoining the big desk. There was a ladder with a padded leather top for getting at the highest books. My father sat on the far side of the desk, obliquely facing the door with, behind him, his bound manuscripts. Since he never varied his practice of writing on unlined foolscap these books were taller than most, and were uniformly bound in grey-green buckram, lettered on their spines in gold.

21

climbing, could locate the special reading needed for say *Augustus*, or even *Witch Wood*. (Margaret Murray's *Witch Cult in Western Europe* belonged, I remember, to the time of the latter.)

JB used to be severe about the mistreatment or misplacement of books, remarking that these were the tools of a writer's trade and must, like all good tools, be respected. Bearing that in mind, however, we were free to take down and read any book we liked, or burrow into the marvellous 1911 edition of the *Encyclopaedia Britannica*, or lie on the floor with the *Times* Atlas, planning journeys perhaps less far-flung than those which, one day, we were actually to take.

Then there were old books, a black-letter Plato among them, more curious than readable, but giving off an appetising dry scent of calf and vellum and old paper. Amongst these was a collection of seventeeth-century works (JB's favourite period), ranging in size from the majestic *Herball* of Gerard to the tiny *Religio Medici* of Sir Thomas Browne, which my father had bought in Bridgnorth for half a crown, and the *Eikon Basilike* published in the year of Charles I's death—*The Portraicture of His Sacred Majestie in his Solitudes and Sufferings*.

Over beside a window, beyond the flower-laden table, shelves were reserved for poetry—sets of Yeats and Kipling and all the volumes of *Georgian Poetry* for the ten years of its life: presentation copies from Walter de la Mare, Henry Newbolt, Gordon Bottomley, Robert Graves; and dozens of obscure slim volumes inscribed by their authors with degrees of fulsomeness more or less varying inversely with the degrees of their merit. Why my father kept these I do not know, except that he had a writer's sympathy with other writers' aspirations, however feeble their achievement, and since they had thought to send him their books he would thoughtfully give them a place on his shelves. There was plenty of room after all, and perhaps, just possibly, some of them, at a later look, and with time and the changes of taste, might prove to have been worth keeping. Meanwhile, of those in places of honour Yeats and de la Mare and Kipling have kept their public, but who now reads Bottomley or Newbolt? And who, much younger than myself, would admit to finding good in *Georgian Poetry*?

One column of shelves—the one containing the more precious items—had a couple of ranks of family books, bound in morocco, blue, black and red. Here were all JB's works he thought deserving of a place, novels and histories in order, flanked by pamphlets and lectures, short scripts, poems and satirical pieces which had seemed worth keeping, if not publishing, either bound or preserved in buckram cases. His sister's books were there, and his brother's and, as time went on, a growing line of works by my mother.

Amongst the taller books on a lower shelf next to Gerard's *Herball*, was the broad-backed, plum-coloured, sumptuously bound copy of *The Seven Pillars of Wisdom*, one of a very few (I think only a hundred) specially commissioned by T. E. Lawrence, and given by him to people for whom he felt a particular gratitude or respect. This book was an expensive as well as a beautiful production, not simply for the splendour of its printing, paper and binding, but for the interleaving illustrations, the Augustus John and Eric Kennington portraits, all commissioned by Lawrence expressly for it. I have a letter signed 'T. E. Shaw' which partly explains how JB came to be the recipient of this gorgeous work. From that it appears that Stanley Baldwin got a less splendid example, although Lawrence-Shaw speaks of him, in the same breath as of JB, as a notable benefactor. The benefaction referred to concerned the necessary arrangements for Lawrence to lose his too-famous identity and sink himself in the ranks of the Royal Air Force.

I.XII.26

Dear Buchan

I go to Uxbridge tomorrow preparatory to embarkation for India. Your copy of my book is not yet ready: it is being rather specially bound.

This copy is one of those which I am giving to the fellows who did the Arab Revolt with me. They are incomplete, in the sense that many plates are missing. I wanted you to ask Mr Baldwin if he would care to accept it. You and he did me the best turn I've ever had done to me, and I think gratefully of you as often as I have leisure to think about my contentment. It is no great return (incomplete copies have no future in the second-hand market) but I'm hardly in the position to make any great return, and if he likes books, as I'm told, he may prefer a broken copy to none at all. The thing is, anyhow, a rarity. If he would rather not be bothered then please return it to Hogarth (20 St Giles, Oxford).

I hope you will like your own copy when it does at last come. The delays of it, due to the little spare time the service gives me, have been unfortunate.

Yours sincerely,
T. E. Shaw

Such books are not for reading. This one was almost too heavy to hold. Children's hands had to be washed, and grown-up supervision invoked, before it could even be opened. It was some years, in fact, before I came to read *The Seven Pillars* in a more workaday version: and I have often wondered what made Lawrence go to the great trouble and expense needed to produce so extraordinary an edition. He spent on it, I believe, a lot of money which had been collected for, or granted to him for his services to his country. The only companion copy of the whereabouts of which I am certain was presented by Lawrence to King George V.

It is not often, nowadays, that I find myself in a private library properly so called. A few shelves and cases of books, a mass of paperbacks crammed into corners—these are about all for which most people can find space. Like many platitudes the one about books furnishing a room is perfectly true. There is something about light falling—daylight or firelight or lamplight—on well-kept bindings, a variety of quiet colours; something about the faint smell of polished leather, and paper and print, that gives a sense of security, a feeling of friendliness and fullness, with no more than a gentle hint that books are not there simply as furniture, but to encourage adventures of mind and heart.

John Buchan's library was entirely the place he had planned, the collection he needed, the inspiration he sought. It was there he wrote books, transacted business, read aloud to his children, entertained his friends, smoked and pondered and made projects. He sat on his side of the desk, writing with a penholder made of a porcupine quill and a Relief nib, regularly dipping into one of the two pots of an eighteenth-century silver inkstand. Sitting on the other side of the desk my mother would write letters, order things from catalogues, organise the affairs of the Women's Institute. The shared inkstand, the shared desk, the shared stock of writing paper in a converted Georgian knife-box, might be taken as symbols of a thoroughly harmonious partnership.

2

COUNTRYMAN

If JB's style of living at Elsfield should seem to anyone, in these restricted days, comfortable almost to the point of luxury, it must be remembered that he needed certain easements to enable him to move about the world like quicksilver and achieve an immense amount of varied and valuable work. He positively needed a stable and well-run household, and people to work for him, and drive him to and from the train. All that he had he had earned and, in addition, he would certainly have agreed with Locke that 'The handsome conveniences of life are better than nasty penury'.

In 1922, when I was six years old, the handsome conveniences of my life began to be curtailed, my totally carefree childhood existence curbed, when I started lessons, for a couple of hours a day, with my sister's governess. But the place remained its complete and sufficient self. Nothing changed. Nothing ran away. I might fret for a while in the schoolroom, sitting cats on mats—actually so, from a Victorian children's 'reader' which seems to have taught me spelling more usefully than any method proposed for my own children—but the garden and the woods and fields were always there, waiting for me to resume an exploration or an interrupted game.

There was so much to explore and so much going on around John Buchan's house to claim a child's attention. The Rev. Thomas Wise's heir, Francis Wise, had, sometime in the mid-eighteenth century, visited, and been much impressed by, the Duke of Buckingham's gardens at Stowe. On a hundredth part of the acreage of that splendid domain, but in sincere imitation of it, Mr Wise planned a garden of classical elegance and romantic surprises. There was little left by the time we came to Elsfield, but enough remained to explore: a pond, a temple, a well. And then there were the two kitchen gardens, the stable-yard, a complex of outbuildings: all of which had an enduring fascination for my brothers and myself. Among the outbuildings were a laundry, a dairy and a brewhouse. I remember the dairy in full use. We had two cows in the field below the garden, and their milk came in pails to be turned into butter, and skimmed for cream, for consumption by the household and all the staff and their families. I loved to watch the butter being pressed into bars, or shaped into thick round pats, to be impressed with a sunflower by a carved wooden stamp. I would also have loved to watch beer being brewed, but the brewhouse was no longer in commission—possibly a diplomatic move on my father's part, for his mother would not have approved.

The way from the house to the garden was through the side door in the hall. From it could be seen the perspective of the high grey wall on the left which flanked the village street, and which ended in the green-black blot of an old yew tree. A flagged path ran parallel to the wall between a long narrow border and standards of rambler roses (Alberic Barbier and Emily Gray alternating) trained over metal umbrellas. On the right of these stood four pointed cypresses, one at each corner of beds of roses enclosing a small lawn, the whole laid on the slope of the hill and extending to the long gravel path which ran from the kitchen garden door at one end, past the house and on to the other kitchen garden behind the yew hedge; a path much used, as can be imagined, by gardeners trudging between the two gardens with tools or barrows or a tall zinc water-butt on wheels. The roses in that garden were mostly pink or red, Zephyrine Drouhin and Caroline Testout certainly, and others that I cannot now remember. The rose beds were underplanted with catmint and the heliotrope which had a special association for my mother.

I can see all this very clearly, and smell roses and mown grass, feel the increasing warmth of an early morning in June, as my father steps out to survey the garden and find himself a buttonhole. He is dressed for London, in a dark suit with a lighter stripe, a double-breasted waistcoat, narrow trousers, with a stiff collar to his shirt, and a tie with a small pearl pin. He sniffs the air and peers, seeks, moving quickly and economically, almost with a fencer's lightness (although this step was learned in boyhood on the Border hills), examines the Alberic Barbier and settles, perhaps for one perfect ivory bud: or moves on, striding over the terrace and down its two steps to the big lawn and the herbaceous border; peers again,

27

bends, comes up with a cornflower, sticks it in to his coat, strides back to the house.

He makes a quick dash upstairs, two steps at a time, to say goodbye to my mother, who is breakfasting in bed; downstairs again he stuffs papers into his briefcase (heavy leather, brass-locked, bearing the Royal cipher, a relic of governmental life in the war), seizes his umbrella—rather a grand umbrella with an engraved gold band and a tortoiseshell handle, most likely a wedding present— from the hall-stand, and walks out to the waiting car. It is to me a proof of JB's grip on life, on things, that whereas I have never managed to keep an umbrella for more than a few months, his had stayed with him since his marriage.

The choosing of a buttonhole was only one of several rituals of choice in my father's life. It illustrated his capacity for absolute concentration on the matter in hand, however apparently trivial. There was, for example, the ritual of the cigarette case. His was round-edged, rather thick, made of silver, a little dented with long use. It held, I suppose, ten cigarettes; but to see JB select one you might think that each had a separate and distinct personality. His hand would hover above the open case for an appreciable time before the choice was made, and the cigarette chosen was by no means always the one at the end of the row. Then followed further actions: the case was closed, the cigarette tapped on its lid until, after perhaps half a minute, it would be ready to be smoked. The same concentration went into choosing a sweet from a box, a process not wholly unlike water-divining, as though a particular sweet might have a particular message for the adept.

Then there was flower arranging. If I call Frank Newall head gardener, this is not to suggest an impressive staff, but simply to indicate that he was in charge of the whole beautiful but demanding garden with sometimes two, sometimes as many as four, people from the village to help him. (My father had his own methods of mitigating economic stress in the village without damaging anybody's pride.)

Frank was a highly trained all-round gardener. He was also an excellent hot-house manager, which is an exclusive art that does not always go with a gift for general planning and management. He had come to us from the service of some millionaire in the north Midlands whose garden staff was about thirty men, and whose hot-houses grew pineapples and bananas as well as more mundane things like grapes and carnations. Perhaps he was glad to get away from such extreme luxury: at all events his was the credit for making the Elsfield gardens at once so pleasant and so productive. His single hot-house produced an unfailing supply of flowers for the house.

Flower arranging was not one of my mother's interests. This was an era before Mrs Spry and others had accomplished a revolution in taste where this domestic art was concerned. My mother had spent most of her life in London, and was in fact new to country-living as distinct from country-house visiting. In the great houses of her parents' relations and friends the flowers were most often 'done' by a member of the staff. Many hands, after all, were employed and work had to be found for every pair. (Staying with a schoolfriend once I thought to compliment my hostess on the flowers which decorated the table at dinner. Their arrangement was truly exquisite, light and graceful and admirably matched for colour. I asked if she had done them herself. 'Oh, no,' she said. 'No one here touches the flowers except Wilkin. He would be most upset if I interfered.')

Suffice it that my mother was not much good with indoor flowers, although in the end she was to acquire great knowledge and skill in growing them out of doors. So my father took over. He liked to see flowers about the place, and not just Frank Newall's pots of schizanthus and lilies, handsome as those were, but cut flowers properly arranged in vases. He arranged them himself, sticking out the tip of his tongue, and arranged them very well, shedding on them the same powerful beam of concentration as he did on any other small job which might be conducive to civilised order and general pleasantness.

My father's hands were mainly for writing. He had little skill with them for anything else, certainly none for anything mechanical. He was a good shot, particularly with a sporting rifle, and an exceptional fisherman. I believe also that, when young, he was rather good at golf. But these are all affairs of the eye, as much as the hand, and I could imagine that he came to them in the first place because of an innate passion for the open air. I suppose I must once have suggested enlisting our father's help over some mechanical problem, because I can remember Johnnie saying scornfully, 'He'd be no use. He can only just about wind up his watch!'

He never really came to terms with the internal combustion engine, never learned or wished to learn to drive a car. Neither did he understand the nature of electricity supply, and he was quite content to leave the supervision of the generator to Amos Webb, his chauffeur. (It was a beautiful engine, with a shining flywheel and much bright brass, its dynamo squatting in front and glass accumulators standing, tier upon tier, in racks against the wall of the stable building where it was housed.)

When, however, it came to some exercise needing strength and persistence and traditional tools, such as tree-felling, or clearing undergrowth, there would emerge quite another being from the dapper, London-bound chooser of buttonholes. Then, with coat and collar off, and sleeves rolled, his breeches held up by braces—I do not think that he ever wore a belt—he would set to with Jack Allam at the two-handed saw while someone climbed a doomed elm tree in the Crow Wood to fix the guide-rope which, when the trunk was all but sawn through, would be pulled on by many hands to make sure that the tree would fall in the proper direction. Such work gave him great pleasure, and much exercise. He would be happy, too, armed with billhook or sickle, attacking brushwood or cutting down nettles. There was no pose in all this. Gladstone's much publicised axework at Hawarden he probably thought silly. He did, as usual, what needed doing, and enjoyed doing it, and equably took the instructions of his men, since he knew that their experience was greater than his.

JB believed in experts. He liked listening to them and, if he sought their advice, usually acted upon it. He once told me that he thought no one could really be a bore on his own subject, by which, of course, he meant that no one who could speak with passion and poetry on his own subject could really bore a sympathetic listener; which may well be true. In any event he was willing to listen most attentively to specialists, and this was perfectly all right so long as the specialists concerned were truly expert and truly disinterested, not always an easy combination to find.

For all that he was a classical scholar, an historian, a man of letters in the traditional sense, as well as a novelist whose work the public was eager to gobble up, JB could comprehend the philosophical side of science without difficulty. He would hardly have become so ardent a follower of Descartes in his university days if he could not. It was simply that applied science, what we now call technology, had no appeal for him. He merely accepted useful benefits such as electricity and motor cars, and left the design and maintenance of those things, with perfect confidence, to the experts.

The results were not always happy. Elsfield, like most old houses, was cold and difficult to heat. The stone floor in the hall, though handsome, had quite soon to be covered with linoleum, for the chill it struck through that part of the house was deathly. My parents' bedroom had five windows, three of them facing east; the morning-room below was the same. The drawing-room had four, and the rooms in the Victorian part were all lit by huge sheets of cold-creating plate glass. With so much exposure and so many doors, draughts were inevitable.

My father and mother must have been thinking about installing central heating when, in August 1924, they went to the United States and Canada. My father had business for Reuter's in New York, and some lecturing to do, but principally, as he said himself, he went for a holiday. He and my mother had many American friends and, as always in that hospitable country, immediately made more. As autumn drew on, they must have been struck by the paradisal warmth of their hosts' houses. Reaching Canada in October, when winter there begins in earnest, they must have been impressed by the universality of means of keeping out the cold. Someone, somewhere, explained (no doubt with the non-boringness of the true enthusiast) a new type of central heating equipment which required neither radiators, nor pipework, or at least no more than one huge zinc tube of about sixteen inches' diameter. The thing was called a Pipeless Heater and it was not very long after my parents' return that a team of experts arrived to install one at Elsfield.

The heat-producing element of this contrivance was something like a very large zinc bottle, standing about seven feet high, and this was set up in the atrium of the cellars. The huge pipe was led along a basement passage and introduced, with really the minimum of structural damage, under the floor of the hall. The outlet for heat was a rather elegant bronze grille, about three feet square, sited at the foot of the staircase. The idea was that a breath like a dragon's should puff up the staircase well, at the same time spreading its heat laterally. There were stipulations, one being that to get the best out of the system all doors had to be left open, so that the heat could penetrate into every room. The immediate result of doing this was that most of the white-painted pine wall-panelling in the morning-room and drawing-room cracked clean down the middle. Tortoiseshell and ivory inlay on cabinets began to buckle. Worst of all was that, unless you leant over the banisters and gazed down at the grille, or stood right on top of it, you did not really feel much warmer. Finally, the furnace consumed an enormous amount of coke every week.

The heater was used, I think, for the space of one winter, and was then quietly forgotten. The apparatus remained, but the furnace burned no more. It was my great pleasure to stand on the bronze grille, while the system was still working, and enjoy the full flow of hot air, until somebody told me that this was a sure way of contracting appendicitis, whereupon I desisted, terrified. Still fresh in my mind was Johnnie's experience, several years before, of having his appendix removed at home, a London surgeon and a nurse, with the local doctor as anaesthetist, performing the operation on the nursery table. In those days, it was not uncommon for operations to take place in the patient's house. JB, too, had been operated on at home, when, in 1917, he had been sent back from the Front with what was diagnosed as a duodenal ulcer.

A child's eye can sometimes see through to truths about people which, later in life, are much harder to discern. A child is obliged to accept appearances as pictures of reality; he has not learned to criticise, or to rationalise, and has little with which to make comparisons. It is therefore, perhaps worthwhile to give this child's-eye view of an extremely complex and daemonic character, if only to note that an underlying simplicity of heart is most readily appreciated by children and by what used to be thought of as 'uneducated' people. These, too, like children, have direct responses founded on their own experience of human conduct; they do not rationalise their feelings nor vitiate an intuitive reaction with sophisticated second thoughts. They like or dislike heartily, not allowing much grey between black and white. No more than children, do they like being talked down to, ordered about, subjected to sarcasm, or ignored. If they have prejudices which are more picturesque than reasonable, they have traditional skills and a collective wisdom as well which it is wise to respect.

Recording a time long past I realise that I shall have to mention things which, nowadays, tend to cause some people's hair to stand on end; domestic service for example, and loyalty and affection between master and man. I expect that I shall raise a crop of thin, disbelieving smiles when I speak of one man's ability to inspire devotion among his employees, when it is a commonplace that such devotion was simply an appearance, a sly form of diplomacy assumed to cover deep resentment at having to give service and respect to another person in return for a necessary wage. I must go further, and offer the opinion that distinction attracts distinction, and that some people have the power quite literally to 'bring out the best' in others.

The fixed stars in our domestic sky were, first, Amos Webb, who, although principally JB's chauffeur, was handy in many other ways, such as managing the electric light plant; then came Jack Allam, whose chief role was keeper, but who helped sometimes in the garden, and looked after the supply of various fuels for the house. His keepering activities varied in scope from the time when my father leased the shooting rights over some local woodland—Pennywell, Little Wood, Long Wood and Woodeaton Wood—in the early days of our stay at Elsfield. This was given up for a while owing, I am sure, to the increasing busyness of JB's life, and then, at a date of which I am not certain, but probably at the end of the twenties, my parents bought Noke Wood, just below the village of Beckley, two miles away. Here there was much to do in the way of ride-cutting and brush-clearing to restore some sporting possibilities to woodland which had been allowed to go wild for many years.

Next was Frank Newall, who lived in the sham-gothic gardener's cottage next to his hot-house and walled garden. There was a groom, Fred Payne, whose domain was the harness-room, who looked after my father's staid old horse, Alan Breck. He had charge also of a skewbald pony called Daisy who pulled, without enthusiasm, the pony trap and also, in summer, had another job hauling the immense lawn mower (an 'industrial antique' of the first order, if one could only find it again), for which she wore shoes of soft leather over her metal ones. Finally, Fred looked after my sister's pony until she gave up riding, and eventually Alastair's black pony Mingo, on which he went hunting sometimes with the South Oxford, being more socially dashing as well as a much better rider than I.

Grooms came and went, and so did gardeners, but Amos Webb and Jack Allam were with us to the last, and I think my father must have counted it an unlooked-for delight of his new home, or as his mother would have said 'an uncovenanted mercy', that two such admirable exponents of the very best in English country life should have come to him with it.

Amos Webb was short and stocky and very strong. He had been born in the same year as my father in one of the cottages belonging to the big house of Woodperry, half a mile beyond Beckley, where his father had worked for Mr Thompson, partner of Herbert Parsons in the Oxford bank of Parsons and Thompson. Webb's family was a very old one in Oxfordshire, and its ramifications extremely wide. It was next to impossible to find a village (and we

33

quartered the county together, taking my mother on journeys to do with the Women's Institute, or out to luncheon) which did not contain a cousin or some other connexion of Mr Webb's.

I always called him Mr Webb, and would find it hard not to were he still alive and in our service (he died in 1940, only a few months after his employer). We were not, as children, allowed to call people by their surnames alone, any more than we were allowed to ring bells, give orders, or in any other way make use of the servants. It would probably not have occurred to us to do so in any case, since, in the world in which we were brought up, children saw more of servants, indoor and outdoor, and of village people, including children of their own age, than they did of their parents. With rare exceptions therefore, such people were our real friends.

Amos Webb was the best company in the world, as my father early discovered. To begin with he knew pretty well everything about the county which was, for the rest of us, new territory. He had shrewd insights, never otherwise than discreetly expressed, into the relative worth of country neighbours, whether long settled or newcomers like ourselves. He had a certain reverence for one or two ancient families (since gone from Oxfordshire) which, in his young days, had seemed to embody what he thought a proper way of living. 'Proper' was a word often on his lips. Passing a long park wall, while out on some excursion, I would ask him whose house lay inside, and he would tell me, with an anecdote or two, often about the owner's grandfather, ending up with the words 'Proper gentleman's place, nicely kep' up.'

He had the countryman's ruddy complexion, with dark hair, and very shrewd, amused brown eyes. He had begun his working life with horses, and there were times when the car—'my car' as he always called it, quite properly, since it was in his sole charge and the cause of a great deal of his labour—was treated somewhat like a horse. Leathering the coachwork after washing it, or going after mud with a long brush between the spokes of the wheels, he would hiss gently, as grooms do when using a wisp to rub down a horse.

Webb was a splendidly safe and careful driver, who never suffered so much as a scratched wing in the twenty years he drove for my father; and those years took him and his car to the farthest Highlands, to many parts of England including London, to Wales and, finally to Canada. He was quite unshakeable. I never saw him respond with anything but calm to a crisis, and he never minded taking a heavy car over drove-roads, cart tracks, even fields, when the family's passion for ancient remains prompted an excursion to a fortified farm or a ruined church. I never saw him more than mildly and humorously irritated by any event or person, certainly never angry.

He was not alone in the world; he had a wife and a family of four children, two of whom, when I first knew him, had already left home. He was, I am sure, an excellent husband and father, but if my own father had found in him a rare spirit, a man to cherish, this feeling was perfectly reciprocated. Their relationship, conducted with delicacy and respect on both sides, was a pleasure to observe: and there was no doubt whatever where Webb's first allegiance lay.

My father not only listened attentively to all that Webb had to tell him about Oxfordshire life, he frequently asked, and took, his advice, having for once found an expert who was both capable and trustworthy. This was usually over matters of usage and tradition. Anxious to fit as neatly and quickly as possible into his chosen new world, the better to enjoy it, JB needed to know what was expected of him, what traditions should be observed, which requests granted, what given or allowed to whom.

One Christmas Eve, for instance, the front door bell rang, quite unexpectedly, and there in the street was a semi-circle of unknown men, perhaps ten of them, each bearing in either hand a small bell held by a leather thong. These were the bell-ringers, of whom we had heard. None of us knew where they came from, or why they had come to our house, but no one who had read Hardy could fail to recognise their visit as a privilege, their art something from an older time, their mere existence already a rarity at that date. We listened entranced to a rendering of carols. There must have been quite a lot of silver in those bells, they sounded so sharply sweet in the frosty night. Afterwards my father made the ringers a speech of thanks and gave them some money. They were not talkative men; they thanked my father and left. Next Christmas we waited eagerly for them, but they never came again.

Something had gone wrong. Webb was consulted, but even he had no ready answer. He had never heard the bell-ringers perform, only of their fame. He thought it possible that they should have been given beer, and perhaps supper, rather than money; but this mystery was never cleared up.

Then there was the summer fête in the manor grounds. This had been a fixed event for many years, and must be continued: and it was the older hands, like Webb and the Allams, who advised on the general organisation, and Webb who had charge of the various entertainments including, most notably, bowling for a pig. Since the pig, in those days, was a really valuable prize, the bowling was

35

not made easy: only the strong and skilful could hope to succeed. While the bowls spun and the skittles clicked and teetered, the pig, in an improvised pen, grunted non-committally nearby. Women might bowl as well, but only for a tea set; their bowls were smaller, the whole thing less strenuous and more elegant.

But, chiefly, Webb was in charge of the motor cars—and over the years my father ran an odd variety of them. When we moved to the country he must have set off, once again, to consult some confident expert as to what kind of car he should get for general family purposes, but principally to carry him to and from the London train. The answer he received was: buy American. This may, in fact, have been good sense in 1920. British engineering could hardly yet have effected the switch back to peacetime production and also, Rolls-Royce and Daimler excepted, the quality of the British motor industry was still highly variable. No doubt, either, that the Americans had seen a chance to gain a foothold in the British market. So JB bought an Overland, what was then called an 'open tourer', which meant that you could drive about in it with the hood down in fine weather, and be covered in dust (since most country roads were still untarred), or you could put up the hood and with it a set of talc and canvas side screens which, while they soon cracked and yellowed so as to impede the view, were powerless to exclude draughts.

The next car was a Dodge, and built to JB's specification. In those days, if you needed a car of any size and comfort you bought a chassis from the manufacturers and sent it to the coach-builders, or got its maker to do this for you. The result of this was that our American chassis, which in its native land would have had one of those boxy bodies familiar from Buster Keaton comedies and period gangster films, wore a stately, if somewhat top-heavy, structure, approximating the Austins and Minervas of our country neighbours. This body, beautifully made by hand, and glossily black, was of a type then known as 'landaulette', which is to say that half the roof at the rear of the car could be unlatched and folded back on itself, being covered on the outside with a waterproof black macintosh, and on the inside with some soft material. Those sitting on the back seat could enjoy the air and the view without any feeling of being cooped up; while those on the strapontin seats (my usual place) benefited also, if to a lesser degree. This landaulette principle gave, when the hood was closed, an odd wrinkled look to the back of the car but, since fresh air mattered more to JB than aesthetics, he caused each new car as it came along to be built in the same way.

The whole business, of course, was really a survival from the days of carriages. It was not until a mass market became possible that coach-builders or, rather, car-designers lost their nostalgic feeling for the horse.

I have a happy, if somewhat bizarre, recollection of driving with my father through narrow Welsh lanes in summer, with the hood down: fitful hot sunshine through green leaves, dust, the slapping of cow-parsley against the gleaming panels of the car, and he sitting bolt upright, wearing a grey homburg hat and a stiff collar, alert as a pointer and thoroughly pleased.

The only criticism I ever had of Webb had to do with my persistent car-sickness. There was a large fur rug which spent almost more time at the cleaners than in the car, because I was sick on it so frequently. There were many causes beginning, I suppose, with some physical intolerance of the car's motion. Other factors came into it. To begin with the car always smelt very strongly of petrol, which nobody but I seemed to mind. Petrol stations, in my childhood, were rare and widely spaced, and so Webb always carried a couple of two-gallon cans, which leaked. In addition, those being the days before a great market had developed in cleaning fluids and detergents, it was his habit to clean spots from the Bedford cord upholstery with petrol. Seated beside my father, who did not scruple to cloud the atmosphere with his very strong Turkish cigarettes, it was never long before the speaking tube had to be seized and Webb urgently asked to stop and let me out. Too often, as I have suggested, such action came too late.

We had two Dodges, I think in succession. I doubt if anybody now uses the word 'dodge' to mean trick, or ruse, or cunning short-cut: it has a distinctly Edwardian flavour. Once, driving to Scotland, we stopped at Broncroft Castle (tiny and delightful) to lunch with F. W. Pember (Warden of All Souls from 1914 to 1932) and his family. As we were leaving, Warden Pember pointed to the car and asked what it was. My father said, 'It's a Dodge.' The old gentleman chuckled. 'I am quite sure it is,' he said, 'but what is its name?'

After the Dodges my father changed to Wolseleys. I think that some outraged caucus of buy-British friends must have brought pressure to bear on him. The Wolseleys, like their predecessors, were built to the landaulette pattern. The last of them went with Amos Webb to Canada in 1935.

Webb enjoyed taking us visiting, the chances being that he would know, know about, or be related to some member of our host's staff. If it was not that kind of visit, then he would disappear to the nearest pub—with much the same result, no doubt. He was an abstemious man, albeit intensely sociable, and one glass of beer kept him going for a long time.

Later on, when I took to going to dances Webb seemed to look forward to those events far more than I. On one occasion when, for once, I was really enjoying myself, I left a neighbouring house rather late; rather early in the morning, in fact. My father was not pleased, and reproved me quite severely for keeping Webb out of bed. Webb either got to hear of this, or simply divined it, for he stopped me next day and said: 'Never you mind how late you stay when we go out, so long as you're enjoying yourself. I had a good time last night with the other chauffeurs. You could have stayed longer and I'd not have minded.' I suspect that Mrs Webb's views on the subject were not canvassed, or if given, listened to.

When I come to write about Jack Allam I must turn to my brother Johnnie, who has written so tellingly about him. The following, in *Always a Countryman*, was published in 1953 while Jack was still alive.

> His gnarled, kindly, even beautiful face is little changed, and in his presence there is ever the homely whiff of country clothes and strong tobacco . . . he looks little different today from my boyhood recollection of him, in the days when the lives of my sister and my brothers revolved round him to such an extent. Though well into his seventies he is still a good shot, a noted fisherman and a first class field naturalist—a countryman with the habit of life of a simpler, sturdier England; above all a kindly man who has always rejoiced with us in our triumphs, and sorrowed with us in our distress.

Johnnie, being older, and the more impassioned naturalist, saw more of Jack than I did, but even if I could not yet go shooting with him I could accompany him on his rounds, to visit rabbit-snares and inspect his forbidding game larder in Woodeaton Wood, where various kinds of vermin—magpies, crows, weasels, jays—were hung up in macabre rows to discourage their fellows. I think of this as a kind of sympathetic magic of rather dubious effectiveness, for when did one live animal ever give a passing glance to a dead one except, perhaps, if very hungry, to eat it?

Jack was thought to be illiterate, but told my elder brother that he could read *reading* but not *writing*, by which he meant that he could read print, but not anything written by hand. Notes from my father, whose handwriting none of us could read, must have been a real puzzle to him.

JB, in Jack, had found another expert, and a true one. He would listen for hours, on long walks through the woods, to Jack's slow Oxfordshire speech. He would learn much from him about old country ways still persisting and, more immediately, about the prevailing state of the local game, the activities of poachers, and what was needed to encourage the wild and unco-operative and, be it said, rather limited pheasant population. Jack taught JB's children a great deal, too—Johnnie again:

> Almost all we learned about birds and beasts, as children, we learnt from him; and not a little of my father's knowledge of natural history came from the same source. We would quarter the hedges in his company. It was Jack who taught us the real art of finding birds' nests. . . . Grouped round the bottom of a tall oak tree we would watch Jack climb to a magpie's or a carrion crow's nest, moving up the trunk by the pressure of his strong knees and elbows.

Ironically enough, since we had been such great egg-collectors, it was to be Johnnie, in the House of Lords, and his wife Priscilla, in the House of Commons, who together put through the Protection of Birds Act of 1954 which made the taking of bird's eggs a felony.

I have dwelt at some length on the characters of Jack Allam and Amos Webb, because I think that they helped JB significantly to an understanding of his chosen corner of England. No doubt, with his acute sensibility and trained habit of finding facts, he would, in the end, have found out a great deal for himself without their help; but they had certain things to impart, which only they knew, and they held certain views and showed certain feelings which, by induction and extrapolation, he could use to comprehend a whole unfamiliar world and its historical perspectives. I think I can say that *Midwinter, The Blanket of the Dark* and even *Oliver Cromwell* owed much to JB's talks and excursions with those two men.

JB, as his writings show, had always been a tremendous walker, but he never walked aimlessly, whether by himself or with his family. Long before, in Galloway, he had once walked eighty miles, spending a night in the heather. Hill-walks of five or ten miles were a holiday commonplace for me when I was only ten. When he walked by himself he would plan a course, say, to Brill by Stanton-St-John and Oakley, then back past Boarstall Castle through the Otmoor 'towns' to Noke and so across the Woodeaton fields and woods to Elsfield again, a matter of at least twenty miles. He found walking then, as he had always found it, far the best stimulus to thinking. Plots and the resolving of situations, whole courses of dialogue, came to him as he walked, while another part of his intelligence was busy with the country round him, noting movements of birds and animals, the weather, the state of the waters and woods.

After the destruction and disorientation of the war, it seems likely that JB found a special kind of repose and reassurance in the small fields with their tall hedges, the neat woodlands, the gentle slopes and secret glades of that unspectacular but intimately beautiful countryside. He quickly came to know the name of every field and copse and stream for many miles around, found time to delve into the history of the land, back to the days when it had been a hunting preserve of kings, and beyond them to the Roman occupation.

Throughout his life he was fascinated by things Roman. Elsfield and its surroundings had been the scene of much Roman activity. A stick rammed down a few inches through the grass and mud of the straight causeway running from below Beckley out into Otmoor would find hard Roman pavement. In the middle of an undulating ploughed field, between Forest Farm and the Islip road, there was a small stand of trees surrounding a hollow. This, the experts said, had once been a factory, producing *fibulae*, the brooches with which Roman togas were fastened. During a strong antiquarian phase I did a lot of digging in that hollow, finding little, however, but the ubiquitous shards of Samian ware which were in every furrow of ploughland, and objects that looked like fossilised sweetbreads which were the slag from the iron-smelting which had once gone on there.

There was a story that a man ploughing at Woodeaton had struck something hard with his ploughshare and found that he had smashed a pot full of yellow coins. When he also found that these would not do as currency at the pub, he threw the lot away. The best I ever found for myself, apart from the occasional flint arrowhead, was the black foot and stem of an amphora.

A mile or so beyond the *fibula* factory, at Beckley, there is supposed to have been a Roman villa; a good place for one, too, protected from north and east, and with a fine view over Otmoor to the west. In *The Blanket of the Dark* JB puts the site of his 'painted floor' (a Roman tessellated pavement) a little nearer, somewhere in the thickets of saplings and thorn and briar on the far side of the Islip road, which was once the road to London from the northern Cotswolds. In a wood nearby, if you can penetrate brakes of bramble and thorn so resistant, so inimical, they might have been put there by an enchanter, you will come out into a small clearing of perfect short turf with a green hillock in the middle, the ideal hideout for a fugitive or for a camp of Midwinter's men.

My father was always powerfully attracted to secret places, whether man-made or natural. He had found many in the Border hills, and his beloved Wood Bush in Africa, and now there were more for him to find in apparently prosaic Oxfordshire. Almost at the end of his life, flying over the mountains on his way back from exploring the Tweedsmuir National Park in British Columbia, he spied just the kind of high upland meadow surrounded by trees and made inaccessible by cliffs of rock which he would have liked to take as the site for a house. This dream had been with him for a long time. It received one kind of expression in *A Lodge in the Wilderness*, and again in the plans he made, when in South Africa, for a domain in the Wood Bush. Now, at Elsfield, he had found his domain, and was content with it; but he liked to play, in fancy, certain games with his settled world, imagining how it would have been to be on the wrong side of Henry Tudor and need obscure friends and safe hiding-places, or to have ridden on urgent and treasonable business through the English countryside at the time of the Forty-five, feeling the same needs.

Walking, its steady rhythm, and the exercise it gives to all the muscles, the gradual change of scene which gives time for both the examination of minute detail and the open contemplation of a grand design, perfectly suited a restless imagination and a strong feeling for logic. (There can be few activities in life more perfectly logical than proceeding from point A to point B by a series of immediately verifiable steps.) In addition JB had never lost what his father had had in such great measure: a capacity for wonder at the beauty and bounty of this world, coupled with a possibly Calvinist and certainly Scottish apprehension of the mutability of human affairs; the stuff, surely, of which good books may be made. Finally, and more practically, it was probable that walking, the exercise and the movement, allayed for a while the almost perpetual nagging pain of his duodenal trouble.

When it came to family walks those were, mercifully, shorter, but no less carefully planned. There might be birds in view, or flowers, or the River Cherwell with, perhaps, a punt trip thrown in; but there was never anything aimless, except on days of really vile weather when, as JB insisted on putting it, we all went out for a 'slog'. I disliked that word very much, it seemed to make a dreary business even drearier, and so I would tag sulkily along in a black macintosh and sou'wester, hating the rain, the wind, the mud and my invincibly cheerful family, my mind set only on getting home to the nursery fire and my paint-box or Meccano set, and the white glare of the electric light. What I should really have liked to have done would have been, in the phrase so often, so scornfully, used by grown-ups, to stay and 'stuff indoors'.

We were lucky in so many ways, in that countryside. Not only was our village, and much of the land around it, safely held by Christ Church, but other colleges were important landlords as well. Both Magdalen and Brasenose (college of my father, uncle and elder brother) owned woodland near Beckley, and more woods and farms beyond. Colleges are, or were, conservative bodies, and in any case their holdings were often immobilised by the terms of their bequests. They were therefore admirable preservers of the status quo.

On Boxing Day in 1979, standing beside Noke Wood with my sons, hoping for a pheasant, I could reflect that more than fifty years had passed since I had first stood on that spot, and nothing whatever in its surroundings had changed. Such a state of affairs might irritate some people, but in the last quarter of this terrifying century I find it reassuring. In any event, it cannot last much longer. I have the impression that nearly three-quarters of our population now live in towns or in urban conditions of some kind. The country has become a peepshow, a curiosity, something townspeople drive out to scratch the back of, so to speak, like a supertax farmer with his pigs.

I have called Amos Webb, Jack Allam and Frank Newall the fixed stars of our domestic life. They were not the only ones, however: indoors were Annie Cox and, most especially, the Charletts, who were invaluable to my mother who was inclined to be bored by domestic details. She had married a writer, and in the liberal and intellectual atmosphere in which she had been brought up, writers were held in high regard. The proper occupation for people of education and imagination, in her view, was writing; she was, however, ideally the wife for a writer such as JB, who was also a man of the world, with interests in other than literary spheres, since she had from her forebears a good deal of political insight and much social experience. But even writers must have homes and, often, families, and these must be made to function smoothly—so my mother accepted cheerfully the administrative duties of running a large household, without giving them any exclusive importance. She was not, however, one to enjoy counting linen, or poring over cookery books, or visiting her children's nursery for more than a pleasurable hour or two each day.

In those days, as I have said, children in that sort of household saw more of their parents' employees than they did of their parents; we were firmly in the charge of our nursemaid and had to fit in to our parents' day as it suited them. Once whisked from bed, washed, fed and generally got ready for the day, I would go to say good morning to my mother. Except when there had to be an early start—say for a trip to London—she habitually breakfasted in bed. The bed seemed enormous to me, and all the paraphernalia of breakfast on it extremely luxurious. Everything was set out on a wicker table with short legs which bestraddled the breakfaster's lap. My mother sat against the high pillows, her cloud of bright fair hair against the blue of the bedhead, surrounded by newspapers and what seemed to me an enviably large post.

Once she was up and about, my mother's day was a full one. All those letters at which I had looked so wistfully had to be answered. Things needed for the house had to be ordered; future entertaining had to be arranged. People came in from the village with problems of one kind or another, many of them to do with the Women's Institute which, rather nervously started by my mother, had settled down to being a valued and popular institution. There were meals to be ordered—a task that I think bored her dreadfully—and conferences to be held with Annie Cox, the housekeeper (who was later to go with my parents to Canada as my mother's personal maid) about the comfort of impending guests. Messages would have to be sent to Amos Webb, concerning things that had to be fetched from Oxford, or journeys to be undertaken; the gardener would come in with flowers for the house, and there would be talk about what was being done in the garden.

It was, therefore, for my mother as for all the rest of us, the greatest good fortune that the Charlett family should have come into our lives. I have already expressed the view that distinction attracts distinction. I would also say that originality appeals to originality, and that the happy conjunctions of personality which we know in our lives are more than just the result of what we vaguely call luck.

Mrs Charlett, a widow with three children, had been left badly off at the beginning of the 1914 war. I do not know by what means she came to apply for the post as cook with my family, but apply she did and, with her two daughters, Elsie and Gladys, she was installed at Elsfield when we opened the house. Old Nanny stayed with us for a year after that, while Elsie was officially nursemaid; then she left us and Elsie, at the age of eighteen, took sole charge of the nursery.

The household staff was usually about seven. Apart from the butler (butlers changed fairly frequently), there were Mrs Charlett, Elsie and Gladys—who, until she left to be married, acted as parlourmaid—a kitchenmaid to help Mrs Charlett, and Annie Cox and a couple of housemaids to help her. Many came and went—sometimes in rather rapid succession—but it was the indomitable Mrs Charlett and her daughters, with their good sense, good humour and steadfastness, who made our world go round.

Our childhood, although it occurred in the reign of King George V, might have been Victorian for its insistence on every sort of education. My father's own upbringing had been, although intellectually exciting and full of family affection, strenuous to the last degree. Even while he was working like a beaver to gain a scholarship to Glasgow University and, later, another one to Oxford, he still had to teach the Sunday School of his father's church, and take part in the numerous functions which were part of the work of a populous Glasgow parish in the eighteen-eighties. It is known that he even wrote a hymn or two, when these were required.

My mother, in 1900, was eighteen years old. This meant that her formative years had been spent in Victoria's reign, and all her friends and relations, governesses and teachers had been brought up in these remarkable years. A Victorian young lady's education, in a cultivated family such as my mother's, included learning languages (in her case French, German and Italian), studying pictures, going to theatre and opera, travelling abroad, and reading, always reading. Charity and public work also played important parts; it was not possible, for any length of time, to moon or dream, or regard living as anything but a very serious affair.

A serious affair it was for her, certainly, but illuminated with an agreeable worldliness, much love and intelligence and a good deal of laughter. My mother never quite got over a tendency to collapse with hopeless giggles when something sparked her idiosyncratic sense of humour. She was once, aged fifteen or so, forcibly removed by uniformed attendants from the sacred precincts of Bayreuth for laughing uncontrollably when the Holy Spirit, in the form of a dove, due to hover over the head of Parsifal, came on upside down with its claws in the air. Only at Bayreuth, at that period, could such an event not have caused the house to explode with mirth. (Stravinsky was also ejected, at a later date, as he relates in his *Chroniques de ma Vie*, for eating a sausage very loudly at some quiet moment of a Wagner opera.)

Our upbringing was, of course, less restrictive. We could play any games we liked, when games were in order, but we were never allowed to be idle. Fortunately, reading, of almost any kind, was not counted as idleness, and, since the house was full of books, and more kept coming at Christmas and on birthdays, one could retire into privacy, at almost any time, with a book.

There was also a lot of reading aloud at Elsfield. When Alastair and I were old enough we were allowed downstairs for this. When my father was at home, and there were no guests—and sometimes if there were—he would read aloud to us, very often from a novel or history in progress or just completed. If he was away, my mother would read, or one or the other of us would take a turn. One rule was rigorously enforced: those read aloud to must have something to do with their hands; fidgeting, sprawling, and gazing vacantly into space were simply not allowed. If one of us had no particular piece of handwork to get on with, he or she was set to making spills. This was an odd economy of my father's. He saved matches by using a spill for his pipe, generally made from a cancelled cheque folded in four and lit from the wood fire in the library, the library being the place for reading aloud.

If there was no home-grown work to be read we had Dickens (probably *The Pickwick Papers* or *Nicholas Nickleby*) and humorous books now, I think, not much read, like *Some Experiences of an Irish R.M.* (Somerville and Ross), or *The Brass Bottle* (Anstey), or also by Anstey, *Vice Versa*, or, better known, *Three Men in a Boat* (Jerome). 'Saki' was another favourite author. None of these last could be called improving works in the stern Victorian sense. They made us laugh and JB, remembering his own childhood, must have remembered how uniting to a family shared laughter can be. Moreover, having stretched his mind, and often his limbs, quite severely all day, he wished to be simply, gently, amused.

Sometimes, if he had reading of his own to do he would sit puffing his pipe, pencil poised to sideline a passage, legs crossed at ease, while my mother read to the rest of us in a lowered voice.

The only other reading aloud that JB did was in church on Sundays or at morning prayers. These took place, as they did in many other conservative households throughout Britain, before breakfast, and only when my father was at home. He would read a passage from a huge old family Bible, and a prayer or two from a handsome eighteenth-century prayerbook, to a congregation consisting of all the children then at home, but not my mother, who almost invariably breakfasted in bed, and such of the staff as could be spared from jobs to do with breakfast or the nursery. Some of the dishes were ready on the sideboard, keeping warm over spirit lamps. Sunday was the day for sausages. During the prayers, while gazing at the seat of a chair from a kneeling position, I received wafts of deliciousness from the food to come. That is why, even now, the General Confession has for me a distinct suggestion of sausage.

Obviously, in rather spacious surroundings, and with other people to help, it is not difficult to bring up a family in a disciplined manner without recourse to a general severity: but it is essential that the parents be themselves fully and usefully occupied, and everyone else about the place likewise, for children to gain the idea that it is better, and happier, to use time for a purpose than to kill it. I should not think this worth writing, except that I remember contemporaries, living in establishments far grander than Elsfield, who yawned through their days, almost literally 'kicking the wainscoat', for lack of any direction or encouragement from stupid or indifferent parents.

We had to be punctual for meals, because unpunctuality was hard on the servants and threw the whole household machinery out of gear. For many years Alastair and I, off together or separately on investigations in the garden, or as far afield as Little Wood or Long Wood, would be summoned to meals, or if suddenly wanted for something, by a police whistle blown vigorously from the nursery window.

I do not suppose that anybody minded working hard for my father, it was so evident to the world that he himself worked harder

46

than most people could even imagine. There was no question, therefore, of anyone's slaving away to minister to a life of idleness or futility. In addition, he was becoming famous, and people who are much in the news probably have less difficulty than most in finding and keeping willing helpers. Apart from anything else, people like JB, who are recognised (as I have recorded) to be important, tend to have important friends. Elsfield was a hospitable house, and those who worked there could be sure of sometimes seeing, close to and in simple humanity, people whose names were household words.

JB had a long experience of English country houses, and a clear idea of what he wanted from his own. He writes of Richard Hannay's house, Fosse Manor, at the beginning of *The Three Hostages*:

> There is an odour about a country-house which I love better than any scent in the world. Mary used to say it was a mixture of lamp and dog and wood-smoke, but at Fosse, where there was electric light and no dogs indoors, I fancy it was wood-smoke, tobacco, the old walls, and wafts of the country coming in at the windows. I liked it best in the morning, when there was a touch in it of breakfast cooking, and I used to stand at the top of the staircase and sniff it as I went to my bath.

Mr Mark Girouard, in his brilliant work, *Life in the English Country House* quotes this passage and comments: 'This kind of country-house romanticism is everywhere in Buchan's books, just as it was everywhere in Buchan's own life, the life of a self-made son of the manse who ended up in his own modest but mellow country house in Oxfordshire.'

'Modest but mellow'—admirably chosen words, perfectly expressing what JB had been looking for. As for tobacco in the air, he could now make his own rules about that. He had suffered greatly in his time from old-fashioned hostesses who would not allow smoking in their houses. He told me once that, staying with Great-aunt Mamie, at Ockham Park near Woking, he had been driven to lying on his back on the floor of his bedroom and blowing his thick Turkish smoke up the chimney.

'No dogs indoors.' Not the least of JB's agreeable characteristics was a tendency, once he had put his foot down firmly, to pick it up again. From the very first, at Elsfield, he had decreed that any dogs acquired—and he was in no way against dogs—must be kept in the stable-yard. Alastair's cocker spaniel, Black Douglas, had his

47

kennel next to the pump. For some time he was the only dog in the family, and indeed was far too enthusiastic and generally scatter-brained ever to settle down in a house.

Then came Spider; I cannot now say from where, nor how, in the first place, he got past my father's guard. Somehow, he was insinuated into the house, and there he stayed, to become the much-loved and pampered pet of everybody, of JB—who put him into *Castle Gay* under the name of Woolworth—as much as anyone. He was said to be a Jack Russell, but whoever called him that could never have seen the breed. He was a cross between a Sealyham and a wirehaired terrier, with a Sealyham's coat and body and the wire-haired's long legs.

He was a ferocious rabbiter, causing many upsets and anxious searches by disappearing during a walk, staying out all night, and coming home the next day caked in yellow mud and no more than formally apologetic. He came to Scotland with us, and to Wales; in fact he made up the party on most excursions. Like all dogs he would rather spend hours in a car than risk being left behind, and, whenever a car appeared, was always first in it.

Amos Webb thought Spider had the makings of a good ratter and so, since there were plenty of rats in the barns and looseboxes, cut his beard close so that he could get his nose into the holes. This gave him an odd and—since he had a black patch over one eye—piratical appearance. Like most dogs who receive a great deal of human attention Spider became a tremendous 'character'. He lived to a fair age, and died much regretted.

Spider's introduction was the thin end of a small wedge. At some point we acquired another species of terrier called Sammy, of whom JB also became fond. It amused him to call this little dog Samuel Johnson, and he would sometimes refer to him as 'The Great Lexicographer'. This title caught on in the family, and was swiftly abbreviated until, in the end, Sammy was answering, when he answered at all, to the name of Cog.

My father disliked rigidity of thought, and had a poor opinion of people who could not be dislodged from a prejudice by valid argument. He used sometimes to quote Emerson—'A foolish consistency is the hobgoblin of little minds'—and the story of the terriers is but one instance of his being persuaded to change his ruling on presentation of fresh evidence, the *de facto* evidence in this case being the dogs themselves.

It was the same with people. He would sometimes express extreme disapproval of a person, perhaps because of something he had written, or because of the company he kept, or for no detectable reason at all. It would then often happen that he would meet one of the people in question, take to him or her, discover a whole range of valuable qualities, and return saying, 'He is really not such a bad fellow, a lot better than those characters he goes about with: it seems he had a wretched childhood;' or, 'She has a remarkable mind, and is really a pleasant woman once you get past that rather grim North Oxford manner.' He was never in the least put out by having to make a complete about-turn; if taxed, he would simply have admitted to having been hasty in his original judgement.

I have said that JB was adept at bringing out the best in people and this, I think, is the reason why he had so few positive and persistent dislikes: he always seemed to manage to find a good point or two, however wilfully concealed. Sometimes I thought, watching him, that he was engaged in the process known to mineral-miners as 'salting'—that is to say he was actually planting gems from his own store which he would then discover and credit to his interlocutor. When this is done with diamonds it is fraudulent, but JB was merely recovering something of his own. However it was, few who spoke with him failed to go away feeling in some way enlarged, exhilarated, and refreshed.

His strong sense of history, coupled with knowledge gained from immensely wide reading, ensured that he could begin a conversation with a stranger and, in no time at all, be immersed in genealogical complexities which the latter, till then, had thought known only to himself. I would see him see *through* some dull, red-faced man in a tweed suit to his Cavalier ancestor, and see the man's beefy, discontented, suspicious countenance take on a momentary look of pride and pleasure, as if carried back to braver and simpler things. All that I am saying, really, is that JB was a true romantic; his rare failures with other people occurred when he came up against a good intelligence frozen by cynicism, iron-bound by some grievance, or distorted by jealousy.

Only once in my recollection was JB deliberately cruel. A certain Dr Frank Buchman, an American, acquired notoriety in the nineteen-thirties when he founded the Moral Rearmament movement which advocated the regeneration of society by 'complete honesty, purity and love', seeking divine guidance in all its activities, and meeting at house parties for mutual encouragement and confession. It refrained from denouncing Hitler's policies. To the great fury of Oxford, he insisted on calling it the Oxford Group. My father was not much amused when an Oxford newspaper, commenting on that movement, headlined an article with the word 'Buchanism'. There was nothing about Buchman's ideas or methods which could possibly have appealed to JB; indeed he found the whole conception nauseating. Nevertheless, when someone begged to be allowed to bring the prophet to tea, JB acquiesced. Buchman was short, plump and bespectacled, and to this day I can remember his limp, damp, handshake. It was a summer day, swimming in heat. We had just set up on the terrace a game of deck-tennis, played with a rubber ring which was thrown from side to side over a high net. My father, after observing his American guest closely, insisted that he should play, and play against an enormously tall and athletic under-graduate who also had come out to tea. Not unsportingly, Dr Buchman agreed to play, and was kept hopping and bouncing in the heat until, near melting, he was reprieved by the gong for tea.

For various reasons, some true, some false and all historical, the Scots and the English tend to be unreasonable about one another, and about each other's countries. I have seen John Buchan's decision to settle in England, to build his life and bring up his family in Oxfordshire, described by Scotsmen in terms which made it seem an irrelevance, almost an affront, something at any rate which no Scotsman (and above all no Scottish writer) should ever do. This kind of chauvinism is regrettably prevalent in Scotland, where it sometimes goes under the name of nationalism. Critics of this order seem to think it a dereliction of duty for a writer to forsake his native land, however compelling the reasons, however essential to his development the mental nourishment he may find in another place. I have no doubt that the same kind of tut-tutting went on when Stevenson took off to Vailima. Certainly, almost identical noises were made in America over the 'defection' of Henry James. Yet James needed Europe for his art, Stevenson the South Seas—for his health as well as his art—and Buchan found the very nourishment he most needed and could best absorb within walking distance of the university town which had first shown him the accessible marvels of the world.

Consider his writing after he had 'taken sasine' of Elsfield: in 1922, *Huntingtower*; 1923, an anthology of Scottish verse: *The Northern Muse*; 1925, *History of the Royal Scots Fusiliers* and *John Macnab*; 1927, *Witch Wood*—arguably his best novel, set in the Scotland of the seventeenth century; 1928, the revised version of *Montrose*; 1930, *The Kirk in Scotland* (with Sir George Adam Smith) and *Castle Gay*; 1932, *Sir Walter Scott*; 1933, *The Massacre of Glencoe*; 1935, *The House of the Four Winds*. All the above are either set in Scotland, derived from Scotland, or concern characters and events in Scottish history: not bad going for a 'denationalised Scot'.

Before taking the plunge and setting up his Oxfordshire establishment, my father must have reckoned clearly how much hard work he would have to do to maintain it, and with it a family of growing children. By that time he was a man of forty-five, already well-known as a writer, mature, at the height of his powers. Having taken on what to some might have seemed intimidating responsibilities, he called on his particular gifts at full stretch to meet them.

He once said to me that only uncreative people ever worried seriously about money, because they knew that, if it dwindled, they would never know how to replace it. I thought, but did not say, that this was all very well for people possessed of his own creative voltage; there had to be other factors as well, not the least being a ready and eager market for the things created. This my father had already made for himself.

Now that television has usurped the 'cultural' place of honour in many homes which once was reserved for shelves of books; now that so many houses quite simply have no room for books, and particularly not for hardbacks, it needs an effort to remember a time when seven and sixpence was about the highest price payable for a new novel. Writers like my father, A. E. W. Mason or P. G. Wodehouse could count upon an educated public with seven and sixpence to spend, and space to store a growing collection. Educated that public certainly was, or anxious to be so—the large number of untranslated Latin tags in *The Blanket of the Dark* caused no howls of resentment that I ever heard of—educated, and alert, and by no means uncritical. If a 'popular' writer such as JB failed to provide his special brand of magic, or went off at some mysterious tangent, or simply became dull, his public's displeasure would surely show itself in the sales of the next book.

My father, by 1929, had a loyal and interested body of readers for his novels. *The Thirty-Nine Steps*, published in October 1915, three months before my birth, had been an instant success, selling 25,000 copies between publication and 31 December of that year.

He had then gone on to produce *Greenmantle* and *The Power-House* in 1916, and *Mr Standfast* in 1919. In 1920 there came *The History of the South African Forces in France*, and during 1921 and 1922 his monumental *History of the War*—a million words written originally in longhand. His public, then, was already a wider one than simply that of a novelist.

Faced with such towering competence, most people can only blink in disbelief. The wider-minded may admire, accepting such a display as evidence of the limitless possibilities of humanity; the narrower will sneer and try to find some way of proving it all a trick, something 'done with mirrors'; which might account for all but one most important thing: the sheer quality of the work itself.

3

THE PEEBLES FAMILY

Until this moment I have been writing about a past of which, even if I do not remember all of it, I was myself a part. Now, for a while, I must launch myself on the treacherous waters of history, for John Buchan was born more than a century ago, and there is today nobody left from his early days to enlighten me about details.

James Robb, a farmer, of Parkgate Stone, near Broughton in Peeblesshire, and his son Alexander left a farm diary, scrupulously kept, with scarcely an omission, from 1819 to 1889. This they called first 'Chronologer' and later, 'Memorandum'. Between the urgencies of farming life, the weather, the price of beasts and fodder, and again the weather, they made succinct notes on local happenings such as weddings and funerals, sermons by visiting clergymen, the success or otherwise of the Biggar Show, and on national happenings and family affairs as well. In August 1875 Alexander Robb, in his clear and beautiful handwriting, penned the following entries:

Memorandum 1875

August

17th—The month thus far has been good as a whole though changeable, crops fast assuming the hue of harvest with every appearance of plenty for man and beast. Cottages and apartments fully packed with summer visitors and the rumble of carriages passing the road scarcely ceased.

23rd—The wife of Rev. John Buchan, Perth, of a son.

31st—The Biggar Farmers' Show came off on the 26th but owing to foot-and-mouth disease among cattle at present no cattle or sheep were brought forward for competition.

Country life does not appear to have been much different in 1875 from the present day, what with foot-and-mouth and summer visitors. (Where did the latter come from, I wonder; perhaps from as far away as Edinburgh or Glasgow, perhaps even from Northern England.) Robb makes one odd mistake. John Buchan was born in Perth, not on 23 August, but on the 26th, the day of the unsatisfactory Farmers' Show.

The matter was of interest to Alexander Robb because his son William was to marry Agnes Masterton, elder daughter of John Masterton of Broughton Green, Broughton, Peeblesshire, and sister of Helen, wife of the Rev. John Buchan and mother of the new-born John.

Helen and her sister had three brothers, whom I remember well, skilled farmers all who, at one time, had considerable land-holdings around Broughton and in the upper valley of the Tweed. Broughton Green, happily, is still in the family and so I have not lost touch with the places and the land which were to mean so much, more perhaps than anywhere else on earth, to John Buchan.

The house of Broughton Green stands, like Elsfield Manor, on the village street, which is also the old southward road from Edinburgh to Carlisle.

Armies had marched along it; Prince Charlie's ragged Highlanders had footed it; in my grand-parents' memory coaches had jingled down it, and horns and bugles had woken the echoes in the furthest glens. . . . It followed Tweed to its source, past places which captured my fancy—the little hamlet of Tweedsmuir where Talla Water came down from its linns; the old coaching hostelries of the Crook and the Bield; Tweedhopefoot, famous in Covenanting days; Tweedshaws, where the river has its source; and then, beyond the divide, the mysterious green chasm called the Devil's Beef Tub, and the Annan and the Esk, and enormous, half-mythical England.

Thus my father, recollecting the Broughton of the late eighteen-eighties.

The highroad, which now glistens with tarmac, was a thoroughfare only for sheep and vagrants and an occasional farmers' gig or tinker's cart. In all its upper stretches, before it crossed the watershed into Annandale, the space between the ruts was shaggy with heather.

The road had changed, but not very significantly, by the time that I first saw it in 1922. Its surface had been metalled by then, and I don't think any part of it was rutted or heathery any longer, but I remember the tarmac as a new thing, and I could still dart out of the house into the road, chased by sister or brother, without much danger from passing vehicles.

Most deliveries were made by horse and cart, although some shops in Peebles had acquired motor-vans, tall, tottering and smelly, but as beautifully painted as the butchers' and bakers' carts they had superseded. Although there were occasional cars, and some horse traffic, dogs could lie safely in the middle of the road, moving slowly only when shouted or hooted at.

When I first saw Broughton Green the farm was still in full swing. None of the family lived there any longer, my aunt and uncle and grandmother being settled in the Bank House, at Peebles. Broughton Green was looked after by Maggie Lorimer, who also ran the farm for my Masterton great-uncles. Maggie, whose Border speech my English-accustomed ear could not always understand, was a robust and energetic person who wore a sunbonnet in summer, was a very good cook, and always welcomed us on our arrival, tired, hot and grubby from a day's train journey, with that phrase which sums up for me the unquenchable Scottish spirit of hospitality: 'Come away in and get your tea!'

After the first war my father took to leasing a house at Broughton called Gala Lodge from his aunt, Agnes Robb, by then a widow. This house, a stone villa of about 1860, is one of a row of houses of various dates, well separated from one another, at the southern end of the long, straggling village, in the part which is called Calzeat. They are mostly on one side of the road and, even as a child, I always thought they should have been by the seaside. Instead of the sea their view is of flat meadows in the valley of the Biggar Water, beside which once ran the railway line to Peebles, and beyond to the prehistoric fort of Dreva and the hills which fold in on one another as Tweed turns eastwards.

On the same side of the road as Gala Lodge and squarely illustrating the schismatic character of the Presbyterian church and the independent-mindedness of the Scots were the village's two churches: one was *our* church, the Independent or Free Kirk; the other the United Free Church. Of these ours was some sixty years older, put up in the eighteen-forties after nearly half the Church of Scotland clergy, led by Dr Chalmers, had seceded—'gone into the wilderness'—over the question of intrusions, or the right of patrons to nominate to livings. That was in 1843, and the Rev. John Buchan, my father's father, born in 1847, had elected to join the secessionist Church. The little church, built with sandstone quoins and colour-washed, with windows lozenge-paned in various pale colours, now lies derelict. The United Free Church stands higher on the hillside, has a short spire and a red sandstone exterior, and is still in use as I write.

Dr Chalmers's was a great gesture, and perhaps more truly in the spirit of Presbyterianism and Nationalism than the work of those who were prepared to compromise; but people who go into the wilderness for a principle are apt to remain there. The firebrands die off and their fire dies with them. Compromise prevails; time passes and religion, or at any rate church-going, declines. The little church at Broughton, built with the subscriptions of only three men, dedicated by the great Chalmers himself, and having once rung with scholarly interpretations of the scriptures and with metrical psalms sung by a congregation certain of being in the right, is locked and empty, with weeds around the door.

I do not know why I should feel a regretful affection for that little church, considering the tortures I suffered there on Sundays as a child. The learned and saintly Dr Forester was minister during my childhood, and he was a preacher of the old school. The points of his discourse were numbered. If I never actually heard him use the famous words: 'Thirty-seventhly and lastly, my brethren', I certainly sat (and fidgeted) under his preaching, on more than one occasion, for a full three hours. My grandmother who, with years of training as a minister's wife, was inured to that kind of trial, had a certain understanding of the constraints it put upon a child. From time to time, she would slip me a peppermint, of the kind that is known in Scotland as a 'pan drop', and these did much to help me endure those truly testing occasions.

Because of Dr Forester's tendency to become rapt away by the matter of his sermons, and his complete indifference to the passing of time, as indeed to most worldly matters, Sunday luncheon at Gala Lodge was sometimes as late as three o'clock.

My great-uncles, John and Jim Masterton, bachelor brothers who lived together in a farm three miles away in the direction of Biggar, would have arrived in their high-wheeled gig in time for the service. Afterwards they would join us for luncheon, where the main argument of Dr Forester's sermon would be gone over (the whole idea of Presbyterianism being that every member of the congregation should be nearly as expert a theologian as his minister), and then the conversation would turn to personalities and, if my father were present, to politics and the international scene. My uncles had loud, deep, resonant voices, as many Border farmers have—due, my brother thinks, to having to call dogs over long distances on the hillside—and they spoke the rolling Border tongue. Their opinions were strong and strongly expressed. Jim was the gentler of the two, but John, whose waterfall moustache considerably thickened his diction, was capable of thumping the table and bellowing, of some local character, 'He's aye a Godless man!'

They were a kindly pair, if stern in certain matters, and visits to their farm were, for all of us, among life's chiefest joys. There was so much to see, so many games to be played in the long, grain-scented galleries of the barns, so much fun to be had with turnip-cutters and cream separators and other strange machines.

With Jim one day I showed myself up badly in my true colours as a renegade Scot, anglicised, corrupted and (to anybody but him) contemptible. In the Scots tongue one widespread usage of the verb 'to mind' means 'to remember', whereas in English it is generally used to mean 'to object to' or 'to resent'. After Church one Sunday, Great-uncle Jim looked down on me kindly and asked, 'D'ye mind the sermon?' To which my regrettable reply was: 'No, not particularly.' The conversation ended in complete confusion.

Those uncles were strong men, tough and shrewd and, in their business, hard: but they were their own men, proud with a pride born of the skill and knowledge coming from many generations following the same calling in the same green valleys and hills. They were narrow and upright and, for certain things, unforgiving. As Janet Adam Smith wrote in her biography of my father:

> A Border farmer [was not] part of such a nicely graded rural society as his counterpart in southern England. In this country-side of farms and tweed-mills where there were few great houses to cast a feudal shadow, the man with John Masterton's eye for sheep stood square on his own skill and had no need to defer to anyone.

It is a pity that none of the formidable Masterton business acumen seems to have come my way. When I first knew the uncles, although you could never have told it to look at them, they were reputed to be very rich. With the disruption of the 1914 war and the general shake-up afterwards, which came to farming as much as to any other industry, they must have seen a new range of opportunities for expansion of their interests which they were not slow to take. After the First World War they began to buy agricultural properties on a large scale, including a property called Carterhope, in the glen of the Fruid Water.

The Upper Tweed valley is edged with glens, steep-sided valleys containing rushing streams. The water of these streams, or burns, when still, is clear as glass, and they tumble in a hundred tiny waterfalls and pools down to the big river from sources high on the hillsides. Nearly all of them are worth trying for trout.

In the early nineteen-hundreds it became necessary to provide another reservoir for Edinburgh's water supply which, till then, had come from artificial lochs nearer at hand than the Peeblesshire hills forty miles away. Talla Water, mentioned by JB in the passage quoted earlier (p. 54), was a larger burn, dignified by the name of Water because of its size, and perhaps because in its early life it falls down a steep rockface in a series of falls, known as Talla Linns, which are impressive. This stream was chosen as the feeder for the new reservoir; the valley was cleared, a dam was built, and Talla Reservoir, two and a quarter miles long, was made. Carterhope lies in the next glen, to the south of Talla, where the farm called Fruid still stands.

Large or small, frowning or friendly, the glens beside Tweed are beautiful, and beautifully unfrequented save by grouse and sheep, and occasionally shepherds. Of all of them, the Fruid glen leading to Carterhope was perhaps the most beautiful and the Fruid farm and the Carterhope rigs the most desirably remote.

I think that JB must have known, by 1935, when he was given a peerage and had to think of a territorial name for it, that his Uncle John intended to leave the Fruid and Carterhope lands to him. He had, therefore, no qualms about taking the name of Tweedsmuir, since the land is in that parish, and so there would be a landowning as well as a profound sentimental reason for doing so. Sure enough, on Uncle John's death in 1938, the land, about 4,000 acres (not a large property in hill country) came to my father.

Unfortunately, for no doubt good reasons, Edinburgh, after the war, began to feel the need for yet more water. Surveys were made, the Fruid valley was decided upon. Carterhope was designated a part of the very extensive catchment area required by reservoirs, and so became subject to a compulsory purchase order: and that was that. The new Fruid reservoir, completed in 1967, is as long as Talla and, in places, broader. The Carterhope burn provides part of the water which it needs. For those who like large artificial lakes this one is a handsome specimen of its kind.

The Royal Burgh of Peebles stands on the River Tweed, just below a narrow defile, where the road twists and turns beside the tall castle of Neidpath. Once past the castle the river broadens, becomes placid, flows through parkland until it comes to a 'cauld', or low weir, and then to the Tweed Bridge. The old town is all on the left bank: on the right are green parks beside the river and, on the steep hillside, looking down on the town, mid- to late nineteenth-century villas. The road which crosses the bridge to the old town turns sharply right into the High Street which is wide and straight, with a view of hills at its end. This view, as in many Scottish towns, gives a slight feeling of foreignness, Austrian perhaps or Swiss, but on a miniature scale. The houses are mostly grey stone, and the place gives the visitor an impression of great neatness and orderly busy-ness, a controlled kind of bustle. If, instead of turning into the High Street, one goes straight on, the road narrows sharply as it passes the tall church and plunges to a bridge over a small tributary of Tweed called the Edlestone Water, but generally known as the Cuddy. Right on the corner of this road and the High Street stands Bank House, the home of my father's family for three generations.

John Buchan's grandfather, another John—as the eldest sons of the family had always been christened—had come to Peebles from Midlothian in 1843 to set up as a solicitor, and also as agent for the Commercial Bank, which had been founded in 1810. He himself was born in 1811 and, by the time he came to Peebles, had been appointed Writer to the Signet, 'the highest stage in Scotland of the Solicitor's calling'. The house was called Bank House because it also housed the bank. Rather as with building societies today, it was common practice at that time to put a bank's provincial business in the hands of a lawyer. Apart from his legal work, my great-grandfather handled the funds and supplied the financial needs of the farmers and flock-masters of the Upper Tweed valley.

Bank House had a small iron gate on the street and a sealing-wax red front door. When I first saw that door I immediately noticed a brass plate, much rubbed but just legible, which said 'Mr Buchan, Writer'. I certainly, and I suppose my sister and brothers as well, for a long time thought that this legend referred to JB (and meant author rather than lawyer). The brass plate is still there, and the law firm of J. and W. Buchan is still very much in business, although none of my family is in it any longer.

Peebles is an ancient town which has touched history at many points. It has always been proud and, on the whole, prosperous. It is the first of the towns in the Tweed valley which possesses mills for making textiles and woollen goods which are world-famous. Tweed's water, flowing from the peaty moorlands to the west and south, is especially suitable for this manufacture, while its hill pastures feed the sheep which provide the wool. The trade has a long history, one firm having been in operation since the early seventeeth century. Peebles is also, of course, the county town ('the auld Burgh toon') of Peeblesshire. When Scotland began to boom as a tourist attraction with the extension of the railways in the middle of the last century, Peebles was discovered as a centre for holidays and a base for fishing on what was then one of the best salmon rivers in Scotland. After the First War, when economic conditions were bad, and the textile industry was suffering, Peebles made a positive bid for the tourist trade. A slogan of the time which appeared on railway posters was much quoted, often with ribaldry: 'Peebles for Pleasure'.

This in the eighteen-forties was a compact community, with many families still living where they had lived for generations. The town supplied the Upper Tweed valley with commerce, banking, medicine, law and, of course, pleasure. There were several inns catering to different classes of customers. The Tontine Hotel, in the High Street, built in the early eighteen-hundreds with the proceeds from that strange form of life-assurance, a tontine syndicate, has at its back, with tall 'gothick' windows facing Tweed, an elegant assembly-room with a musicians' gallery and some delicate plaster work. Here, in wintertime, the townspeople and the local lairds, with the farmers and graziers and their wives and daughters, would amuse themselves at cards or dancing or suppers in ways little different from those of English county towns at the same period.

Professional men stood high in Scottish life in the mid-nineteenth century, as indeed they still do. The lawyer, the doctor and the minister were figures that received much public respect, but, since this was Scotland, never dared to think themselves immune from criticism. When a lawyer was proved highly capable as such, he was on an eminence, and in a position of influence, which demanded a high sense of responsibility, much hard work, and a more than ordinary ability for diplomacy. That the scope of his activities was small by metropolitan or national standards meant little: people being people, although the canvas was smaller, the skill required was the same—even perhaps greater, since, on a small canvas, mistakes are not so easily concealed.

I wish that I could see my great-grandfather more clearly. In his day country lawyers in Scotland did not often have their portraits painted and, although photography had become fairly usual, certainly by the seventies, photographs of that period are generally stiff and unrevealing. That he was a 'douce' (agreeable) man I somehow know; that he was an able lawyer and banker and a good administrator seems clear.

An elegant silver snuff-box is in my possession, on which is engraved 'To John Buchan Esq. for services efficiently performed'. The date is 14 October 1865. There is no mention of its donor or donors, whether it might have been a satisfied client or a gratified Town Council who thought John Buchan's services worth rewarding. The inscription is so wonderfully discreet, it might equally well refer to getting someone out of legal hot water or shipping someone else's scapegrace nephew off to the colonies: this is likely to remain for ever a mystery.

John Buchan can scarcely have known his grandfather, who died when he was eight years old: and if he remembered him at all it can only have been as a broken and melancholy old man—for, shrewd and upright as he certainly was, he had been the victim of what even now seems a most monstrous piece of bad luck. In 1878 came the crash of the City of Glasgow Bank, an event which had disastrous effects all over Scotland, and particularly for him. I quote from an obituary article contributed to a local paper at the time of his son's, my Great-uncle Willie's death in 1906. (Willie, who had studied law at Edinburgh, had returned to Peebles to help his father in the lawyer's office: he is the 'W.' in J. and W. Buchan).

Business did not absorb his whole activities, and there was much time for volunteering [military training], for angling, and much other open-air life, and, above all, for continued study in the humane subjects of which he was so fond. Then came a time of gloom when his father's whole means were swept away in the disaster of the City of Glasgow Bank, not for an investment he had made, but because he was a trustee, although not an executor, of an estate which had held shares, and he had cashed dividends. It was one of the hardest cases of many. A heavier burden now fell upon the son to exert himself to the uttermost, and in paramount filial duty to soothe the cares of his father, broken alike in fortune and in health.

The rather rhapsodical prose of the above extract should not obscure the fact that this was, indeed, one of the hardest cases to result from the failure of the City of Glasgow Bank. My great-grandfather and his son fought desperately, and with all their skill. The case went right up to the House of Lords where, although genuine sympathy was expressed, nothing could apparently be done to improve matters. My great-grandfather was found liable to repay a prodigious sum of money. That this tragedy shortened his life there seems no cause to doubt. He worked grimly and furiously to repay the debt. He did repay it: and within five years he was dead from the effort.

My great-grandfather had three sons, and two daughters. Of the sons, my grandfather, John, was the eldest, Tom the next and Willie the youngest. Of Great-uncle Tom there are many legends, too highly coloured to be easily believable, but one thing is certain: Peebles was not big enough to contain him. Of the story that he killed a man in a fight and had to flee the country I am more than doubtful, but I have no doubt at all that somehow he made his native town too hot to hold him. He probably drank too much, and behaved in a riotous manner unbecoming in the son of the town's leading lawyer, who was in any case generally thought to have had enough trouble without having to endure a troublesome son. However things may have been, we know that Tom went off to sea and was not heard of again for a long time.

It would have been totally unlike the Buchan family not to regret the loss of a member by any means, and not to pray that such a brand might be saved from the burning. When he died in Australia Tom's name was added in proper form to the obelisk over the family grave in Peebles churchyard. I think myself that Tom probably had a good deal of the insouciant charm shown by all young Buchans, but was perhaps not very bright. The youthful devilry of the others, particularly his nephews, modulated early enough into serious intellectualism and high-minded responsibility. If Tom was not clever, and had perhaps too much charm and devilry, and too little self-discipline, it is easy to see how he might have become unmanageable in a God-fearing, step-watching, rather stuffy small town. There can, however, have been no absolute rupture with him (who often, it seems, referred to himself in later years as a black sheep) because in the summer of

1893 we find him home again on some sort of holiday and visiting Bank House.

It is to Great-uncle Willie that I feel most drawn. JB's sister, Anna describes him as looking like the large parrot which he kept as a pet, and certainly he seems to have been thin and slight, and perhaps rather birdlike, with the usual long, enquiring Buchan nose but, unlike the others, who were all clean-shaven, he had a neat small beard and moustache.

He was born in 1851, the year of the Great Exhibition, and died at Bank House where he had been born, in 1906. Unlike most of his family he was a rather delicate boy. If I return to quoting from the anonymous obituarist, it is because his article on Willie, although the style may now seem quaint, is written with great percipience and affection. It is, in any case, the best source at my command.

> Less robust than the average boy, and impelled also by natural inclination, Willie took early to books. There the impressions made on his mind by his mother, and by his old French tutor, M. de Chastelaine, himself connected with the Knights of Malta, stimulated him towards history of all nations, folklore, antiquities, genealogies, heraldry, and French language and literature, of which subjects throughout his whole life he remained a student, and in which he attained a scholarship beyond that of the mere amateur.

I think that Willie Buchan was a wise man. Knowing the limitations of his physical strength and at the same time judging accurately his own abilities, he knew that he could do his work in Peebles to everyone's satisfaction, and yet have time for all the things which were closest to his heart. He belonged to that honourable company of country lawyers, doctors and clergymen who have extended their interests beyond their calling into archaeology, genealogy, botany and horticulture, to the great benefit of scholarship and scientific discovery.

The Town Clerk to a burgh is a kind of General Manager; there is nothing to do with the well-being of the town and its people that does not come under his eye. William Buchan became Town Clerk in 1881, and so remained for the twenty-five years until his death. In that time the Borough grew in extent, in population and in business. It was his task to keep the administration abreast of this. Big schemes such as the supply from Manor Water, pavements, the taking over of the gas and the building of the new gasworks, the widening of Tweed Bridge, were taken in hand and carried through in William Buchan's reign.

Gasworks and Maupassant, main-drainage and heraldry, railways and folk-lore—these in the right combination were perhaps the formula for a happy life, for a man who loved all good things in the world: who was clever and honest but not ambitious; and who knew exactly what to do with his spare time.

Great-uncle Willie's main enjoyment was his annual tour abroad and I like to think of him on his travels, darting about, admiring, enquiring, putting up cheerfully with a hundred small setbacks and irritations, surprising people by his command of French and entering into talks in cafés, extolling the 'auld alliance' between Scotland and France. I like to think of him inspecting the coats-of-arms of kings and bishops, and visiting the castles of Touraine. I imagine that by the time that he had money and leisure to travel, the worst upsets in Paris were over—the Siege, the shelling, the suppression of the Commune. If they were not, then he would not have been the first Scotsman to look on at such events with sturdy, if sympathetic detachment.

It was he who interested my father in French literature, and it was to hospitable Bank House that JB liked to go at some point in every vacation from Oxford, to be lapped in luxury by his maiden aunts, to enjoy his uncle's excellent food and wine, his library and, above all, his conversation.

For William Buchan's elder brother John, my grandfather, life was to be viewed and lived on very different terms. Unlike his younger brother he was tall and strong, but no less douce and appealing to his fellow men. It is clear that he was born with a strong religious gift—a gift as definite and compelling as that of music or painting—and that, from his earliest age, his life had been governed by his sense of the wonders of the Creation. Great-uncle Willie, on the other hand, was not, I suspect, religiously inclined beyond the observances becoming to one continually in the public eye. One clergyman, pronouncing a eulogy at Willie's funeral, seemed to indicate this when he said: 'As a member of this church I always found him loyal and true-hearted, a generous supporter when any special cause was brought before him. There was about him in religious matters a certain reserve but when one got a glimpse beneath this reserve, one found his religious instincts to be very real.'

I think that one tended to find what one was looking for. That reserve, I can well believe, masked a profound distaste for a certain religiosity which sometimes showed itself among adherents of the Presbyterian Church. I am quite sure that my own father felt the same reserve, and that, in removing himself from the narrow, if devoted, evangelism of his family life, and the lip-tightening and head-shaking and general nosy-parkering of some who thought themselves 'the Elect', he was obeying instincts which more readily responded to a cool classicism than to the heats and ferments and immoderation of his native Church.

These feelings are made plain enough in *Witch Wood* and *Montrose*, which both deal with a period in Scottish history, the seventeenth century, when the Kirk was guilty of appalling wrongs. 'The prime defect of the Kirk was intolerance', he wrote in *Montrose*, and although the Kirk had gone through many vicissitudes since then— and although by the nineteenth century it had shed many of the worst excesses of the seventeenth-century divines—enough of their spirit remained to be irksome to a deeply tolerant man.

There was nothing intolerant or cruel about my grandfather. He was, in the best sense of the phrase, a simple soul, full of the love of God and of his fellow mortals. I count it a misfortune to have been born too late to have known this John Buchan, who died in 1911. He was born at Peebles in 1847, and went to school there, then to Edinburgh University. His must have been a happy childhood, a happy growing-up, for he loved the Tweed valley, was devoted to the two family passions, fishing and walking, was a keen naturalist and a poet. Quite clearly, from an early age he had begun to lean towards a career in the Church; already, at nineteen, his evangelising spirit had caused him to help found the YMCA in Peebles. From Edinburgh he went to the Free Church College and, at the age of twenty-six, he was ordained.

It is extraordinarily difficult, at this moment in history, to realise the influence of the Church upon every aspect of daily life in Scotland a hundred years ago. It may be that the poor of the ever-expanding industrial towns were too harassed by their bitter struggle for survival to count much on help from ministers who could only tell them that such consolations as they could find for themselves in this life would condemn them to eternal fire in the next. But, for the burgesses, the professional people and the country dwellers, and certainly (although sometimes for unacknowledged reasons of politics) for the lairds and the great nobles, religious observance and the application of the scriptures to daily living were more or less universal. Further, a tide of evangelism was flooding throughout the English-speaking world, and in a less sophisticated age than ours, amongst people whose sole reading was the Bible and whose only regular entertainment was the pulpit, what Americans then called a 'hot gospeller' would have had a good chance of a hearing, and very probably of many conversions.

Family testimony should always be taken cautiously, and I am quite aware that this must apply also to my own. It is only human nature to remember the best, the golden aspects of a personality, to be governed somewhat by a feeling of '*de mortuis*. . . .'. Nevertheless, the testimony of my father in *Memory Hold-the-Door* and that of his sister in *Unforgettable, Unforgotten*, where it concerns their father, agree at every point. Perhaps my mother was the most useful witness. Coming from a different world, unbriefed and unprepared for the kind of family life she was about to enter, she warmed immediately to this intrinsically happy man, to his wide knowledge and his great simplicity. In his long experience of pastoral work he must have met with every manifestation of misery, crime and despair, yet nothing had impaired his belief in the goodness of God, nor his certainty that all was somehow tending towards the best.

Speaking in his father's old church, the John Knox Church in Glasgow, JB said: 'He had his troubles like other people, but his message to the world was always one of serious joy. His optimism was never assumed; it flowed naturally from the benignance of his heart and the sureness of his faith.'

My mother came swiftly to love her father-in-law. Noting his high seriousness, and the respect and affection in which he was held outside the circle of his family, she could also enjoy his liking for simple pleasures, how he told stories and sang and recited ballads, and played delightfully on the penny whistle. (Only recently looking it up in a dictionary of music, I found that the penny whistle, which I had always thought one of those squeaky, tin things I could buy at the village shop, is in fact a respectable instrument, for which serious music has sometimes been scored. This modest musical talent of my grandfather's was not transmitted to his eldest son.)

My grandfather, although his nature was truly poetic, never quite succeeded as a poet. His book of verses, *Tweedside Echoes and Moorland Musings*, celebrates the countryside which he loved so dearly, and certainly found an appreciative public in its own time. His verse too often inclines to the banal, and is better in the vernacular than in English.

★

The year, 1873, in which my grandfather was ordained was the year of a visit to Scotland by the American revivalists Moody and Sankey. The Rev. John Buchan was, as the Americans might have said, immediately 'swept in'. That winter he was in charge of the Free Church at Broughton, during the absence abroad of the Rev. William Welsh, the minister—in Rome, of all places—and there he introduced the Moody and Sankey hymns which were to have immense popularity in Nonconformist circles all over Britain. The young enthusiast held nightly meetings which drew people in from the farthest Tweedside glens. As I have said, the pulpit was almost the only respectable source of entertainment, and in any case religion, at that time, was a very real force in the lives of the Peeblesshire farmers, shepherds and lairds. The young minister must have been gratified by the strong response to his efforts, and his congregation must have been more than pleased with him, for they gave him, at the end of his three months' stint, a fine gold watch. (Where the legend of the meanness of the Scots has come from, I cannot tell: not, I think, from the Borders.)

During his time at Broughton he saw, and at once fell in love with, Helen Masterton. My grandmother-to-be was famous for her long mane of bright golden hair, and this seems, first and last, to have been the physical attribute dearest to my grandfather. I have a manuscript poem, one of a series he wrote to his wife for her birthdays, which reads:

> Hair once so bright in hue
> Shining like gold:
> Eyes of the sky's deep blue
> Fair to behold.
>
> Hair now all lustreless
> And thy cheek wan:
> Such brings life's pilgrimage
> To wife and man.

Not even loving kindness can subdue the Scot's fondness for plain speaking, nor his consciousness of mortality.

Helen was the youngest daughter of John Masterton, farmer, of Broughton Green. When my grandfather first saw her she was sixteen years old. She was in her eighteenth year when they were married at Broughton Green on 2 December 1874 by the Rev. William Welsh.

That year the Rev. John Buchan had been called to Knox's Free Church in Perth, and after their marriage the young couple left for Perth, where, in 1875, a week after Helen's eighteenth birthday, my father was born. They had been in Perth only a year when my grandfather accepted a further call, this time to the West Church at Pathhead near Kirkcaldy in Fife.

For anyone unfamiliar with the workings of the Presbyterian Church it should be explained that a new minister is not imposed upon a congregation by the patron of a living—strife about this very issue was the cause of the Disruption—but called for by the elders in council, or Kirk Sessions, of the parish concerned. The elders are guided in their choice by the candidate's reputation and, of course, his qualifications. Of the latter my grandfather had plenty, and even at the age of twenty-seven his reputation as an inspiring preacher had already gone before him.

I do not know whether the shortness of his stay in Perth had any significance. Perhaps a rare access of ambition, a desire to test his powers to the full, caused him to accept the call to Pathhead, one of the largest congregations in the Free Church, and one of highly varied composition. At all events he went to Pathhead and stayed for thirteen years.

When a few months old I was brought by my parents to a little grey manse on the Fife coast. It was a square stone house standing in a big garden, with a railway behind it, and in front, across a muddy by-road, a coal-pit and a rope-walk, with a bleaching works somewhere in the rear. Today industry no longer hems it in, but has submerged it, and a vast factory has obliterated house and garden. The place smelt at all times of the making of wax-cloth; not unpleasantly, though in spring the searching odour was apt to overpower the wafts of lilac and hawthorn.

One of Kirkcaldy's principal manufactures was linoleum, and the smell of this was as much associated with that town as the smell of fish with Grimsby.

I have a photograph of that little house, where my grandparents lived for thirteen years and reared five children. It is a neat stone villa of about 1830, probably built for some worthy citizen of Kirkcaldy while the land around it was still green, and before the helter-skelter, unconsidering industrialism of the mid-century had covered the fields and poisoned the streams which ran down the 'dens' (dingles) nearby. The children seem to have been almost ideally happy there, for, with their mother's instinct for comfort indoors, and a big garden to play in, they were in the situation which always suited them best—in one another's company and a little away from the world. In those days the insalubrious surroundings could quite soon be left behind, and expeditions made along the seashore to the many little fishing-ports which nibble the Fife coast, or inland to invade the demesne of an old country house.

This coast and the life of the children are described at the beginning of *Prester John*. The theme of that book, to be developed many years later, must have set its seed in the mind of the child JB, when a black clergyman came to preach at Pathhead.

My grandmother must have been in her element. Thoroughly well trained by her own mother, she could make sure that the house was as clean and comfortable, the fires as warm, the food as good as she, a perfectionist in such matters, could manage on her husband's stipend. More, and at how young an age, she had a manse of her own, healthy children, and a minister for a husband, a minister who had already made something of a stir in the, to her, immensely important world of the Free Church.

I have noticed that the phrase 'son of the manse' is often used in such a way as to sound derogatory, belittling, as though the word 'manse' itself created visions of something canting, stuffy, convention-bound, out of date and faintly ridiculous. This, at least, is an impression I have gained from reading or hearing English people on the subject. It is not, perhaps, wholly surprising. The manse has produced a significant number of ambitious, clever, highly effective people, who have made a name for themselves, and perhaps a fortune, with a degree of energy and high-mindedness, or in some cases simply energy, which has not wholly endeared them to their fellow-men.

Besides my father, I can think immediately, of four sons of the manse who made a powerful impression on the world: Cosmo Lang who joined the Anglican church and finished up as Archbishop of Canterbury (having, on the way, as Bishop of Stepney, married my father and mother); Lord Reith, who may fairly be described as the father of the BBC, and whose odd ambition it was to march up the aisle of his father's church in uniform, wearing spurs (he published his memoirs under the title *Wearing Spurs*); Alexander Fleming, the discoverer of penicillin and Lord Beaverbrook. The latter's manse was a Canadian one, certainly, but his family name was Aitken, his origin was Scottish, and I think the principle still holds.

My grandfather's manse differed from many others, perhaps from the majority, in at least one important way. The proper discharge of duties and a really solid diet of church-going on Sundays apart, his children were never kept down at home. They could, and did, talk freely to their parents; they could, and did, make jokes about their father's parishioners; they did get up to a great deal of serious mischief which might have turned a more conventional parent's hair white. My grandmother's mother, a strong character in many respects, and sometimes severe, was toler-ance itself with children. Her favourite phrase was: 'Never daunton youth' and she often repeated the text: 'Fathers, provoke not your children to anger, lest they be discouraged.' This scarcely tallies with conventional ideas about child-repression in Victorian times. I think that her daughter might have preferred a little more decorum, but she had bred a highly gifted, highly energetic family which was, quite literally, irrepressible.

In spite of what may have been said since, by Scottish Separatists and others, against the Act of Union of 1707, the fact remains that its chief effect was to end the poverty-stricken condition of the Scots. This effect was not immediate but, by the end of the eighteenth century, it was evident in vastly improved agriculture, better roads, new and more commodious building, and above all in the nation's intellectual life, which had come far since the ironbound days of the seventeenth-century presbytery. That pride which had once been almost the Scotsman's sole possession was swelled by the universal recognition of certain Scottish excellences—although many English people still found the Scots priggish, conceited and thrusting, and many Scots detested the English as having been the chief cause of their historical woes, and an ancient obstacle to prosperity.

Whatever an increasing ease of life might have brought to Scotland, and whatever flights of speculation might have soared from philosophers in Edinburgh, nothing happened to diminish the Scottish interest in religion and the condition of its Church. Nothing diminished the Scottish passion for education, nor caused the Scots to lose interest in the doctrinal subtleties and reaffirm-ations of their faith. Of the Kirk in Scotland in the seventeenth century JB wrote, in *Montrose*, 'In principle it was a noble demo-cracy. The Kirk made no distinction of class; the ministry was not a hierarchy, but issued from the ranks and could be reduced to them again; an educated laity therefore became the pre-condition of an educated ministry.'

We might add to this G. M. Trevelyan's remark in *English Social History*: 'Some critics of the older Calvinism have said in their haste that the Scots were a "priest-ridden people". It would be truer to say that theirs was a "people-ridden clergy". The Zealots in the congregation kept a close eye on their minister's orthodoxy.' If that was true in the eighteenth century, it was still true in the nineteenth, and even in my own time, as witness the Sunday conversation of my great-uncles John and Jim Masterton.

It follows from all this that the manse must be an important focal point in the life of a parish. At the time of my grandfather's ministry, in such places as Perth and Pathhead and Glasgow, the manse was not only the fountain-head of religious orthodoxy, but also a political and social centre of great importance. People went to it for worldly as well as for spiritual advice, for guidance on their children's careers, for comfort in bereavement, for help in every kind of trouble. It was the co-ordinating agency for charity, the centre of evangelism and religious education, and the provider of innocent entertainment. The minister was respected for his learning and his spiritual quality; his wife for her practical good sense and her tireless work among the poor and the sick; his children were approved of for the work they did for the parish, for the help they gave at home, for the promise they showed of growing up to be worthy of their parents and their well-wishers. In every country parish, especially those in the Borders, like Broughton, where there was no great landed proprietor, but a scattered community of minor lairds, shepherds and farmers, the manse and its inhabitants, so long as nothing was said or done to upset settled religious opinions, received a meed of respect not generally granted, at any rate in Scotland, to ordinary human beings.

It was not surprising, therefore, that the children of a manse— any manse—should grow up with a slight but definite sense of being set apart. That this condition required of them extra high standards of conduct, especial displays of diligence, must also have been borne in on them at an early age. Some it irked extremely: those were the ones who broke away, sometimes disastrously, more often to follow a profession as far removed from their father's as possible. For those who, like my father and his brothers and sister, were genuinely devoted, and grateful, to their parents, the path of diligence, the road of good conduct, were clearly their only choice. Not that these roads were severely circumscribed. There was a wide variety of professions and vocations which, if followed by their children, would have caused no real pain or even regret to their parents.

Only my grandmother, who had already achieved her own highest ambition—to be married to a minister and have a manse of her own to run—would have liked to keep all her children within the safety of a limited world, and in the embrace of her own Church. There is no doubt that she would have wished all her sons to be ministers, and to have manses of their own. I think that she must have cherished dreams of seeing her brilliant eldest son one day in knee-breeches and buckled shoes, as Moderator of the General Assembly of the Church of Scotland. In her view there was no earthly pinnacle more exalted than this; beside it all other attainments were insignificant.

Given the kind of children she had mothered, there was little hope of an enclosed and tranquil world for my grandmother. When I first came to know her well, that is to say to detach her from the general ruck of grown-ups (only perceptible to a small child as varying degrees of warmth or cold, attention or indifference) and, so to speak, see all round her, I found her enigmatic and rather depressing. There was all that business about church to begin with (pan-drops notwithstanding) and not playing anything but 'Bible games' on Sundays, and rounds of questions about what one was going to be when one grew up; and edifying stories of the general brilliance and exceptional virtue of my father and his family at my age; and further stories about Scottish contemporaries of my own who were already showing signs of remarkable brains or even saintliness. It was all rather tiring. I was off my own ground and, faced with statements and questions and propositions quite different from any that I ever heard at home, I fear that I came off badly, seeming perhaps frivolous, rebellious, inattentive, all kinds of things that might be expected from someone who was half English, and a highly suspect kind of English at that.

We called her Gran, and she and Uncle Walter, my father's youngest surviving brother, and Aunt Anna—who wrote successful novels under the name of O. Douglas—were all the Buchan family in Scotland, as far as we were concerned. My grandmother had reason enough to be melancholy. Her younger daughter Violet, born in 1888, the year before the family moved to Glasgow, died at Broughton when she was five. This was the first of many blows and possibly, being the first, the most painfully remembered. The child was buried in the old churchyard at Broughton where, as in so many Border churchyards, there is only a fragment left standing of the old church which had seen so many burials of her forebears.

Her younger son, Willie (after whom I am named) began what looked like being an exceptional career in the Indian Civil Service. My grandmother had not wished to let him go to India, had indeed, to my father's annoyance, lamented loudly on the subject. JB tried to persuade her that she would be as close to her children, or even closer, if they went away to do worthwhile things in the great world, than if she kept them near her, living in the next street: but I doubt very much that she was ever so persuaded. At all events Willie went to India in 1903, came home on leave for six months in 1909 and was back again on leave in 1912. He had contracted some illness, never at that time fully diagnosed. He returned from India unwell, grew worse, and died in a Glasgow nursing home at the age of thirty-two.

The year before, my grandfather was setting out with my grandmother, Anna and Walter, for a holiday in Switzerland, when he had a heart attack in London and was ordered home for rest and quiet. My grandmother then became seriously ill with a disease which involved high fevers and extreme depression. She recovered slowly from this, only to have a severe relapse in October 1911; and then three weeks later, in November, my grandfather died.

There was even worse to come. My youngest uncle, Alastair, born in 1894, after the family had settled in Glasgow, went to the war, was given a commission in the Cameron Highlanders, and transferred to the Royal Scots Fusiliers, of which Winston Churchill was for a while Colonel. Alastair, the one who seems to me to have been untouched by either his mother's melancholy or the *gravitas* of his elder brothers, the one in the old photographs who has always a wide, schoolboy grin—one of his last letters from the Front accompanied a photograph with the words 'Toujours Smiley-Face!'—died of wounds on 9 April 1917 after the battle of Arras. In his letter of condolence Churchill wrote: 'a most charming and gallant young officer . . . simple, conscientious and much loved by his comrades'.

Of Gran, my sister Alice wrote, in *A Scrap Screen*: 'My grandmother's personality affected me like a piece of grit in the eye.' Although a past mistress of the arts of creating comfort in the physical sense, our grandmother was adept at creating moral discomfort over almost any matter, however small. Yet, she was shrewd and experienced and, except where religious propriety forbade it, capable of seeing the funny side of our conduct. For a

Bible game, for instance, we chose, one Sunday, to play the story of
Noah. This involved filling the bath at Gala Lodge, and letting the
water overflow down the stairs and through the drawing-room
ceiling on to a tea party of ladies in hats. There were official ructions
because, apart from anything else, the laws of hospitality had been
transgressed; but it made my grandmother laugh, later on, when it
was safe to do so. She was, as my father said, a diplomat.

> My father was a true son of Mary: my mother own daughter to
> Martha. Had she had his character, the household must have
> crashed, and if he had been like her, childhood would have been a
> less wonderful thing for all of us . . . my mother was married at
> seventeen, and had at once to take charge of a Kirk and a manse,
> to which was soon added a family. A Scots minister must be
> something of a diplomat if he is to keep his congregation in a
> good temper; my father had about as much diplomacy as a
> rhinoceros, for he was utterly regardless of popular opinion, so
> my mother had to be ceaselessly observant, and an habitual
> smoother of ruffled feathers . . . successive congregations were
> handled so adroitly that my father's defects in tact were covered,
> and the charm of his personality given full play.

Although I should like to think that the rules of Christian conduct
were generally followed at Elsfield, the minutiae of
religious observance—texts, and Bible-readings, extra services,
and much illustrative quotation—were not part of our lives there.
Family prayers apart—and these were sporadic, depending on my
father's presence—and counting attendance at morning service on
Sundays at the village church, and enjoyable readings from *The
Pilgrim's Progress*, we did not live in continual anxiety about Grace,
nor with any strong sense of what was owed to Omnipotence in the
daily round. My grandmother, however, was, as JB said, 'a rigid
specialist'.

> Her world was the Church, or rather a little section of the
> Church. Her ambitions were narrowly ecclesiastical. . . . She
> had a passion for church services, which were to her a form of
> ritual; so many in the week were a proper recognition of the
> claims of religion. So was the reading of the requisite number of
> chapters from the Bible and other devotional literature.

I once amused my father by saying to him, when my grandmother had just left us after her usual spring visit: 'Look what Gran's left behind—a couple of lethal tracts and a chunk of Holy Writ!' My father must have been very like his own father in one particular—tolerance. He did not think the utterances of children, when ribald or impertinent, a certain sign of their being already half-sold to the Devil. Like his father, he taught by example rather than precept. We learned early, therefore, to respect his beliefs and principles, and usually did our best not to offend them.

Writing of his mother, he sometimes sounds drily amused; often, in life, she made him impatient. Yet there was a strong bond between them. She was, after all, only eighteen years older than he: she could, on those terms, have been an elder sister. He was, beyond question—and in spite of much doubt, misgiving and even alarm at the breadth of his ambitions and the speed of his career—the dearest and most admired being in her life.

She was a possessive mother and fiercely maternal. The bodily and spiritual well-being of her flock were never out of her mind. She nursed its members devotedly through their illnesses, and my carriage accident, which involved nearly a year in bed, must have taken severe toll of her strength. She lived in perpetual expectation of disaster, not to herself but to her children, and wore out her strength with needless anxieties; but when disaster did come, she faced it with coolness and courage. . . . Her success was largely due, as I have said, to a rigid specialisation on two things, family and Church. In a bookish household she alone was totally uninterested in literature. Public affairs only affected her if they affected her kirk. . . .

In the ordinary business of life she was apt to deal in moral and religious platitudes and in the prudential maxims which the Scots call 'owercomes' and which flourished especially in her family. . . . She had a wild subtlety of her own which gave her a wide prospect over human nature, and she could assess character with an acumen none the less infallible because charity was never absent. My one complaint was that, in practice, she was too charitable. No tramp was ever turned away from her door, and her tenderness towards bores was the despair of her family.

The reference by John Buchan to his carriage accident is a casual remark about a matter of great significance. When my father was five years old he fell out of a carriage and, somehow, a back wheel went over his head. (Sixty years later, in Canada, he was to meet a retired minister who, as a young man, had held the fracture closed until a doctor could be fetched.) My grandmother was so distraught by what had happened that she threw all Scottish proprieties to the winds, dashed into a strange cottage and rummaged in drawers and dresser until she found linen to tear into strips for bandaging John's head. Once home, the little boy underwent a trepanning operation—an operation which John Buchan was to discuss many years later, in Canada, with the famous neuro-surgeon Dr Wilder Penfield. Neither then knew that Penfield, before very long, would be fighting day and night to save JB's life after another such operation.

The immediate result of this childhood accident was that JB had to spend a year in bed. He had to learn to talk all over again and was forbidden to learn to read. When he was up and about once more, he taught himself to read from posters and advertisements in the Glasgow streets. Commenting in her biography on the accident, Janet Adam Smith wrote of the deep scar which it made on the left side of his forehead which 'enhanced the lean, Red Indian character of his face'. She continued: 'A more important, though secondary, effect was the striking change in his general health made by the year he had to spend in bed . . . after it he was tough and hardy, and never had a serious illness until 1911.' JB himself remarked that previously he had been a 'miserable headachy little boy'.

JB wrote to his mother every day of his life that he was away from her, or as nearly as the exigencies of war and travel would allow. When absent from home, he also wrote to my mother every day. He wrote to a great many people, and I think that letter-writing, even more than literature, turned his handwriting into the appalling cryptogram that it soon became. In the end, in Canada, and to my relief, he took to dictating his private letters along with his official correspondence.

In *Memory Hold-the-Door* my father's portrait of his mother is loving and sympathetic, and this he would certainly have thought is how a memorial should be. Nevertheless, she caused him, besides the anxiety during her very real illnesses, and sorrow with her in her bereavements, a great deal of not always minor irritation. Some of her attitudes and actions, particularly where my mother was concerned, caused him on one or two occasions to be very stern with her indeed. Generally, though, he put up with her admonitions, intimations of disaster, regrets and repinings, with perfect good humour. He was careful, too, not to upset her unnecessarily. For instance, there was the brewhouse at Elsfield to which I referred earlier—unused probably in deference to Gran. Sometimes I wonder whether my father regretted this incompletion to his then almost complete domestic economy. He had nothing against beer—indeed, an enormous cask stood always outside the cellar for household use and he would often drink it at luncheon from a silver mug. But, never having quite persuaded his mother that to attend the languid Anglican services in Elsfield Church was not necessarily to fling oneself into the arms of the Whore of Babylon, he very likely decided that it was simply not worth another running fight, over alcoholic beverages brewed on the premises, just for the pleasure of drinking his own brand of beer.

As I have mentioned, it was scarcely possible for the children of the manse not to grow up with a feeling of being somewhat set apart. When you add to that a particularly joyous family circle where the rigorous demands of duty in daily life were mitigated by omnivorous reading, the recital of ballads and stories about the great people and great moments of Scottish history; where highly imaginative and intelligent children acted and re-enacted in their play the cherished romantic past, it would not be surprising if that little band grew away from its contemporaries, grew more into itself, and came in the end to accept, and even to relish, an increasing sense of difference.

My father's youngest brother Alastair was, from the beginning of his twenty-three years of life, devotedly loved by this uncommonly affectionate family. When he was little they gave him the Gaelic name 'Mhor'—the Great One—and would have spoiled him completely had his been a nature capable of being spoiled. At the age of five or thereabouts he is said to have made a statement which perfectly contains the essence of his family's feelings about itself: 'We is the Buchans'.

Because of the clan system, which exists in the Lowlands also, although in a different form from the Highlands, there are few Scots who cannot claim a connexion, however far-stretched, with some noble or at least long-established family. This is one of the reasons for the abiding Scottish passion for genealogy, for noting and collating relationships into the farthest reaches of cousinage. It is, in my view, a perfectly harmless and even fortifying exercise, which only becomes snobbish or unpleasant when used as a ground for needless boasting or for claims of superiority over others.

In *Memory Hold-the-Door* JB wrote:

Like most Scottish families we believed ourselves to be gently
born. A certain John Buchan, a younger son of the ancient
Aberdeenshire house of Auchmacoy, came south in the beginning of the seventeenth century and was supposed to have
founded our branch. There was a missing link in the chain, and an
austere antiquary like my uncle would never admit that the
descent had more than a high probability; but we children
accepted it as a proven fact, and rejoiced that through Auchmacoy we could count kin back to the days of William the Lion.
So in the high story of Scotland we felt a proprietary interest.

The link must, in fact, have been satisfactorily dealt with because
Mr William Buchan, of Peebles, (the 'austere antiquary') applied to
the Lyon Court (the highest heraldic authority in Scotland) in 1895
for leave to use the arms of Auchmacoy, and these were granted to
him only slightly differenced. The sunflower crest of Buchan
which, for Auchmacoy, has two flowers, came to Great-uncle
William with one. When JB was made a peer his arms continued the
same, with the addition of supporters (a stag and a falcon) and a
rather stiff-looking sunflower, with one pair of leaves. Now, if
William Buchan was an austere scholar, so was his nephew John,
yet as far back as I can remember the sunflower and the family
motto were in evidence: on my father's gold half-hunter, on his
signet, and on his bookplates in various guises. Our motto, sometimes held up to me in my early youth as an essential rule of life,
always struck me as rather priggish, at least in one interpretation.
Non Inferiora Secutus: 'Not following meaner things'. It might also
be interpreted, in a less moral, more worldly sense, as going firmly
for the top.

The district of Buchan in Aberdeenshire contains a great many
people called Buchan; on the war memorial in one small fishing
village near Peterhead there are no fewer than fourteen. Nearby,
at Auchmacoy, in a late Georgian house not far from the square
keep of the old castle, lives the 'chief of the name', Buchan of
Auchmacoy.

The Buchans consider themselves a *clan*, not a sept. They are the
old 'tribe of the land' of the province of Buchan, and since the
Comyn, on marrying the heiress [at the end of the twelfth
century], did not take her name and arms, the tribe continued as a
clan under their own chief. In 1830 the family and name of
Buchan were received in Lyon Court as descendants of the

78

ancient Celtic Earls of Buchan . . . and Buchan of Auchmacoy, in Aberdeenshire, as being the chief of the name of Buchan. The family has held that estate (part of the old earldom lands) from the dawn of history, and tradition says that the Buchans, unlike the Comyns, were loyal to the Bruce, and therefore allowed to retain their patrimony.*

I mention all this to show that romance and a devotion to 'old, unhappy, far-off things' were bone of the bone of my father's family, and contributed to its members' sense of being set apart. For many generations after John Buchan the first had left Auchmacoy, thought to have gone as Master of the Horse to King James IV at Stirling (told to go out and seek his fortune, I imagine—too many mouths to feed at home), that particular lot of Buchans lived on in Stirlingshire, at a place called Ribbald of Polmaes, getting some sort of a living and approximating to Trevelyan's 'out-at-elbows gentlemen' who had little but their pride to sustain them: their pride and perhaps their brains. The brains certainly showed up in the early nineteenth century when two lawyer cousins set up their practices in Edinburgh and Peebles. The pride, as we have seen, was never lost, and perhaps it was his sense of being settled squarely in his country's most exciting history which gave the Rev. John Buchan his individual style. In these days of anguish about 'crises of identity' it is pleasant to contemplate a man who had no doubts whatever as to who he was, nor what he was supposed to be doing here below.

It is possible to wonder, considering the reputation of my father's family for being 'douce' whether the early Buchans had some of the same, somewhat other-worldly quality. This seems unlikely in medieval Scotland, although intelligence and foresight they may have had in greater measure than others of their time. The fact remains that of the three generations which I have been able to study at all closely, the quality mentioned appears in every single member, and is remarked on again and again. This in itself is odd. Odd also is the fact that they seem to have been so little inclined to marry. My great-grandfather had three sons and two daughters. Only the eldest son married. He in turn had four sons and one surviving daughter and, of these, only the eldest married. Had JB not married, that small section of the Buchan clan would have come to a full stop. It has since expanded: JB has fifteen grandchildren.

*Frank Adam, *Clans, Septs and Regiments of the Scottish Highlands*.

4

THE SPELL OF OXFORD

I have never been perfectly satisfied by the phrase 'a self-made man', applied not only to JB but to any successful person. Obviously it is a useful description of a man's success in changing, by his own efforts alone, his fortunes and his social influence, but it tends to give a merely two-dimensional appearance to the person so described. The self-made man seems too often to be seen as having sprung from nowhere into the life of the world, fully armed for the struggle and without antecedents, yet this can never be the case. Most often I think he is the culmination, the point to which generations of his forebears, consciously or unconsciously, have been tending, the final result in a long and detailed chain of experiments.

It is as though an ancient blade, roughly made and notched by toil, has been hammered and smoothed, ground and polished down the generations to the point where, finally, bright as a diamond and sharp as an epigram, it is ready to cut a straight swathe through the musty fields of convention and habit and received ideas.

The career, then, may be self-made, but the man himself is made by other things. Part of John Buchan was made by Scottish history, part by his upbringing, with its insistence on the need for effective living, its strong emphasis on scholarship, and its coloured groundwork of fairy story and historical romance. There was, in addition, nothing mean nor impositive in the personalities among whom he came to manhood, nor in the world outside the charmed circle of his home. He was born at a time of national ferment over the future of the Kirk. Religious controversy raged round his youthful head, and even his gentle father who, in Church politics, belonged to the extreme conservative wing, delighted, when a member of the Annual Assembly, 'in stirring up all the strife he could by indicting for heresy some popular preacher or professor'. JB was, therefore, from the beginning, no stranger to the battles of the world and its conflicting causes, nor to the idea of going out himself to put things right.

Scotland was then producing, as she still does, a great number of skilled professionals—lawyers, clergymen, doctors, surgeons, engineers—far greater than could possibly be absorbed by Scotland's economy alone. The British Empire, in spite of some ominous setbacks, was still a *stupor mundi*, and it is hard to see how it could have been kept going so successfully for so long without its complement of energetic, high-principled, adaptable, self-exiling Scots. The idea, then, of going out into the world to seek a fortune—or at least to make a living—must have been powerfully in the air throughout JB's childhood and youth. Further, we might think that continual exposure to the teachings of the Bible, continual reminders that 'Faith without works is dead', constant repetition of the Parable of the Talents, would have provided a strong stimulus to endeavour in any normally affectionate and dutiful boy—if it did not have the opposite effect of sending him rapidly and gleefully to the bad.

The clue to JB's astonishing single-mindedness—and whether admired or not it is still astonishing—lies in this early discipline, his family's and his own. To the strict observances of religious life, the irrefragable demands of Church and charity, must be added the bracing, striving atmosphere of Hutchesons' Grammar School and Glasgow University, in what was probably the heyday of Scottish education.

From an early age he had been one to set himself goals, and there exists a 'List of things to be done in the next 4 years', written on his twenty-first birthday in 1896. This was divided into Literary (for instance, 'Arrange for serial and book rights of *John Burnet of Barns*'), Academic ('Get the Newdigate' 'Get the Stanhope', etc.), Probable Income, and Practical ('Take strong interest in politics', 'Be called to the Bar'). What he did not achieve, he crossed out—and there are comparatively few crossings out. Another list he drew up was 'Honours Gained and to be Gained', the honours in question being mostly publications—starting with that of a selection of Bacon's essays which John Buchan edited and wrote an introduction to at the age of nineteen—literary prizes (including the Newdigate and the Stanhope) and positions of academic eminence.

If I find these ambitions both impressive and touching, I am aware that others do not. Concentrated ambition (except in commerce) and the pursuit of excellence (except, perhaps, in the theatre and sport) are suspect at present. The thought of someone deliberately setting out to excel, to discern great heights and determine to climb them, seems to the present generation in some way excessive, out of measure, going altogether, and perhaps unfairly, too far.

Having known the man, and knowing a good deal about his beginnings, I can only watch with sympathy the lonely, intrinsically lonely boy in Glasgow, poised on the threshold of an extraordinary career. Cribbed by a dearly loved but necessarily circumscribed way of life, and even though surrounded by intelligences almost as lively as his own, at a moment in history, and in a place where hard work and high endeavour were admired rather than despised, he yet knew that he must find his way out into a greater world, a larger and more demanding sphere. The way out, for such as he, must be through the intellect, and through work and yet more work. This is not to suggest that he was in any way what his Oxford contemporaries would have called a 'grind'. Simply, he was what I have always thought of as a *directed person*—I have not known many—one who would not, could not in fact, fail to follow what seemed a pre-ordained path.

There was an old nurses' saying—'Your eyes are bigger than your stomach'—which came into use when appetite for food failed after a too enthusiastic start. JB's eyes were certainly big where intellectual achievement and the prizes which confirm it were concerned: but his stomach, in the old sense of a repository of courage, was greater still. I have sometimes thought that a very rough division might be made between those who, throughout life, carefully avoid biting off more than they can chew, and those who gallantly learn to chew what they have been impelled to bite off.

It would be wrong to think that the sharpest spur to success in the young John Buchan's life was need of money, but it must certainly be counted in. His father, least worldly of men, had probably never come to terms with economics; it was left to his brisk and capable wife to bring up and somehow feed, clothe and educate five children on what was provided by his stipend and the 'sustentation fund' of various parishes. In any event the family, though deeply united and generally, sometimes uproariously, happy, and lacking nothing needed by the mind and heart, was decidedly short of cash. John, as the eldest, seeing his parents growing older, and his father tiring from overwork, and his highly gifted brothers and sister in need of the same chances of self-fulfilment as himself, knew that somehow he must bring some ease to their circumstances, and that as soon as possible.

None of this, of course, explains the powers of concentration, and the ability to organise his time, which JB exhibited at so early an age. The spurs were there, the needs were evident; but 'between the desire and the fulfilment falls the shadow . . .'; not everybody would have been capable, first of seeing what had to be done, and secondly of devising an effective form of self-discipline, nor would have had so fine a sense of priority, so acute and exact an awareness of his own powers. The talent for organisation, brought out, perhaps forced, so early was to show up again in JB's work for Milner in South Africa, in his creation of the Department of Information towards the end of the 1914 war, and in his various highly successful publishing ventures for Nelson's in the first years of his married life.

When JB got a bursary to Glasgow University in 1892, his seventeeth year, he moved into a world more intellectually stimulating than any he had so far known. The University, the second oldest in Scotland, had at that time occupied its monumental gothic buildings, designed by Gilbert Scott, for only five years, and was at one of the most brilliant moments in its long and distinguished history. Edward Caird, later to be Master of Balliol, was Professor of Moral Philosophy, A. C. Bradley Professor of English and, perhaps most important for JB, Gilbert Murray, then only in his midtwenties, had just become Professor of Greek. With such teachers as these the still adolescent Buchan's questing intellect found much to consider in fields far beyond the scope of the manse in Queen Margaret Drive.

The influence of Gilbert Murray on JB was very great, and their friendship lasted all his life. My father was never to become what is called a pure scholar, or else no doubt he would have ended an honourable career in classical scholarship with a chair at some university, and that would have been that. But what the young Murray found in the even younger Buchan was a splendid brain, a truly enquiring turn of mind, a seemingly unlimited capacity for absorbing knowledge and, above all, a romantic imagination and a poetic sensibility equivalent to his own.

It must have become apparent quite early in JB's Glasgow career that this was not to be his ultimate aim. He must, quite soon, have set his sights on Oxford, and those—they are mainly Scottish—who think this ambition in some way belittling of the great institution of Glasgow miss the point, I think, completely.

JB took all that Glasgow University had to give him and was

grateful for it; but his appetite had grown with the diet he had there; he thought that there were certain things that he needed to learn, not all of them academic, which only Oxford could teach. He had begun already to want a future in politics; he had started to write, and to take writing seriously; whatever the virtues of Glasgow— and they were very many—he felt that he would never reach his true self-expression there, or even perhaps in the Scotland of his time, dear as it was to him.

Janet Adam Smith has suggested that these new horizons for JB caused certain tensions at home. JB's parents must have felt that their oldest child was growing away from them, especially his father, to whom philosophical speculations were alien, and who positively rebelled against intellectual criticism which tended to call in question beliefs and traditions which he thought immutable. 'It was odd that he should have been by profession a theologian, for he was wholly lacking in philosophical interest or aptitude,' JB wrote in his autobiography, and earlier, with a very young man's impatience: 'My good father has not the proper turn for speculation. He cares too little about logic and sees things in a pictorial way.'

I return to my own, possibly Calvinistic, definition, a *directed person*, in considering JB at this stage. Already he had had a book published: his *Essays and Apothegms of Francis Lord Bacon* appeared in 1894. He was to say, nearly fifty years later: 'Looking back, my industry fills me with awe.' Those were days at a Scottish university when the work was done in one solid, six-month 'session' from October to April.

Things have changed now, but in my day a Scottish university still smacked of the Middle Ages. The undergraduates lived in lodgings in the city and most of them cultivated the Muses on a slender allowance of oatmeal. Every morning I had to walk four miles to the eight o'clock class through every variety of the winter weather with which Glasgow fortifies her children . . . fog like soup, drenching rains, winds that swirled down the cavernous streets, mornings that dawned bright and clear over snow. . . . My summers were spent in blessed idleness, fishing, tramping and bicycling up and down the Lowlands. But my winters were periods of beaver-like toil and monkish seclusion. I returned home early each afternoon and thereafter was at my books until midnight.

John Buchan, Esq., Writer to the Signet, JB's grandfather. An able and well-liked lawyer and banker, he lost his money in the 1878 crash of the City of Glasgow Bank, and died a broken man in 1883.

JB's Uncle Willie—'"equable, alert and gay", no one enjoyed the good things of life better than he'; from him John Buchan inherited interests wider than those of his background.

John Buchan aged four, before the carriage accident that disfigured his forehead.

'We is the Buchans'—*left to right*: Anna ('O. Douglas'), Walter, their mother, Helen, holding Alastair ('Mhor'), JB, Willie, and the Rev. John Buchan.

John Buchan while at Brasenose, 1895–9. 'I felt that I had been pitchforked into a kindergarten . . . I must have been at that time an intolerable prig.'

Oxford friends—the 'revenants from the Augustan age': *top left*: Auberon Herbert (Bron Lucas); *top right*: Raymond Asquith; and Tommy Nelson (*below*). All were killed in the Great War, to JB's lasting sadness; he saw them as being 'now part of that immortal England which knows not age or weariness or defeat'.

Lord Milner, the 'seer of Empire', in Johannesburg: he sought to recruit 'young men with energetic and unconventional minds'—the famous 'Kindergarten'. JB joined him in South Africa in October 1901.

'I have ridden many miles, faster than I cared, to avoid losing my breeches to a commando whose clothing had given out . . .'

An informal picnic in the veldt, JB, seated, wearing a disreputable hat. 'I would have been content . . . if I had a chance of making a corner of the desert blossom and the solitary place glad.'

Susan Grosvenor. 'John thought me haughty, while I thought him conceited and difficult to talk to.' They married in July 1907.

On honeymoon on the Lido, still being transformed from a small fishing village.

Left: The rising writer and publisher skating with Susan.

Above: Walking was one of John Buchan's passions. For moments of true informality he wore rough old tweeds and an extraordinary shapeless hat which gave him a strangely raffish appearance.

JB with his first child, Alice, born in 1908—one of the rare photographs that show him smiling.

Lt-Col. John Buchan during the Great War. 'The war left me with an intense craving for a country life. It was partly that I wanted quiet after turmoil . . . it was also a new-found delight in . . . small homely things after so many alien immensities.' Many of his closest friends were dead, as was his youngest brother, and his health was irrevocably breaking.

'So I sold my house and bought the little manor-house of Elsfield . . .' With its purchase a dream began to take shape, but even so my parents must have had to weigh its advantages against any ideas of an architectural gem that they might have been cherishing.

John Buchan's library at Elsfield was entirely the place he had planned, the collection he needed, the inspiration he sought. Behind the desk are his bound manuscripts.

It is hard to see what could have stopped the young John Buchan from proceeding to a rocketing career. Marcel Proust once, in a letter to his mother, said that he wished he could break a leg, be confined to his room and prevented from going to parties, and thus be obliged to write. His asthma, in the end, did the trick for him. It would be interesting to speculate what JB might have done—not by breaking a leg: he would quickly have accommodated that—if some really crippling ailment, such as asthma, had come along to slow him down. Turned in on himself, prevented by the sanctions of illness from pursuing a life of action, his imagination working outwards from a fixed point, he might have produced a very different kind of fiction. At least two of his works show that he had a capacity for profundity and for acute psychological perception. He might have been a more 'serious', and, therefore, to some critics more acceptable, novelist; but, as a person, he might have been less interesting.

The university had little social life. Those who were far from home lived, for the most part, extremely frugally in lodgings; those whose homes were in Glasgow probably had more of the normal pleasures of youth; but not JB. That he was something of a disappointment to his brothers and sisters and their cheerful contemporaries comes out in their writings about him. That he was something of a prig he has himself acknowledged.

Most people know the much-repeated lines of Milton which begin 'Fame is the spur . . .' and end 'To scorn delights and live laborious days.' It seems to me that JB's spur, to begin with, was not to seek one particular kind of fame, to be clearly envisaged and single-mindedly pursued; rather it was the instinct for excellence, the desire to excel. With excellence of the right kind, fame would accrue in any case. He was also, as we have seen, in no doubt about the need to make money. One thing is sure, however—there was to be no sporting with Amaryllis in the shade. During the session he scorned even the most innocent of delights, and his days were indeed laborious.

A golden reward awaited him. He must have heard many things about Oxford, from his professors or from other young men who had gone there from Scotland. All other considerations apart, the very idea of a university divided up into colleges, each a manageable cosmos on its own, and offering to an undergraduate the luxury of rooms all to himself, must have seemed little short of paradisal. Further, Oxford had bred in the past, and still contained, men whose minds enormously appealed to JB, and chief of these, the one he dearly wished to approach more closely, was Walter Pater, then a Fellow of Brasenose.

JB has written much about Oxford, but perhaps the most telling passage describes his first visit when, in 1894, he went there to sit his scholarship examination.

It was, I remember, bitter winter weather. The Oxford streets, when I arrived late at night from the North, were deep in snow. My lodgings were in Exeter College, and I recall the blazing fires, a particularly succulent kind of sausage, and coffee such as I had never known in Scotland. I wrote my examination papers in Christ Church hall, that noblest of Tudor creations. I felt as if I had slipped through some chink in the veil of the past and become a mediaeval student. Most vividly I recollect walking in the late afternoon in Merton Street and Holywell and looking at snow-laden gables which had scarcely altered since the Middle Ages. In that hour Oxford claimed me, and her bonds have never been loosed.

When JB went up to Brasenose in 1895, he was twenty years old, at least a year older than the majority of freshmen coming from English schools. He was also very poor. His accounts for his first year at Oxford show an anxious frugality—seeing these, even the stoniest-hearted enemy of success might think twice before grudging him the financial ease which he was to create for himself later. 'For two years I could not afford to dine in hall.' Dinner in hall cost about two shillings. 'My Oxford bills for the first year were a little over £100, for my second year about £150. After that, what with scholarships, prizes and considerable emoluments from books and articles, I became rather rich for an undergraduate.'

It might be interesting to speculate what courses John Buchan might have followed had his grandfather's fortunes not suffered so from the crash of the City of Glasgow Bank. That his own father was famous for his total disregard of money was due principally, of course, to his preoccupation with higher things. Nevertheless, even he must have realised, however vaguely, as a young man, that he stood to be very comfortably off at his father's death. Accordingly, his natural inclination 'to take no thought for the morrow' may have been reinforced by the knowledge that the morrow had, so to speak, been taken care of. One of his obituarists, who had studied with him at Edinburgh, wrote: 'At the New College, where we were students together, he was a decidedly religious character; while something in his appearance suggested that he had been brought up in less straitened circumstances than the majority.' The straitened circumstances were to come: but supposing they had not; supposing John Buchan the writer had had a sound financial backing, what other road might he have taken?

He would undoubtedly have travelled farther afield than Switzerland or France, and his fondness for, and considerable skill in, mountaineering would very likely have impelled him to the Himalayas or the High Karakoram. His delight in remote places and unconventional people might have led him to spend himself in odd byways of reasearch. However, if my grandfather had indeed inherited money, he would almost certainly have given the greater part of it away, probably to the Kirk, and my father's situation would in the end have been very much the same.

As things were, JB started life like his hero, Sir Walter Scott, who was the son of an Edinburgh lawyer, related by blood to an ancient Border house: 'I was born a Scotsman, and a bare one. Therefore I was born to fight my way in the world.' That sentence says more about the Scots of the nineteenth century than volumes of sociological study. Its logic, stern but irrefutable, has inspired many Scotsmen to extraordinary deeds, both in their own interests and those of their fellow-men.

JB might have fallen for ever in love with Oxford at his first visit, but when once he got there he found plenty to criticise.

> My first impressions of Oxford were unhappy. The soft autumn air did not suit my health; the lectures which I attended seemed jejune and platitudinous, and the regime slack, after the strenuous life of Glasgow; I played no game well enough to acquire an absorbing interest in it. Above all, being a year older than my contemporaries I felt that I had been pitchforked into a kindergarten. . . . I must have been at that time an intolerable prig.

There were some who, for a while, must indeed have thought him so.

It was always axiomatic that a gentleman should learn to hold his liquor: if he could not hold it, then he must not drink. The young freshmen of BNC, freed from the restrictions of home and school, and with money of their own to spend, were busy making their first experiments in drinking. JB, reared in a totally abstaining household—partly because a manse, in those days, could scarcely be otherwise; partly because, in a poor parish, the heartbreaking effects of drunkenness were a daily spectacle—was not inclined to be tolerant of inebriated adolescents. 'Paper-faced babies,' he once told me, still scornfully, 'puking all over the chapel steps.' One night, in the old Presbyterian tradition of 'testifying', he waded into a crowd of those infant pukers, who were demonstrating against the College Principal, Dr Heberden, whom JB liked and admired, and made them a speech not unworthy of John Knox at his most trenchant. Nobody attacked him. Nobody seems to have told him to go away and mind his own business. The crowd, half-stunned by alcohol, was further stunned to silence by a torrent of Scottish eloquence. From being a totally obscure young man, John Buchan became the talk of the university. No doubt the story of that night lost little in the telling. No doubt some people were affronted; but the general feeling must have been that someone truly original had come to Oxford, someone who would have to be reckoned with.

It was not that JB was puritanical about drinking. All he asked was that it should be done with civility. A phrase of his that I remember was 'Hopeless head for drink: gets drunk on the sniff of a claret-cork.' His own head was strong, and though abstemious all his life, he was certainly no spoil-sport at the parties of his Oxford friends.

John Buchan wanted to go to Brasenose because Walter Pater was a Fellow, but, sadly perhaps for both of them, Pater had died in 1894, the year in which JB sat for his scholarship. It had been Pater's *Plato and Platonism* even more than *Marius the Epicurean* or *Studies in the History of the Renaissance* that had caught his imagination and won his respect. Brasenose, otherwise, was not a conspicuously intellectual college. Its record for games and sports was impressive, and it produced some highly able and even famous people; but what JB found in it to love, apart from its small size and ancient history, was its Englishness. The scholars came mostly from grammar schools and the lesser public schools; the commoners largely from the county gentry of Lancashire and the North. 'The average Brasenose man was very close to English soil, and from him I learned some of the secret of the English character, that hardly communicable thing which even a Scotsman born in the same island understands only by slow degrees.'

Let it be said that a great many Scotsmen, then as now, would not even have tried to understand the English character, fearing perhaps to weaken a comforting sense of ancient wrongs. It should be put to the credit of the English that they were willing to welcome and immediately accept this forthright northern romantic, recognising with a shrewdness which may have come from country breeding that here they were confronted with a rare and rewarding personality.

One important quality of my father's was in evidence for all his life: a really outsize gift for friendship. This seems to have declared itself first at Oxford. Although, on his long idyllic spring and summer holidays, spent in Tweeddale and involving, with every year that passed, explorations farther and farther afield, he made friends as he went with shepherds, farmers, roadmenders, bag-men—everyone who came his way—he probably did not give of his best to his Glasgow contemporaries. The reason for that was the Herculean schedule of work to which I have referred, and which led to the Junior Hulme Scholarship at Brasenose.

In the softer air of Oxford, among people who astonished him by their maturity, their elegance of mind, their scorn for the very go-getting which was (as it had to be) a strong feature of Scottish life, another part of JB's nature expanded joyfully. He had possibly never imagined that such beings existed in his own century. He gave them the treasures of his learning, his wit and his imagination, and, for all his life, a part of his heart. They, in their turn, admired him, cherished him, frequently teased him, and predicted great things for him not, oddly enough, in literature but in politics or the law.

Brasenose is well placed for visiting the other colleges which line the High Street or are to be found clustered around at convenient distances; it could well be at the very centre of collegiate life, being only a few yards from the Radcliffe Camera and close to the University Church. From such a centre it was easy for JB, moving at his habitual high speed, to exchange visits with friends in other colleges or join them for festivities in their numerous clubs.

'I have a great many so-called friends,' he wrote to his sister, a few years after leaving Oxford. 'I haven't very many real ones,' and went on to give a short list. Of JB's closest circle of friends four were Scottish: John Edgar, whom he had known in Glasgow, Johnnie Jameson from Galloway, and Stair ('Sandy') Gillon and Tommy Nelson from Edinburgh. He lived on the same staircase in Brasenose as Taffy Boulter, and, when, in his fourth year, he went out of college into rooms in the High Street, he shared these with Boulter and Johnnie Jameson. The other members of JB's set were Cuthbert Medd, Harold Baker, the two Herbert cousins, Aubrey and Auberon, and Raymond Asquith, who came up in 1897.

The fact that most of his friends were from other colleges—seven of them from Balliol alone—did not mean that he was not firmly established in Brasenose. There also he had many friends, especially among the rowing fraternity, who liked him so much that they would frequently interrupt his highly-geared working schedule by coming to gossip in his rooms.

Although the principal bond between most of this group of young men was intellectual, and although each was hard-working and academically successful, they had enough spare energy to excel at games and sports, or go in for bold and imaginative adventures. Besides Tommy Nelson, who was to become famous as a Rugby player, Johnnie Jameson boxed for the university, Sandy Gillon captained the New College Fifteen, Raymond Asquith captained the Balliol football Eleven, and Auberon Herbert rowed for two years running in the Oxford boat.

The two friends, Asquith and Baker, who had come to Oxford from Winchester, impressed JB particularly with what he was later to call their 'amazing maturity'.

> They seemed, while still in their teens, to have covered the whole range of human knowledge. Their urbanity put to shame my angularity. Their humanism confounded my dogmatism. They were certain of only one thing—that all things were uncertain. They were interested in the value of things and not the prize.

The inner circle of this close, small world of friends comprised JB, Raymond Asquith, Cuthbert Medd and Harold Baker. They were the real high-flyers. They might not have been narrowly bent on prizes, but they won them just the same. All four left Oxford with firsts in Greats; and all but Cuthbert Medd has been President of the Union. Harold Baker became a Fellow of New College, while Raymond Asquith and Medd won prize fellowships to All Souls. JB won the Stanhope and Newdigate prizes, Asquith the Ireland and Craven, and Baker the Gaisford and Craven.

The star of stars in John Buchan's Oxford galaxy was Raymond Asquith, eldest son of the Liberal Prime Minister. JB had a highly developed sense of veneration: when he found a worthy object for it, his affection and appreciation were unstinted. Of Raymond Asquith much has been written, but no one, I think, has celebrated better than JB his particular magic. Brilliant Asquith undoubtedly was but his brilliance, combined with great handsomeness, an apparently effortless skill in all kinds of achievements, and a certain quality of aloofness, might have made him somewhat forbidding. The close friendship he had with JB was, in many ways, an attraction of opposites. For instance, he was often unkind, something which was nearly impossible for John Buchan.

Let it be admitted—there were times when he was almost inhuman. He would destroy some piece of honest sentiment with a jest, and he had no respect for the sacred places of dull men. There was always a touch of scorn in him for obvious emotion, obvious creeds, and all the accumulated lumber of prosaic humanity—that was a defect of his great qualities. He kept himself for his friends and refused to bother about the world. But to such as were admitted to his friendship he would deny nothing . . . it was the relation of all others in life for which he had been born with a peculiar genius.

Cuthbert Medd died of typhoid in 1902, just as it was being arranged for him to join JB on Milner's staff in South Africa. Aubrey Herbert, the far-travelled, the mysterious and unpredictable, upon whom JB based the character of Sandy Arbuthnot, was wounded in the Great War, and twice taken prisoner, but survived to be offered the throne of Albania. His cousin Auberon (Bron) inherited the ancient barony of Lucas, went to South Africa as *Times* correspondent, was shot in the foot and lost a leg. In spite of this he continued the sporting life that he loved and, when the 1914 war came, found his way into the Royal Flying Corps, became an exceptional pilot, and was finally shot down and killed over enemy lines. Raymond Asquith was killed in September 1916 when his battalion of Grenadiers advanced on Les Boeufs.

Our roll of honour is long but it holds no nobler figure. He will stand for those of us who are left as an incarnation of the spirit of the land he loved. . . . He loved his youth, and his youth has become eternal. Debonair and brilliant and brave, he is now part of that immortal England which knows not age or weariness or defeat.

JB, all his life, made a firm differentiation between games and sports. Sports, for him, were shooting, fishing, hunting, sailing, rock-climbing, walking—all occupations where people were competing against nature. Games were competitions between people. This distinction seems nowadays to have disappeared completely.

At Oxford he tried his hand at most games, without much success. What he really enjoyed were the wild and testing adventures, for no known reason called 'booms', which he and his friends would undertake together. These were competitive, in a sense: to walk the eighty miles from Oxford to Cambridge, for example, within twenty-four hours; to make long canoe trips up the tributaries of the Thames; and, most hair-raising of all, to ride point-to-point in a straight line, over a course ruled on a map, and negotiating such obstacles as lakes, woods, farmyards and gardens on the way. These exploits sometimes brought them to the doors of the police court. In the evening the friends dined together and told their adventures.

Of the friends who were closest to him during his time at Oxford, JB also wrote:

In that circle there was no pose, unless it be a pose in youth to have no pose. The 'grand manner' in the eighteenth-century sense was cultivated, which meant a deliberate lowering of key in professions, and a scrupulous avoidance of parade. A careless good-breeding, an agreeable worldliness were its characteristics. It was a very English end to strive for, and by no means a common one, for urbanity of mind is rarely the aim of youth. It implied, perhaps, an undue critical sense, and a failure in certain generous foibles. . . . To think of a career and be prudent in laying its foundations was, in our eyes, the unpardonable sin. It was well enough to be successful if success could be achieved unostentatiously and carried lightly, but there must be no appearance of seeking it. . . . It was our business to be regardless of consequences, to be always looking for preposterous adventures and planning crazy feats, and to be most ready for a brush with constituted authority. The peculiar feature of our circle was that this physical exuberance was found among men of real intellectual power. . . . In the world of action we were ripe for any venture; in the things of the mind we were critical and decorous, chary of enthusiasm—*revenants* from the Augustan age.

If, as was so frequently remarked by critics and commentators at the time of the centenary of his birth, 1975, John Buchan 'worshipped success', the lines quoted above make interesting reading. I think that this particular objection is based on an over-serious reading of JB's popular novels, the ones which he called 'shockers' and we should call 'thrillers'. Writing what was often a not very plausible story, drawing rather heavily on coincidence, and needing to seize and hold his reader's attention at the outset, and to engender that 'willing suspension of disbelief' on which the success of his story depended, he thought it as well to make his characters as portentous as possible—they were generally the 'greatest living' exponents of something. This seems to me to have been shrewd, given the terms of the game (for to him it was a game, even though he allowed seriousness its place from time to time), and few of his readers can have objected to being let in to the company of exalted people, almost always the first in their field, in exalted places, doing rather high-flown things. For the most part, as we know, they lapped it all up.

In 1968 Mr Alan Bennett wrote and produced a revue in London, called *Forty Years On*. In that there was a gently satirical and very funny sketch based on JB's characters, and containing some such line as 'He's the finest philatelist west of Bournemouth.' When I told Mr Bennett how exact I thought this was (my father would have said 'what good spoof') he replied: 'We vary it on most nights. The third best theologian in Lincolnshire was another one we tried.'

Some of JB's Oxford friends came from rich families, but by no means all of them, or even the majority. Some had family businesses where a place was being kept for them. Some were nearly as poor as he. But in those comparatively unstressful days, before two great wars, and their attendant disillusionment; before the vast growth of populations and the extension of easy travel, the world still appeared an uncrowded, exciting and mysteriously promising place. It was still possible for a young man to believe that, with brains and effort (and of course the prizes which would proclaim these), a useful and rewarding career after university was well within his grasp.

JB's friends were much amused, as well as impressed, by his ability to be at once severely practical and wildly romantic. His practical good sense, and his pursuit of opportunities beyond Oxford, with London editors and publishers, improved his financial circumstances out of measure so that, by the end of his third year, he was better off than any of his friends. Such success would not have won their admiration if he had not seemed to achieve it so effortlessly and with it a number of university prizes such as the Stanhope, the Newdigate, the Senior Hulme scholarship at Brasenose, and a first in Greats.

It was his ability to apportion his time, to accomplish what he wanted within it, and then to be free to join in all the fun that was going, which seemed to his friends so astonishing and so admirable. If those friends were intellectually mature, JB, with as good mental equipment, was more mature than they: he was already making, and paying, his own way in the world.

My father several times remarked to me that the eighteen-nineties were a wonderful time for an aspiring writer. He might have added that they were days of high opportunity for any brilliant young man at Oxford or Cambridge who meant to make an impression in London. Politics, literature, the law, the sciences, diplomacy, the Church, colonial administration—all were interested (in varying degrees) in recruiting fresh talent. Worldly dons dined out in London and gave their hostesses news of the high-flyers shortly to appear on the London scene. Publishers and editors were ready to encourage good young writers, to commission articles and book reviews, to consider seriously stories and novels.

Certain hostesses had considerable political as well as social influence. Money still ran deep and strong in a narrow stream. Entertaining was lavish and continual during the Season in London: out of season it took place in country houses, where long weekend parties were given, or whole weeks devoted to racing or cricket or, in Scotland, to fishing and shooting. The tendency to divide people into 'age-groups' had not yet asserted itself and so, at a dinner party for twenty or thirty, there might be cabinet ministers, people from high society of all ages (some famous for wit or beauty), writers, explorers, soldiers, the young lion just down from university, and the youngest débutante enjoying (or otherwise) her first Season.

While JB was racing through his final year at Oxford, driving four-in-hand, inventing clubs with ever more arcane rules and rituals, speaking at, and in the end presiding over, the Union, he was being watched with interest by a number of London people whose power and position might have caused even his eager heart to miss a beat.

For anybody who has only known Oxford since the Second World War, it must be next to impossible to imagine what university life was like in the eighteen-nineties. In the nineteen-twenties, the time of my childhood, a good many of the old Oxford ways remained and, even in the thirties, when my brothers and I were there, and in spite of unpleasant and menacing noises from the world outside, it was still possible to consider it as an enclave of civilisation, a protected place.

When JB went up to Oxford its atmosphere, for all that four women's colleges had already been established, could still fairly have been called monastic. 'I had the privilege of knowing some of the bachelor Fellows of the old regime, "characters" all, who kept the monastic flag flying in spite of the new domesticated Oxford of the Parks.' ('The dons were scattered over North Oxford, at gay, contentious little dinner-parties,' Evelyn Waugh was to write in *Decline and Fall*, thirty years later.)

To all intents and purposes, Oxford in the nineties was still a unisexual society. The women's colleges tended to keep their inmates to themselves; the latter in any case, were not made welcome by the more conservative members of the university who felt that they were out of place in an entrenched and comfortable masculine world.

With rare exceptions, the male undergraduates, freed at last from the straitjacket of the public school and enjoying their freedom, had no desire to complicate their lives with emotional entanglements, however romantic, nor to be forced into serious intellectual dispute by 'intense' young women. There would be time enough for such things after they had left the university. Women—represented for many of them by dominant or plaintive mothers, moralising maiden aunts, bossy sisters, nurses and governesses—may well have been a feature of life which, for the time being at any rate, they were glad to be allowed to avoid.

'The great point of Oxford, in fact the whole point of Oxford, is that there are no girls.' Compton Mackenzie, who went up to Oxford three or four years after my father had gone down, wrote in *Sinister Street* (published during the First War) what JB considered a good description of an Oxford sufficiently like his own. His record of the anxieties and general commotion attending Eights Week, when mothers and sisters had to be invited down and entertained by their sons and brothers, gives a delightful picture of a leisurely, self-regarding, rather indolent body being prodded into unwonted brisk activity by a sharp social stick.

It would be pointless to try to make any kind of comparison between the Oxford of then and now, where relations between the sexes are concerned. Too many, too profound changes have taken place. But to assume—as some critics seem disposed to do—that because Oxford was unisexual, or only just post-monastic, in JB's day; because he and his friends were so obviously devoted to one another, and so unregretful about the absence of women in their lives, therefore the university must have been given over to homosexuality is, in my view, a serious misreading of social history. To begin with, though cheerful bawdry was acceptable, sexuality in practice was considered to be 'bad form', and worse form still if recounted, discussed or bragged about. Furthermore, young men of my father's generation had been brought up to 'respect' women. (The women of their world, a much more conventional, close-knit and controlled world than could be found anywhere nowadays in the West, had a vested interest in that particular piece of propaganda. Much depended on it, including the stability of marriage itself, and the safeguarding of virginity, still thought indispensable before marriage.)

Those young men knew much in theory about mortal love, read their poets, accepted without blushing the stories of Suetonius and Petronius, gravely discussed Ovid's *Ars Amatoria*, or Martial's *Epigrams*, but amorous activities performed in a dull contemporary, rather than in a golden and classical, light very probably appeared to them as sordid, unaesthetic and dangerous to health.

If their opportunities for sexual expression were severely limited, however, they were at least spared the continual bombardment by advertising, books, cinema and theatre which serves (sometimes for the most calculated commercial reasons) to keep the sexual temperature high. Obvious and intrusive stimuli were lacking. If it was in some ways a more hypocritical, it was also, for many people, a more comfortable world than our own and, in certain ways, decidedly more innocent. Only innocence could have allowed the almost rhapsodical expressions of friendship between those young men; today we are far too self-conscious and psychologically knowing to expose our feelings in such ways, unless we are making a positive statement of sexual preference. Oscar Wilde, whose trial occurred in JB's first year at Oxford, had gone up to Magdalen the year before he was born. No doubt but that his special interests had been rumbled at Oxford by one or two shrewd observers, even if their suspicions could not at that time be expressed except by words like 'unhealthy'. Obviously, in spite of the shattering Wilde scandal, some homosexual practices at Oxford must have gone on in my father's day, and some heterosexual ones as well. But—I find myself coming back to that useful old phrase—such practices were certainly considered 'bad form' and, equally certainly, our young Augustans would have coldly disapproved.

Young unmarried women of the more prosperous classes were

rigorously protected from sexual adventure, and the males of their families were enjoined to help in that protection. My father once, speaking of a famous literary man, said that whilst he admired much of his work, he disliked his practice of 'having affairs with girls of good family'. That remark underlined rather well what must have been a prevailing sentiment of JB's youth. If you must have affairs, then you must go as far away as possible to pursue them, either abroad, or into the *demi-monde* which is never far below the surface of any settled *monde*. What you must not do is carry your sexual adventuring into the lives of young women brought up to look forward to a respectable marriage and nothing else. 'Free love', as it was beginning to be called at the end of the Victorian age, belonged still to the relatively unpeopled littoral of Bohemia, or to the aristocracy, whose activities were hidden in clouds of glory well out of sight of the groundlings. That the 'girls of good family' quite often made the running in a love affair was a fact my father could not contemplate.

The best illustration of the attitudes which I have tried to describe is contained in a story told me some years ago by a much younger friend. At that time there still lived in London a very old gentleman, Mr Stone, the proprietor of Albany, who, in his day, had been a great dandy and man-about-town. Then in his late eighties, and physically infirm, he kept the pleasant custom of champagne in the morning in his splendid set overlooking the courtyard of Albany. My friend used to visit him fairly regularly, to cheer him up and to give him the gossip of the town. One day his host asked him to describe the sexual scene in London, with some such question as 'What do you young people get up to nowadays, eh?' My friend replied that, in this respect, London had become a pretty general free-for-all and went on to give one or two examples. The old gentleman's face lengthened. 'What!' he said 'You don't tell me——you can't mean——fellows with fellows' *sisters*?'

Coming, as most of them did, from stable and well-run homes, JB and his friends saw little charm in settling down early to a quiet domesticity. No doubt they vaguely thought of marriage as something which might have its attractions one day, but not until the world and its multitude of exciting possibilities had been explored. For all the talk going on at that time about the New Woman, and although each young man probably knew girls at least as clever, brave and venturesome as himself, the idea that women in some way slowed things down was probably still strong. People are fond of quoting Bacon's lines: 'He that hath wife and children hath given hostages to fortune'—but do not always remember the rest of the quotation: ' . . . for they are impediments to great enterprises, either of virtue or mischief'. JB and his friends might have professed to despise ordinary careerism, but almost every one of them had the possibility of great (and virtuous) enterprises in mind.

In his various lists of things to be done and goals to be attained, John Buchan never mentions marriage. His letters show a certain rather gloomy jocularity whenever he is obliged to face the fact that someone of his acquaintance contemplates the fatal step. There is nothing especially significant in this, since lists and letters belong to his early twenties, before he had encountered real discomfort and danger, human tragedy and mountainous administrative problems, with Milner in South Africa; before, in short, he had matured. I have already remarked the non-marrying tendency of at least three generations of Buchans. JB's family was solidly coherent and almost voraciously affectionate. The only women, probably, that he knew really well, were his mother and sister, and both must have been continually glaring over the Border at their adored son and brother, alert for the first signs of an 'entanglement'. Small wonder then that, given the terms of his time and his intentions, the word marriage should not have appeared on his 'List of things to be done in the next 4 years', written on his twenty-first birthday. Moreover, at that period, marriage was not even to be thought of by any principled young man as even a remote possibility until he had achieved sufficient fortune to be a reasonable prospect for an anxious parent. JB no doubt well understood the difference between earning enough to live comfortably and achieve mobility as a bachelor, and the kind of income required to support a family while retaining any kind of freedom of action.

5

LOFTY AND SANGUINE DREAMS

In 1899 John Buchan got his First in Greats, but failed to win a prize Fellowship in history at All Souls. He wrote to Gilbert Murray, 'I am rather cross just now, for I have been rejected at All Souls, where everybody thought I was safe. I hate not to do the things I am expected to do.'

A second attempt to live up to expectations, in 1900, also failed, to JB's particular chagrin a man he despised becoming a new Fellow of All Souls. He was disappointed and hurt, but would not allow the rejections to rankle, writing to his brother Willie not long after: 'I felt annoyed at the time but have forgotten it now.' Nevertheless he decided it was time to leave academic life.

> Had I wished it, I could have stayed on and taught philosophy. But at the end of my fourth year I had come to feel that I was not sufficiently devoted to any branch of learning to give up my life to it, either as don or professor. I wanted a stiffer job, one with greater hazards in it, and I was not averse to one which offered bigger material rewards. The supreme advantage of Oxford to me was that it enabled me to discover what talents I had and what I really wanted to do. Horizons had extended and revealed a surprising number of things which woke my curiosity. I wanted to explore the wider stages of life. Besides, I had become attached to the study of law. . . . So I decided that my profession should be the Bar.

By January 1900 JB was settled in London and working for a firm of solicitors. While serving his apprenticeship he supported himself by writing articles and reviews for the *Spectator*, indeed eventually becoming 'a sort of assistant-editor'. Fresh from an Oxford which had seen scarcely any social change for a century, and with eyes a little dazzled by scenes and people of kinds quite new to him and seemingly changeless in their elegant assurance, the young John Buchan took them as he found them, more or less uncritically. He enjoyed his legal work and his journalism, and came to love London for its mixture of splendour, filth and cosiness, its solid comforts and its ancient survivals.

> Fleet Street and the City had still a Dickens flavour, and Holywell Street had not been destroyed. In the daytime . . . I penetrated into queer alleys and offices which in appearance were unchanged since Mr Pickwick's day. On foggy evenings I would dine beside a tavern fire on the kind of fare which Mr Weller affected. Behind all the dirt and gloom there was a wonderful cosiness, and every street corner was peopled by ghosts from literature and history.

Stevenson, too, had been strongly attracted by the same snugness, the contrast between the 'dirt and gloom' and the creature comforts to be found within.

JB remarks in his autobiography that he fell easily, during his first years in London, into comfortable urban habits. 'I who had begun by regarding life as a strenuous pilgrimage, and at Oxford had come to interest myself in the environs of the road, was now absorbed by the wayside gardens and inclined to dally at the inns.' We can take that, I think, with a pinch of salt; strenuousness can never have been far from his thoughts. It is pleasant, though, to see him as a young man, enjoying both the high and the humble pleasures of London life, his health good, his intellect fully occupied by the law and journalism, possessing many friends of all sorts and ages and continually making more. He shared a rod with Andrew Lang (the Scottish writer and scholar) on a dry-fly river in Hertfordshire. 'He used to laugh at my new-found enthusiasm for lowland waters, as he jeered at my absorption in the law. He thought it a sad descent from the Borderer and erstwhile Jacobite.' At one time JB kept a boat on the Blackwater, in Essex, and would go off for sailing weekends with a couple of companions.

I do not know how good my father may have been at sailing small boats. He would typically have set himself to learn the theory of the sport quite exhaustively, would have familiarised himself with the techniques of navigation, but how he was at actual boat-handling I cannot say. Many years later, in 1926, the family spent a week at a house called Inchmery, on the Beaulieu River in Hampshire. It was

Cowes Week, and there was much activity to do with boats. JB had a friend staying, a politician, and something prompted them to enter a boat belonging to our host for one of the races. The boat was of a class then known as International Racing Dinghy. Its crew had probably not seen the inside of any such thing for more than twenty years. The two of them had much to discuss and, after a successful start, and running with a fair wind, they settled down to talking. Conversation must have been absorbing for, about half way round the course, they fouled a buoy. Deciding, with no great regret, that they had disqualified themselves, the pair set sail for home. Officials, seeing their dinghy spanking across the finishing line, naturally supposed that they had won the race, and in a remarkably fast time too. Flags were dipped, guns were fired, and JB and his political friend had some apologising to do.

JB may have felt himself settling down, becoming *rangé*, as he approached his twenty-seventh year, but somewhere at the back of his mind—as always throughout his life—there must have glimmered the possibility of challenge, of radical change, of something which would (as one day it would for Richard Hannay) 'jog him out of his rut'. Such challenge was to come to him, in fact, three times in his life; the first time was to be very soon; the second was when, in 1914, the Great War gave him work of high importance to do, while fundamentally damaging his health; the third was in 1935 when, at the age of sixty, he was appointed Governor-General of Canada.

We are not always prepared for the high challenges in our lives, or do not immediately see them as such, but when, in August 1901, John Buchan received from Lord Milner the offer of a post in his South African Secretariat, he lost no time in accepting it. 'I had only met Lord Milner once before, but the name had been long familiar to me, for at Oxford men spoke of it reverentially. He had won every kind of academic honour and had impressed Jowett as the ablest man of his time.'

When further trouble was coming to a head between the British and the Boers in the eighteen-nineties Milner, who, at the age of forty-three, already had much experience of the upper reaches of public service—at the Treasury, as Under-Secretary for Finance in Egypt, as Chairman of the Board of Inland Revenue—was sent out to South Africa as High Commissioner. He went with the goodwill of both political parties, but soon became 'the most controversial figure in the Empire, applauded by many as the strong man in the crisis, bitterly criticised by others as bearing the chief responsibility of the war'.

I can see my twenty-six-year-old father almost frantic with excitement at this new turn in his career. 'I love seeing the world and I much prefer politics to law!' he wrote to a friend at the time, and to his mother, who was vocally opposed to his going: 'I think it is a great chance, an interposition of Providence, but *you* must be considered.' His invocation of Providence, perhaps a shade disingenuous, comes at the end of a letter setting out the advantages of the new post and crisply disposing of his mother's objections.

Once again, and as with Oxford in the nineties, it is necessary to make an effort to catch the atmosphere of a time made remote by more than the passing of the years. When the Boer War broke out in 1899 there were many in Britain (JB among them) who were doubtful of the justice of the British cause. Some thought that Britain had gone to war to protect the fortunes and the future gains of the mining millionaires on the Rand, and that to fight the Boers over land which they had so hardly won for themselves showed the worst kind of colonial greed. Dreams of Empire and of further colonisation were already being questioned, and by no means only among cranks and 'Little Englanders'. When the Boers proved to be hardy fighters who, knowing their own territory perfectly, could run rings round Britain's professional army, inflicting heavy casualties, defeat and disgrace, there were many who despaired at Britain's miscalculation, and some who felt inclined to cheer.

To many it appeared that Milner's intransigence on behalf of the British in South Africa was a contributory factor to the outbreak of war in 1899; but by 1901, with the end of the fighting in sight, Milner's energies were turned towards the reorganisation and reconstruction of the two new colonies of the Transvaal and the Orange Free State, the former Boer republics. For this work he was anxious to recruit young men with energetic and unconventional minds . . . 'There will be a regular rumpus and a lot of talk about boys and Oxford and jobs and all that. . . . Well, I value brains and character more than experience. First-class men of experience are not to be got. Nothing one could offer would tempt them to give up what they have. . . . No! I shall not be here for very long, but when I go I mean to leave behind me young men with plenty of work in them.'*

*Janet Adam Smith, *John Buchan: A Biography*.

L. S. Amery, by then an old friend of John Buchan's, was among the first to be invited to join Lord Milner. He could not be released from his post on *The Times*, so suggested JB instead. Milner, who has been impressed by an article about South Africa in the *Spectator* written by JB, and who had heard many good things about the young man from English friends during his visit home in 1901, decided to accept the suggestion. On 7 August John Buchan was summoned to the Colonial Office where Lord Milner offered him the appointment.

He was to go out to South Africa for two years. 'I am to be paid £1,200 a year—out of which I suppose I could save £600,' he told his mother. After a hectic few weeks settling his affairs, and saying farewell to his family in Scotland and friends in London, he sailed to his new adventures on 14 September.

When John Buchan speaks of 'politics', it is important that this word should not be taken in its narrowest, its party–political sense. For that, as I shall try to show, he had no commanding aptitude. Politics, for him, was an affair of wide imagination, of grand designs, of the application of humane principles to the welfare of peoples, to the furthering, in short, of civilisation as the Romans understood the word. The tasks which awaited him in Milner's South African administration, where the immediate aim was to restore health to a country ravaged by war, and the ultimate to create a society where Dutch and British and native Africans could live prosperously in amity, lay directly in the field of his most ardently cherished beliefs. Early in 1901 he had written in the *Spectator*:

> We believe that . . . the Dutch and British in South Africa will be fused into one loyal and prosperous people. If we did not believe this, we should regard the war as indeed an unqualified disaster . . . we must make the Colony, not a wilderness where fortune-hunters may find gold, but a civilised and united nation. And to do this we must work alongside the Dutch.

The young man who had so often proclaimed the principles of leadership, who himself was always ready to be led by someone whom he could truly respect and admire, had found almost his ideal in Lord Milner. Much has been said and written about Milner, both in his lifetime and since his death, a great deal of it unsympathetic if not positively hostile. In *Memory Hold-the-Door* John Buchan devoted several pages to the analysis of this apparently austere, Olympian person whom he came so quickly to revere as much for his gentleness and courtesy as for his high visionary aims and superb practical ability.

It was truly a strange world in which JB found himself when, after a three-day journey from Cape Town, he found himself in Johannesburg, raw and clangourous, part shanty-town, part nascent metropolis. He was at once thrown in at the deep end.

> In that strenuous time it was a case of all hands to the pump, and I was given a series of emergency tasks which were intended to prepare the ground for a normal administration. Since the War had smashed the old machine it meant starting at the beginning and dealing in bold improvisations. . . . My first job was to take over on behalf of the civilian government the concentration camps for women and children established by the army.

The words 'concentration camps' have, in our time, become so infamous that it is worth noting that the original official description in South Africa was 'refugee camps'. The *Spectator* article that aroused Milner's interest was probably a second one on South Africa which John Buchan wrote in June 1901, explaining how the camps had come to be established. In the extremely fluid terms of the fighting—which terms were largely imposed by the Boers—women and children were left alone in isolated farms on the veld when their men went off to join the fast-moving Boer commandos. The refugee camps were, at least in part, intended as a measure of protection for the civilian population. There is no doubt that in the early days they were horribly mismanaged.

John Buchan embraced his new task in October 1901, when there were 118,000 white and 43,000 coloured inmates of the camps. The death rate was at its highest—nearly 35 per cent. The suitability of JB for this particular work is best commented on by himself:

> Not many young men with an academic past are given such a chance of grappling with the raw facts of life. . . . It was a queer job for a young man, whose notions of hygiene to begin with were of the sketchiest, and to whom infantile diseases were as much a mystery as hyper-space. The word of a bachelor carried no weight with the Boer mothers, so, in order to speak with authority, I had to invent a wife and numerous progeny.

In January 1902 he wrote to Lady Mary Murray, wife of his Glasgow professor and a staunch friend.

> The refugee camps have made my hair grey . . . I shall never forget going through the hospitals three months ago, when the children were dying like flies. We have now revolutionised the whole system, and the death-rate is down to something nearly normal. . . . It has been a hideous grind for everybody, but I think we are all better for having gone through it. I say nothing about the original policy of forming camps: it was certainly not wise: but everyone who knows the country admits that it was humane.

JB might have escaped from a London grown over-familiar, into a life where each new day brought excitement and heavy demands, to a country whose very air was electrifying, but he had reckoned without his family. Hardly had he settled into his new life, and the company of new and congenial friends, than word came of a visit to South Africa by his parents. His father had agreed to take over for nine months the work of a minister in Port Elizabeth, and in spite of anguished letters and cables intended to discourage them, his father and mother and brother Alastair, then aged eight, arrived in December 1901. The presence of half his family in a country still under martial law must have added greatly to JB's anxieties; worse must have been the feeling that his first steps in the great world had to be taken, like his first steps in the nursery, under the eye of his mother.

If his work for reconstruction and the example of Lord Milner were powerful influences on JB, the country itself took a strong hold on his imagination. He came to see a lot of it. Even while he was struggling with the problems of the concentration camps, he was drawn into the urgent business of the land and its future, of settlement and resettlement, of the framing of an agricultural policy.

> I had the problem of the land squarely on my shoulders, and had to spend much of my time on the road. Long before the War ended I was travelling far and wide, often in areas where fighting was going on, and I was fairly often in difficulties. I have ridden many miles, faster than I cared, to avoid losing my breeches to a commando whose clothing had given out. . . . Those were

wonderful years for me, years of bodily and mental activity, of zeal and hope not yet dashed by failure. I learned perforce a little about a great many things and a good deal about one or two things. . . . I had to be in some degree a jack-of-all-trades— transport-rider, seedsman, stockman, horsecoper, merchant, lawyer, not to speak of diplomatist. . . . I trust that my work was of some benefit to the country; it was beyond doubt of enormous benefit to myself. For I came to know and value a great variety of human beings, and to know and love one of the most fascinating lands on earth.

His beloved Borders apart, JB wrote of nowhere more lyrically than he did of South Africa. As a small boy growing up he had ventured every year a little farther away from the settled surroundings of Broughton into the hills and moors of Tweeddale, seeking far-off glens, and hidden streams. He had early felt the haunting contrast between 'the desert and the sown', between the secure and orderly and the wildness beyond. His strong sense of place, always an integral part of his writing, must have been established in childhood; in South Africa it found much on which to work. Since his duties took him from end to end of the new territories, he saw every variety of scenery from the gently pastoral to the fiercely dramatic. He was greatly taken by his first sight of the Wood Bush in Northern Transvaal, where the high plateau, with its big timber trees, its arum lilies and agapanthus lighting the meadowland, its 'streams of grey-blue water, swirling in pools and rapids like a Highland salmon river', lies between stony uplands and the malarial bushveld below. It was precisely this kind of contrast which appealed most to JB. He meant, he said, to come back one day and build a house in the Wood Bush, a true 'lodge in the wilderness'.

About JB's South African years a whole book could be written. He was to come, in the end, to the sad recognition that those high and sanguine dreams, those magisterial abilities, those lofty and unshakeable principles which sustained Milner and Rhodes and his own colleagues, had not produced the results so hopefully and confidently proclaimed. But when he left South Africa he was on fire with thoughts of an ideal commonwealth.

Of his experiences in South Africa, the result, JB wrote, was that:

My notion of a career was radically changed. I thought no more of being a dignified judge with a taste for letters, or a figure in British politics. I wanted some administrative task, some share in the making of this splendid commonwealth. I hoped to spend most of my life outside Britain. I had no desire to be a pro-consul or any kind of grandee. I would have been content with any job however thankless, in any quarter however remote, if I had a chance of making a corner of the desert blossom and the solitary place glad.

Returning to England, John Buchan hoped to go at once to Egypt, to take up a financial post under Lord Cromer. The vacancy, however, did not occur. My father felt restless now, no longer uncritical of London life.

South Africa had completely unsettled me. I did not want to make money or a reputation at home; I wanted a particular kind of work which was denied me. I had lost my former catholicity of interests. I had no longer any impulse to write. I was distressed by British politics, for it seemed to me that both the great parties were blind to the meaning of Empire. London had ceased to have its old glamour. . . . Something, too, seemed to have happened to London society. I had now acquired a large circle of acquaint-ances, and had become an habitual diner-out, but it was in a society with little charm for me. The historic etiquette was breaking down; in every walk money seemed to count for more; there was a vulgar display of wealth, and a *rastaquouère* craze for luxury. I began to have an ugly fear that the Empire might decay at the heart.

The death of the old Queen and the accession of her son had loosened bonds which, in JB's early London days, had still been holding fast. It is probable, however, that signs of the changes just mentioned would have been there to see, even in the nineties. The currents and counter-currents of optimism and apprehension associated with the ends of centuries were there to be felt. Standards were changing, even then, at every level of society.

Returning from South Africa in August 1903, my father had behind him two years of grinding hard work, discomfort and danger, during which he had seen much human misery, defeat and death; he had had to take rapid and far-reaching decisions affecting the lives of many people; he had worked in the company of able and mature men under a master whom he positively revered. He was only just twenty-eight years old at the time of his return, but we may believe that if London society had changed by then, the former cheerful young lawyer, littérateur and man-about-town had changed even more radically.

For the next couple of years JB continued with the legal work and journalism he had been engaged upon before, but he no longer wished to go on with his career as a barrister. He had had too vivid, too active, an experience; he had been given vast scope for action and a degree of authority not often, in peacetime, to be had by a man in his twenties. So, when, in 1906, Tommy Nelson, one of JB's Balliol friends from Oxford days, offered him a partnership in the family publishing firm, which already had offices in London and New York and was expanding fast, he accepted gratefully.

After his return from South Africa, JB may, as he proclaims, have lost interest in writing. Nevertheless, in 1903 he published *The African Colony*, a study of various aspects of South African life, on which he had begun to work while serving with Milner. He also wrote a law book, choosing, on Lord Haldane's advice, 'that intricate and evasive topic, the liability to British tax of income earned abroad'. The book, which came out in 1905, was called *The Law Relating to the Taxation of Foreign Income*, and was for many years the only work on the subject. 1906 saw the publication of *A Lodge in the Wilderness*, at first anonymously, but soon with JB's name attached. This was not a novel so much as a symposium on the theme of Empire, a subject upon which JB's thoughts had crystallised during his term of practical imperialist activity in South Africa.

I suppose that one should not blame the journalists who wrote and re-wrote the story of JB's career, even before he was thirty, with such repetitious enthusiasm. A young man who had made a name for himself as a writer before he had even left university; who had his own entry in *Who's Who* at the age of twenty-three; who had played a part in Milner's famous 'kindergarten' of brilliant young men who, whatever their critics or his might say, had worked with real devotion at the task of South African reconstruction; and who was also a rising barrister, was bound to be a useful source of copy about his achievements, and of speculation about what he might do next.

His life in Temple Gardens—an attractive cubby-hole of old London later to be destroyed by bombs—where he was looked after by an extremely gloomy manservant called Mole, must have been a model of bachelor comfort. If his care for his appearance in later life is anything to go by, he must, as a young man in London, have been almost finically elegant. Like many men, he liked to dress up (or down) to his various parts. A photograph taken in about 1907 shows him in a braided frock-coat, with a high-buttoned striped waistcoat and striped trousers. Part of his political conservatism being enshrined in the phrase 'if change is not necessary it is necessary not to change', once he had found a good thing he was inclined to stay with it. Thus he stayed with the same tailor (Norton, then of Conduit Street, W1) for the whole of his adult life.

There are many snapshots of him from that period, of such variable quality as to make me wish exasperatedly that the science of photography could have made more rapid strides. Those taken in the country show him dressed for various occasions—skating, for instance, or motoring—in tidy and appropriate clothes; but for moments of true informality—walking, fishing, climbing, picnicking—he wore rough old tweeds and an extraordinary, shapeless hat, which gave him a strangely raffish appearance. In London he wore the high, stiff collars which were the fashion of the day: in pictures these tend to disembody his head, making him look constrained, uncomfortable, yet they remained his choice. In the country he preferred striped shirts, whose detachable collars were starched and those he often wore unwilted on the very hottest days.

I can piece together, from odd remarks dropped at wide intervals, something of the pleasures which my father enjoyed in his London days. He had, for instance, certain happy memories of food. It was probably the continuous strain of his South African work—long hours at a desk, varied by exhausting treks all over the country, a scrappy diet, much anxiety—which began the digestive trouble which was to loom ever larger in his life over the next thirty years. At the time of which I am writing, however, he seems to have kept himself fit, in spite of his habitual load of work, and to have had a good appetite for many things which, later on, he was going to have to forgo.

For example, he loved oysters. Sweeting's Oyster-Bar in Queen Victoria Street was a regular port of call. He liked suppers at Romano's or at the Savoy Grill, where his particular dish was devilled kidneys swimming in mustard. Sometimes after a dance, he and his friends would take hansoms and drive down to Greenwich for a breakfast of whitebait at the Trafalgar Inn. '*Nessun maggior dolore. . . .*' Paraphrasing Dante we might think that there were few greater sorrows than the recollection of good food when a man is inhibited by duodenal trouble from eating anything but poached eggs.

Again and again in JB's books we are given descriptions of meals, beginning with the ham and eggs and oatmeal scones of a shepherd's cottage, reward for a particularly gruelling walk or climb and eaten with the healthy undiscriminating appetite of youth. Dr Johnson (who figures in *Midwinter*) had once been very poor and when food became plentiful he would attack it with desperate gusto as if each meal might be the last before privation again set in. He was particularly fond of veal pie with plums and fish sauce. In *Midwinter* he dines with Alastair Maclean, the hero, in an Oxfordshire inn:

> There was thick hare soup, with all the woods and pastures in its fragrance, and a big dressed pike caught that morning in the inn stew-pond. . . . Then came roast hill mutton which [he] highly commended. But he reserved his highest commendations for a veal pie, made with plums, which he averred was his favourite delicacy.

In *The House of the Four Winds* there are two descriptions of meals eaten in Evallonia, one simple, one elaborate, but each excellent in its way.

> Jaikie had eaten an admirable supper on a corner of the table, a supper of cold ham, an omelet, hot toasted rye-cakes and a seductive cheese. . . . He had concluded with coffee and cream in a blue cup as large as a basin.

And, later on in the book:

> The dinner was all that the landlord had promised. There was trout from the hills—and a pie of partridges slain prematurely—and what Archie pronounced to be the best beef he had eaten outside England—and an omelet of kidneys and mushrooms—and little tartlets of young raspberries.

There is nothing exotic about this menu, nothing there that could not have been achieved by a good English cook—in fact the sort of fare which JB might have been offered in an English or Scottish country house where most of the ingredients would have been found 'on the place'. For my father it is clearly one special kind of happiness recalled in misery.

In *Memory Hold-the-Door* John Buchan described the London of the end of the nineteenth century, before the changes which came to it with a new reign.

London at the turn of the century had not yet lost her Georgian air. Her ruling society was aristocratic till Queen Victoria's death, and preserved the modes and rites of an aristocracy. Her great houses had not disappeared or become blocks of flats. In the summer she was a true city of pleasure, every window-box gay with flowers, her streets full of splendid equipages, the Park a showground for fine horses and handsome men and women. The ritual went far down, for frock-coats and top-hats were the common wear not only for the West End, but about the Law Courts and in the City. On Sunday afternoons we dutifully paid a round of calls. Conversation was not the casual thing it has now become, but was something of an art, in which competence conferred prestige. Also clubs were still in their hey-day, their waiting-lists were lengthy, and membership of the right ones was a stage in a career. I could belong, of course, to none of the famous institutions; my clubs were young men's clubs, where I met my university friends. One was the Cocoa Tree in St James's Street, a place with a long and dubious history, of which the bronze cocoa-tree in the smoking-room, stuffed with ancient packs of cards, was a reminder.

This was an appropriate club for the young JB, the former Jacobite, since in 1745 it had been the meeting place of the Jacobite party.

After his South African experience, the warier, more mature John Buchan was, as we have seen, less in a mood to be delighted by all aspects of London life. Nevertheless, he dined out frequently, went often to the theatre and enjoyed close and fruitful intellectual relations with certain seniors, such as the great lawyer Haldane, who was to be Minister of War in the successive administrations of Campbell-Bannerman and Asquith. His early leaning towards politics had now taken a definite direction, that of a highly imaginative, expanded idea of the British Empire and its possible future role.

His dream of this future had been set forth in *A Lodge in the Wilderness*, in which a number of influential, high-minded and highly articulate people of both sexes meet in a luxurious mansion,

Musuru, built in wild African highlands by one of JB's most romantic inventions, a virtuous millionaire named Francis Carey. I can imagine JB discoursing on, endlessly discussing, this theme, himself alight with the passion of his enthusiasm, delighting—if not always convincing—more sceptical and earthbound listeners.

> These were the days when a vision of what the Empire might be made dawned upon certain minds with all the force of a revelation. Today [1940] the word is sadly tarnished. Its mislikers have managed to identify it with ugliness like corrugated iron roofs and raw townships or, worse still, with a callous racial arrogance. . . . Phrases which held a world of idealism and poetry have been spoilt by their use in bad verse and in after-dinner perorations. . . . Something like the sober, merchandising Jacobean colonial policy has replaced the high Elizabethan dreams. But in those days things were different. It was an inspiration to youth to realise the magnitude of its material heritage, and to think how it might be turned to spiritual issues.

Forty years on, the Empire is finished. Only a somewhat fissile body called the Commonwealth remains. Unfaithful to our past, we beat our breasts about the misdeeds of our forebears, forgetting that what is ugly is always remediable, but that the vision of great things, of true civilisation, once lost, is hard to recover. Minds like John Buchan's, idealistic and sanguine, may have been wrong to praise the civilising mission of the Anglo-Saxon peoples, but one quality must be allowed them, a complete and selfless sincerity.

John Buchan's theories of Empire were in no sense jingoistic; indeed he hated the cant and mawkishness which had grown up to obscure what he thought best in the imperial idea: a recognition that what the British had got, materially, from their Empire obliged them to give much more in return, and not only in a material sense.

> I dreamed of a world-wide brotherhood with the background of a common race and creed, consecrated to the service of peace; Britain enriching the rest out of her culture and traditions, and the spirit of the Dominions like a strong wind freshening the stuffiness of the old lands. I saw in the Empire a means of giving to the congested masses at home open country instead of a blind alley. I saw hope for a new afflatus in art and literature and thought. . . . The 'white man's burden' is now an almost

meaningless phrase, then it involved a new philosophy of politics, and an ethical standard, serious and surely not ignoble.

There is no need to enumerate the many ways in which this conception, indeed not ignoble, came to be falsified. JB then, as later on, seems to have had one or two curious blind spots. He never, for example, in all the wide-ranging discussions of *A Lodge in the Wilderness*, mentions India. His concern seems always to have been with the white Anglo-Saxons, with Canadians, Australians, New Zealanders, the Dominions rather than the Colonies. About the future of the black races he is respectful but rather vague.

He takes no account of revolutionary movements in Europe, yet the events of 1848 occurred less than sixty years before the date of his book. He does not seem to regard as important the successive industrial revolutions which followed our own, nor to see how being first in that field might not have been to our best advantage. He seems to have had no anxieties about the growth of that urban proletariat which would one day provide material for the experiments of Lenin and the German and Italian dictators. Yet the evidence of urban discontent and deracination was already to hand. In fairness, it must be remembered that, in 1905, the possibility of a world war was hardly imaginable. Thoughtful, gradual change still seemed possible. Only a handful of people who were in no sense idealists, whose vision was not lofty, and whose ears were close to the ground, heard, and correctly interpreted, certain tremors. If they spoke of their apprehensions, few listened except another handful of people for whom a world war was desirable as the essential means to revolutionary ends. In fairness, also, there were some consequences of war, and its scientific and technical needs, which nobody, probably, could have imagined: the tremendous technological advances which would be achieved with a speed impossible under ordinary industrial conditions. What the First War did for the aviation and automobile industries, the Second did in far greater measure; and the advances in electronics made during the last war have probably more radically altered life for the majority of people than any discovery since the invention of printing. Nuclear fission has posed a perpetual threat which is always at the back of the mind. But then, as we have seen, technology was not JB's strong point.

If it was, or could be, an inspiration to British youth to realise the magnitude of its material heritage, there were others in the world who felt very bitterly about it. The French, the Dutch, the

Portuguese, from whom in the past we had wrested considerable material advantages, looked at the British Empire, generally, with narrowed eyes, as, for other reasons, did the Americans. It was good of Santayana to say that the world had never seen so sweet, so just, so boyish a master, but there were those in India, Africa and other places who remained unmoved by this conception: who did not, in fact, want a master at all.

In my teens—and possibly because Europe seemed generally to be left out of my father's view of the world—I laid myself open to European influences. It was very likely the need to find some small corner in which JB had never been either interested or effective which led me in this particular direction; that and a strong feeling for France and for French literature. Travelling in France, however much I might be among friends, I could not help being aware of the acid of envy underlying the kindness of my hosts, the only half-friendly jocularities about my powerful passport and strong money. *Autre temps.* . . . Much of that has changed. It is long since anybody envied an Englishman for those things.

Paradoxically enough, there are quite a lot of people in the world who now regret the passing of the British Empire, and they are often to be found in the places where once we were indeed the masters. What I could see in the nineteen-thirties, although my father could not, or would not, was that, where the Empire was concerned, we had lost our nerve. That essential belief in our right to be where we were and do what we did, which perhaps received its first debilitating jolt from the Indian Mutiny in 1857, had been a casualty of the First War. We had seriously begun to doubt our right to go charging about the world, imposing ourselves; more important, we had ceased to want to. Late in 1944, I had a conversation in Calcutta with a senior official of the Bengal Government, an Indian of great charm and wisdom. He pointed a finger at me suddenly, and said: 'You British! Either you stay or you go. But if you stay, for God's sake *rule!*'

The arguments in *A Lodge in the Wilderness*, for anyone interested in the history of ideas, and not too conditioned to reflexes of horror where words like imperialism are concerned, are well worth examining, not only for the texture of the dialectic, but for their freshness, their romantic optimism, the sense they give of poetry and, above all, of generosity.

6

A MARRIAGE OF TRUE MINDS

I have seen it suggested from time to time that John Buchan 'made a good marriage', as if that had been part of a careful political and financial calculation. It was indeed a good marriage, but not in the worldly sense, except in so far as it brought the perhaps rather lonely young man a new world of relationships which he very much valued.

The young Scotsman had no need to marry into a noble English family to prove that he had 'arrived'. Long before he thought of marriage he had arrived on his own. His already considerable reputation, carried ahead of him from Oxford, and enhanced by his work in journalism, his books, and his exciting career in South Africa, would have opened any door to him that he would have thought worth entering.

One evening in 1905 John Buchan was taken by a friend to dine with Mrs Norman Grosvenor. A few days later he called at her house, No. 30 Upper Grosvenor Street. Years later my mother was to write about this occasion in *John Buchan by his Wife and Friends*.

> The polite fashion of the time was for a young man to come and call several days after the dinner-party had taken place. On this particular afternoon my mother was out and I gave the visitor tea. We conversed with difficulty and in an intermittent and stilted manner. This was all the more curious as both of us had usually a great deal to say. After we became engaged, and in later years, we discussed our first meeting. I found that John thought me haughty, while I thought him conceited and difficult to talk to. Why we should have belied our real characters in this way I cannot imagine.

What an excellent scene for a novel that first encounter might make in the hands, say, of a Henry James. I feel that I can see it clearly: my grandmother's drawing-room with its dark green walls, its Morris chintzes, its Chinese porcelain, the Burne-Jones of naked nymphs parading down rocks which my grandfather had bought at the studio sale after his friend's, the artist's death. I suppose that my father, as was customary, took his top hat with him in to tea, set it beside his chair and dropped his gloves inside. I can imagine that conversation for both young people was inhibited by something more than shyness. I am even prepared, for this occasion, to believe in love at first sight.

Thereafter the young couple met often, and exchanged letters, ideas and books. After he had proposed marriage to Susan Grosvenor, and had been accepted (with her mother's proviso of a year's engagement), JB wrote to her: 'You are the only woman I have ever been in love with, and ever shall be in love with.' In this, as in so much else, John Buchan knew his own mind and his own capacity. My parents were married at her family's church, St George's, Hanover Square, on 15 July 1907 at 2.30 p.m. The day was a Monday, which fact says much about the leisurely existence then possible for many people in London. It was a hot sunny day and my mother travelled in slightly queasy state in the Grosvenor family coach, lent by her cousin Westminster.

Newspapers had more room in those days for recording social events, and that particular wedding seems to have created a lot of interest. Most of the descriptions of the wedding, and the lists of the good and great present in the church, read like a syndication, but several editors left the path of straight reporting to write about the bridegroom and his remarkable career.

Marriage then was expected to be permanent. Wedding presents, accordingly, were solid and carefully chosen; if their donors were well off they were sometimes very splendid. The young couple received, according to one newspaper, which faithfully listed most of them, more than four hundred presents. Among them was a diamond tiara, subscribed to by several members of my mother's family. This was an item then considered as indispensable as, say, a car would be today. There was other jewellery as well, and much silver, including a whole flotilla of sauce-boats. Nowadays we are sympathetic to young marriages, but doubtful about their permanence. Some table mats or a wastepaper basket will generally be thought to fill the bill: and nobody publishes our thoughtful generosity in the press.

John and Susan Buchan left London by train for Hampshire. Her travelling dress was of blue crêpe-de-chine bordered with Irish lace tinted to the same shade of blue; with this she wore a blue straw hat to match, trimmed with ostrich feathers. The first week of the honeymoon was spent at Tylney Hall, lent to them by Lionel Phillips, a Rand millionaire with whom my father had made friends in South Africa—one of the few of whom he approved. Tylney was luxurious: the baths ran pink, scented water. There was a huge staff to look after the young couple. At the end of their stay JB felt obliged to tip the butler twenty-five pounds, in those days a very large sum.

My parents' marriage was the union of two radically different strains, two nationalities, two Churches, and many centuries of diverse influences, all equally powerful and peculiar. My mother, it is true, had some Scottish blood through her own mother's family, the Stuart-Wortleys, the Stuart in their case coming from that Lord Bute whose disastrous administration of 1762–3 lost Britain the American colonies. John Buchan had no English blood whatever. Their alliance in no way responds to the metaphor of new wine and old bottles: it was rather the mixing of two different kinds of very old wine. How the children of it would fare in life could have been a matter for speculation.

If, through marriage, JB had been seeking fortune and access to political influence he would have had to look elsewhere. Susan Grosvenor's father, the Hon. Norman de L'Aigle Grosvenor had been the younger son of a younger son,* and so some distance from the mainstream of the Grosvenor wealth. Her mother's father, James Stuart-Wortley, also a younger son, had been Solicitor-General under Palmerston in 1856. His career—he was to have been Speaker of the House of Commons—came to an end with a riding accident which broke his back. His father, Lord Wharncliffe, had been Lord Privy Seal in Peel's administration of 1834. Both families had made their best effects in politics in the eighteenth and nineteenth centuries; by the time my father came to know them they had turned their attention to other things.

It seems likely that by 1905—the year of the 'Liberal Landslide' and Campbell-Bannerman's administration—the more knowledgeable and reflective members of the ruling classes had begun to feel a certain unease, to hear sullen rumblings both at home and abroad, to be aware of an atmosphere of shift and change. The

---

* His father, Lord Robert Grosvenor, made Lord Ebury in 1857, was the younger son of the Marquess of Westminster, and uncle of the 1st Duke.

South African war, with its almost incredible reverses had seriously undermined national confidence, and social upheaval was much in the air. To the more radical such changes as they foresaw might have seemed desirable; the more conservative may have thought it sensible to welcome into their ranks people of ability from other spheres, who would increase their mental alertness and at the same time let in fresh air to a scene which too many years of national power and prosperity had rendered stuffy and stale. JB was not the only young man to rise by his own talents and be welcomed warmly by families which, fifty years before, might have looked doubtfully on anyone not possessed of known relations and a settled fortune.

In her book *The Edwardian Lady* (published in 1966), my mother wrote of the betrothal:

> Aunt Mamie [Mary, Countess of Lovelace] was not very pleased about my engagement to John Buchan. She had hoped for a nephew who possessed a large country house standing in a park. But both my husband and she could recognise qualities of heart and mind, and they became fast friends.

Great-aunt Mamie was my grandmother's eldest sister. Like my grandmother she had trained as an artist with Sir Edward Poynter. Realising, with rare self-criticism, that she would never be a first-rate painter, she concentrated on helping other artists. She married Ralph Lovelace, Byron's grandson, and threw her considerable energy into managing and improving his estates. Not all her improvements, notably those entrusted to the architect, C. A. Voysey, were entirely happy. I still think with a shudder of the looming black basalt chimney-piece in her drawing-room at Ockham which he substituted for an eighteenth-century original. At Ockham she entertained largely, and it was there that my father first met Henry James.

Aunt Mamie's initial response to my mother's engagement came from the conservative and traditionalist side of her nature. She managed to combine—and this was in no way unusual in that generation—strict Tory principles with a lively interest in new movements in the arts. JB's conquest of his aunt-to-be, which was swift and permanent, may be taken as the pattern for many other conquests of the same sort; he had only, so to speak, to be seen to be believed. The first and, of course, most important person, after my mother, to place her complete trust in him, was my grandmother.

After that, and since in an unobtrusive way she had considerable social influence, all was plain sailing.

The world in which my mother grew up was a small one, sharply defined at its edges—so small, in fact, that it was not usually necessary to perform introductions, since everyone knew everyone else, or had no difficulty in 'placing' a new face. 'This is Caroline's eldest girl', my mother told me, was generally an adequate introduction when she was first brought out into Society. (I use the capital letter advisedly. You were either 'in Society' or you were not. Once in, only the most eccentric misconduct, or a personal choice of reclusion, could put you out again.)

John Buchan was never to know his wife's father, who died at the age of fifty in 1898, but it is possible to believe that they would have found much in common. When her father died my mother was sixteen years old. She had loved him dearly, looked up to him—in every sense, he was so immensely tall—and was never, perhaps, to recover completely from his loss.

Norman Grosvenor was one of a scattered but in no way despicable band of rebels in the Europe of his day, aristocrats of wide and liberal sympathies who were impatient of the rules and sanctions, the constraints upon social action, of their own world. He was deeply sensitive, a fine musician, and a composer of music who somehow never quite reached the heights at which he aimed. His relations thought him a dangerous radical, a leveller, a traitor to his class. In fact he was a gentle and liberal-minded man, intelligent, serious and kind-hearted, through whose nature ran a consistent strain of melancholy and a vein of romantic idealism which made him especially susceptible to the ideas of William Morris and his school.

I like to think that it was of him that Sir William Rothenstein once told me this story. Dining one evening in the eighties, in all-male company, Rothenstein found himself next to a very tall, elegant, rather sombre man who turned to him and said abruptly: 'You're a painter, aren't you? I suppose you think I'm just another damned Philistine?' Sir William thought he remembered that the young man's name was Grosvenor: the remark itself would have been perfectly in keeping with my grandfather's intense annoyance at being continually cast, because of his social position, as an immutable type.

By the time of my father's first momentous visit to Upper

Grosvenor Street, my grandfather had been dead for seven years. I feel sure that he would have admired and approved of his son-in-law as enthusiastically as did the rest of my mother's family, and I know that JB would have found much to love and respect in him. Music need not have been a fatal division between them, since JB respected devotion in any form. He would have seen how hard Norman Grosvenor worked at his music, and how unremittingly he struggled for a perfection that he never quite achieved. His sympathies would have been warmly engaged by this man who wished, with such desperate sincerity to make a better world for everybody, when he might so easily have accepted his own privileged situation and let the rest go hang. Above all, with his strong feelings on the subject of popular education, my father would have wholeheartedly approved Norman's work in bringing serious music to the people.

In the eighteen-seventies he had founded The People's Concert Society for which he was solely responsible.

> In the early days of the People's Concerts admission was by programme costing one penny: the quality of the music depended on the generosity of musicians who gave their services. The running costs came out of the individual pockets of a committee of which Norman was chairman. The Society threw its net wide over Barking, Bermondsey, Canning Town, Somers Town, Poplar, Wandsworth, and kept going for fifty-seven years, long after Norman had died and Hubert Parry had succeeded him.*

My grandmother, after her marriage, was to live all her life in grace-and-favour houses on the Grosvenor's Mayfair estate. My grandparents had two daughters, Susan and Margaret and, when their first house in Green Street became too small even for this small family, moved to a much larger one, No. 30 Upper Grosvenor Street, the house where my father met my mother and where, ten years later, I was to be born. It was one of many fine, commodious eighteenth-century houses which were demolished in 1929 when the Duke of Westminster sold the large site bounded on the east by Park Street and on the west by Park Lane, to allow the building of the Grosvenor House Hotel. It stood beside the courtyard of old Grosvenor House, the town house of the Westminsters, and its

*Alice Buchan, *A Scrap Screen*.

back windows looked down into their leafy garden. When the house was demolished my mother was allowed to have two pretty eighteenth-century marble chimney-pieces which were then installed at Elsfield, one in the library and one in the drawing-room.

After No. 30 had gone my grandmother moved house, but not very far, merely up the street to No. 2, on the north side, a few doors short of Grosvenor Square. Of that house I remember every detail. It was the goal of my first visits, by myself, to London and, at all times until the last war, the rallying place of the family when any member was in London, either to stay or in transit. In 1937, when I was living alone on Campden Hill, I used to walk across the Park to Upper Grosvenor Street for tea with my grandmother on a Saturday or Sunday. By then she had lived in Mayfair for nearly sixty years, and was inclined to discount residence anywhere else. People who lived outside Mayfair, even in Belgravia, must, she pretended to think, 'live in filth and squalor'. I tried in vain to explain to her the difference, social and architectural, between Campden Hill and Camden Town. She had often visited the latter, on charitable errands, and concluded that filth and squalor must indeed be my own portion. When my parents left Bryanston Street for Portland Place, my mother felt obliged to apologise to her in an anxious letter explaining that it was not really so very far away.

During the years of her marriage, and for the early years of her widowhood, my grandmother spent several months of the year at Moor Park, near Rickmansworth in Hertfordshire, home of her husband's parents, Lord and Lady Ebury. My mother and her sister had perhaps the happiest times of their childhood there, but my grandmother found life in the Palladian mansion, with its rules and routines and formalities, somewhat stifling, as her daughter was to recall in *The Edwardian Lady*.

> My mother loved the months during which she lived in London in her own house. She was devoted to her husband's family, but she found the give and take of family life at Moor Park trying, and her boredom at having no household of her own to look after filled her with a sense of frustration . . . when my grandfather died we lived entirely in London and after my father's death we went less and less to Moor Park.

That park is now a golf course, and the magnificent, glacial house is possibly the most inappropriate club-house in the world. I never tired of hearing my mother's stories about it, she had loved it so.

The heliotrope underplanted in her little rose-garden at Elsfield was there to remind her of hot summer days at Moor Park.

After her husband's death my grandmother took to letting her house for long periods and travelling abroad with her two daughters. Thus my mother spent seasons in Rome and Florence, and others in Germany. She had particularly liked Dresden, where the King of Saxony still reigned within the framework of Bismarck's empire. She would describe to me evenings at the opera when the king was present with members of his court—jewels, magnificent uniforms, but something of homeliness about it all as well. She once remarked that everybody in places like Dresden had an official position of some sort, even if it was only deputy under-park-keeper, and that nearly everybody had a uniform. This system, she thought, suited the German temperament perfectly.

> The girls of my generation were supposed to marry and to marry well—i.e. some man with money and a country estate. They were still supposed to fill up their time with a little painting, a little reading, some music; to stay about in country houses, go to dances, and generally play a sort of waiting game until the right (or wrong) man came along. It seems incredible (nowadays) but it was so, and it had the result that some of us wasted those precious years of youth.*

I do not think that my mother wasted very much of her youth. Her readings in Pascal, her devotion to Amiel, her struggles with Hegel, and her courageous attempt to teach herself Greek, were all tending towards the intellectual support and illumination which JB himself was going to bring to her. Moreover, although bookish, she was no blue-stocking, as she herself said in *The Edwardian Lady*.

> For all my philosophical readings I was the product of my world and the circumstances of my life. I soon developed a love of social life with parties and dancing. I even enjoyed what was then called 'a Drum', a sort of party where men and women were crowded together in a room and tried to talk to each other. It was held late in the evening, after dinner, and was considered by most people a boring duty, a sort of sweep-up of acquaintances. But Drums had their points all the same—at least to a young person who was eager to see people, coiffures and clothes, and not to be called upon to make much contribution.

*Susan Tweedsmuir, *The Edwardian Lady*.

There can hardly ever have been two people more widely different from one another than my Scottish and English Grandmothers. My father's mother was tiny, my mother's tall and straight as a grenadier. My Scottish grandmother (Gran) despised women whose housework was done for them by servants, although she had admirable servants of her own, with whose work she constantly interfered. My English grandmother (Tin), an artist and writer who was also much occupied with public service, would have been as helpless without servants as a Manchu princess. Gran lived her days truly in the fear of the Lord, but not without a comforting sense of being one of the Elect; she thought all matters not connected with the Kirk trivial if not actually wicked. Tin was an agnostic, chiefly out of loyalty to her beloved Norman, and not, I think, without occasional misgivings. Gran had an extremely poor opinion of the English, a race of which, until my mother appeared, she had hardly known a single member. Tin's experience of Scotland was confined to visits to country houses and castles, and it is doubtful whether she had ever seen the inside of a Scottish kirk. What both had in common was great kindness and hospitality, a strong interest in family affairs, and a long widowhood: each was to outlive a husband by many years—Gran by twenty-six and Tin by forty-two.

All through my childhood and adolescence, up to her death in 1940, Tin was a stable point in my life, a kind and wise counsellor and, on occasion, a severe and impressive critic. It would be unfair for me to make comparisons between the two grandmothers in terms of affection. I saw less of Gran than I did of Tin and, although Gran had much to offer where holidays and hospitality were concerned, Tin was near at hand, readily accessible, not only during my holidays, but when, later, I went to work in London. I saw very much more of her than I did of my Scottish relations and it would be useless to deny that I felt happier in her company than I did in Gran's.

My Scottish grandmother's view of my mother was for long to be conditioned by the kind of misconceptions so obstinately cherished about one another as much by nations as by different ranks of society. She had probably never seriously envisaged her son's marrying, and if she had, it would certainly not have been to an English girl, and one whom she probably thought of as a 'social butterfly'. It cannot be denied that, from the moment of learning of her son's intentions towards my mother, she behaved with a stark ungraciousness which must have been as bewildering to her future daughter-in-law as it was painful to her son. Fortunately my mother was deeply and truly in love, and so able to face treatment by my grandmother of a kind that she could never even have imagined, in her own kindly and graceful world. Their fearsome encounters, however, must have had their comical side. My mother, on her first visit to Peebles, to meet her prospective husband's family, was urgently enjoined by Anna not to bring a maid. So JB had to make a special trip from Edinburgh, where he was working, to conduct his fiancée, who had never before travelled alone, to Peebles.

No words of praise could be high enough for my mother's demeanour during what must have been in many ways a mystifying as well as a trying experience. It was the greatest good fortune that she and Anna became at once, and remained always, firm friends. My uncles loved and admired their sister-in-law from the start; and my grandfather and she appreciated one another deeply. Only Gran remained aloof, glowering and reciting texts and generally having the vapours, and that must have been one of the occasions on which JB was obliged to be unusually severe with her.

If my mother ever complained about my grandmother's behaviour, she did so in private, and to JB's ear alone. In later life she often defended Gran to me, pointing out her good qualities, gently playing down her more tiresome ones, reminding me of many kindnesses that I had had at her hands. Gran did have one true and proper grievance with which I entirely sympathise. When the marriage finally took place, the Church of England, still pre-ecumenical in its attitudes, refused to allow my grandfather to take part in the service. While I suppose this was part of the rules then obtaining, it still seems to me singularly cruel, and moreover guaranteed to confirm my grandmother in her dislike of all things English and particularly of the English Church.

In common with many men, my father's first idea on marrying was to introduce his young wife to his favourite outdoors sports. Accordingly, part of their honeymoon was spent at Cortina d'Ampezzo in the Dolomites, where they set off to climb on Monte Cristallo. My mother quickly realised that this pastime was not for her. She was not reassured by their French guide, who urged her to 'put her feet in the void'. So JB, ever adaptable, gave up trying to teach her to climb. The young couple left Cortina for Venice and spent happy days splashing about on the Lido, which was still being transformed from a small fishing village to the smart resort of palace hotels and beach cabins so hauntingly described five years later by Thomas Mann in *Death in Venice*. They returned to set up house in Edinburgh, so that my father could go every day to the Parkside printing and binding works of Thomas Nelson and Son, having taken over from Tommy Nelson during the latter's absence on holiday. After that there was a period of house-hunting in London which ended in their taking a lease on No. 40 Hyde Park Square. They were, on the whole, to be happy years for my parents, those seven years between their marriage and the outbreak of war. JB still had his health; he had an interesting and inspiring job, which he worked hard to make even more so; and his young wife and he were much sought after, both in Edinburgh and London. They dined out continually, stayed in various country houses, and entertained modestly themselves.

In the following year my sister Alice was born. At that time John Buchan was extremely busy, on top of all his other work, with raising a fund to buy a portion of the Plains of Abraham, the site of the Battle of Quebec, for a public park. In that battle, which won Quebec for Britain, both Wolfe and the French commander, Montcalm, lost their lives. The park was to be a memorial to both armies. 'Canada has always been a hard country to govern for the reason that it consists of two nations—French and English,' said Dr Parkin CMG, a Canadian, speaking at the Mansion House when a committee was formed to advance the project. 'There is nothing that could consolidate the *entente* in the great Dominion more than the conservation of the Plains of Abraham, as it would be the means of wiping out the past animosity of the two nations'. This event is worth recording, since it gives one of many examples of the selfless effort JB was capable of putting into any cause that appealed to him, and because it is one of the now obvious steps on the road which was to lead him, one day, to practical experience of the problems of *entente* in Canada.

My sister's birth came at a sunny moment. She was much photographed—Kodaks, then almost a generic term for cameras, were becoming ubiquitous—with all the members of the family back to her grandparents' generation. There are pictures of JB holding her gingerly, looking, like most newly made fathers, as if he thought she might explode; and others of my mother looking mildly surprised. The nurse whom I was to know as Old Nanny came to my family at Alice's birth. She must have been thought thoroughly trustworthy because my parents felt able to go away on several extended holidays, besides their regular yearly visits to Scotland.

In 1910 they went to Constantinople by the Orient Express, there to join Gerard Craig-Sellar on his steam yacht *Rannoch* and make a tour of the Greek Islands. They touched at Lemnos, landed at Thermopylae, and, again, one evening, on one of the Petali islands.

> Some way back from the shore, standing in what appeared to be walled gardens, stood a long, low house with a mellow red roof. It was shuttered and impenetrable. We stared at it hoping that someone might emerge from it who would tell us who lived there, but no one came, and we had to content ourselves with walking along a carefully made road fringed with bushes which dipped and wound round hills and promontories. We returned to the yacht still burning with curiosity about the history of house and island.

All that is strange, original, secret, out of the rut, is grist to a writer's mill. JB's short story 'The Lemnian' (which appeared in *The Moon Endureth*, 1912) belongs to that holiday: the shuttered house on the island is the sinister house of Plakos in *The Dancing Floor* (1926).

The following year they went to fish on the Leardal in Norway. There they lived in a farmhouse, a *saeter*, and that and the Norwegian landscape are re-created in *The Three Hostages*. On another occasion they stayed at Rosensee in Bavaria, fishing, boating and walking in the woods, in territory which would later be used in *Greenmantle* and *A Prince of the Captivity*.

John and Susan, like most young couples, revelled in the discovery of one another, the exchange and adjustment of each other's experiences and opinions, the joyful sense of setting out on a joint adventure. This comes out strongly in their early letters, which are full of absurd nicknames, shared jokes, shared ambitions and anxieties. My mother had never ceased to mourn her father, whose death when she was sixteen had removed a most comforting, stable point in her life. There were only seven years between her and JB at the time of their marriage, yet I believe that the return of a competent and reassuring masculine presence, an alert, practical and perceptive mind, while it brought to her much that she had never known, served also to restore an element sorely missed.

Wherever they went on holiday, JB usually found comic situations, invented serial games, composed stories and poems to heighten the pleasures they and their friends found together. He was never very good at drawing, but tried his hand at it just the same, sometimes decorating his letters with sketches, once or twice producing pages of pictures to illustrate the comedies of travel abroad. He could provide comic verses at very short notice. Travelling with my mother in a New England bus, at the time of their first visit to America in 1924, he was confronted at the entrance to a village, with a large notice which read: 'You are entering ——home of the author of "We are lost!" the Captain shouted as he staggered down the stairs.' Delighted with this, JB caused scandal in the bus by rather loudly completing the couplet: 'For the hired hand's got the whisky and the wasps have got the pears!'

I have mentioned that JB had failed to dazzle his young wife with the pleasures of mountaineering, but he did not abandon this interest. It was a sport which perhaps gave him more pleasure than any other.

> A long rock climb is a series of problems, each one different from the rest, which have to be solved by ingenuity of mind and versatility of body. I was fortunate to have the opposite of vertigo, for I found physical comfort in looking down from great heights. Bodily fitness is essential, for there are always courses which you must have the strength to compete or court disaster. . . . I know no physical well-being so perfect as that enjoyed by the mountaineer.

I have to say, with sorrow, that here is one of the places where I part company with my father. As in so many other things he soars away from me, while I remain earthbound. JB's children probably disappointed him in several ways, although he would never have admitted this, but it must have been vexing to find that all four of us suffered acutely from vertigo at no greater height than the top of a church tower. The same was true of my mother. If this disability can be inherited it must have come to us from her, since my father's sister and brothers happily accompanied him on many climbs, both in the Cuillins and in the Alps.

JB did several more climbs between his marriage and the outbreak of war; indeed, in *The Scottish Mountaineering Club Journal* of 1940, his old friend and climbing companion, Stair Gillon, speaks of him as being at his best in 1913.

When I knew him his methods were original, unconventional, individualistic, but his movements were sure, decided, purposeful, and invariably he finished his climb. His assets were strong fingers and arms, rather short legs of enormous lifting power, an enviable poise, and a body that had limpet qualities. . . . His physical reserves were enormous. I never saw him tired. Mentally he had purpose indomitable, patience, courage, calm, self-control and, nerve.

My father made at least one 'first ascent' in the Cuillins, towing behind him his rather stout younger brother Walter, who at one point became seriously stuck in a crevice. Many years later Uncle Walter said to me: 'I don't think you younger ones realised quite what an exciting person your father was. If he proposed something, however dangerous or difficult, we simply could do nothing else but follow him. He kept our hearts in our mouths half the time!'

In 1926, when I was ten, we spent a part of our holidays at an inn at Chapel-le-Dale in the West Riding of Yorkshire. The hills in that region are a little like the Border hills. They have glens, and green pastures and sheep, but they differ in that there are also towers and buttresses and outcrops of limestone rock, excellent for an unambitious sort of climbing. Few of the rock formations near at hand were high enough to bring on vertigo, and my brothers and I had a good time scrambling about on them. There were places where streams (called 'becks' instead of 'burns') had carved their way through limestone beds to make narrow gullies with sheer sides. That part of Yorkshire is, of course, famous among pot-holers. Alum Pot and Gaping Ghyll (as frightening as its name) were not far away, and each rock-face above a low-running beck was riddled with holes and passages.

My father thought it would be a good idea to teach his sons something about rock climbing, so he got a length of rope and we set off for one of the limestone ravines to try a climb. JB put himself in the middle of the rope, with Alastair behind him and myself in front. I was then popped like a ferret into a rock-corridor and told to go ahead. The passage was narrow, but I elbowed my way along towards a circle of daylight. When I reached it I looked over the edge and did not like what I saw. The rushing beck seemed to me to be a thousand feet below—I do not suppose it was more than forty—the sides of the ravine were sheer and offered, as far as I could see, about as good a foothold as plate glass. My father's tones of encouragement had turned to vexation. Slim as he was, he was too big for the passage. He was stuck. I was terrified, and therefore furious. I announced in fairly sharp tones that I did not wish to continue this foolhardy exercise, and demanded to be withdrawn from my dangerous perch. Eventually, after much patient wriggling, my father extricated himself and me. With his usual equanimity he seemed to accept at once that rock climbing *en famille* was not a practical proposition. Harold Nicolson's Miss Plimsoll in *Some People* said, 'We must be careful, we must be very careful not to become a muff!' Where rock climbing was concerned I fear that muffs were exactly what we were.

JB had one more try at interesting us in climbing. In the early summer of 1934 Johnnie left England for Africa. He had been accepted for the Colonial Service the year before, and now he was on his way to take up the post of Assistant District Commissioner in Uganda. This first departure, prefiguring others, was a shock to the family organism. My mother liked to have her family around her at all times—in this one respect resembling Gran—and had never taken kindly to the absence of any one of us, even on short visits away. She was so unhappy, as indeed were we all in varying degrees (I alone envying Johnnie his chance to travel, to go far away) that JB swallowed his dislike of Europe, put away the evil memories of France he had from the war, and took us all to Talloires on the Lake of Annecy in Haute Savoie. There we lived in the house of a doctor, having our meals under the vine trellises of a small restaurant down the road. We rowed on the lake and swam in its cold, clear water, and went on the steamboat down to Annecy, to Duingt or Menton, to see castles and churches and eat marvellous *pâtisseries*. We dined, unforgettably, on *poulet à l'estragon* at the Restaurant Marius Bise.

JB had chosen Haute Savoie for two reasons: if he had to go to Europe, he preferred to go somewhere which had happy memories of his climbing days, and none of the war. We were not far from Chamonix, and somewhere in the ranges behind Talloires stood the great mass of Mont Blanc; also, at that time, he was seeing a lot of Stanley Baldwin, whose habit it was to spend some weeks every summer taking a cure at Aix-les-Bains. My father proposed to Baldwin that they should use the opportunity of being in the same territory to meet and talk about certain matters in complete secrecy. JB was much taken by the idea of 'two men meeting at a country inn': it made the whole business of going abroad more purposeful and, I suspect, more interesting. As I have suggested, he found family holidays a little difficult to manage. Alice was then aged twenty-six and married, I was eighteen and Alastair fifteen. With such a spread of ages, temperaments, tastes and interests—some aspects of which he must have found mystifying, unworthy or plain futile—he may well have found us insufficiently clear-cut to fit into the kind of categories which he would have preferred for us.

We went to Chamonix on a blinding hot day. The little town which JB remembered as a village was noisy, dusty, ugly and commercial. The great glacier, the Mer de Glace, looked yellow and dingy. Our expressions of polite boredom must have been exasperating.

The village of Talloires lies on the northern shore of the Lake of Annecy at its farthest end. Above it woods and upland pastures rise steeply to the stone towers of the Dents de l'Anfan. JB soon grew restless. Pottering, swimming, eating and visiting castles, which suited Alastair and me well enough, did not satisfy him. There had to be an expedition of a more strenuous kind, and so we rose very early one morning and set off upwards towards a pass from which we should be able to see the dawn over Mont Blanc.

The expedition was not a success. All went well to begin with, as we climbed through dark pinewoods and traversed dusky meadows, with the rock peaks high above us. The valleys were still full of night, while the uplands were beginning to be touched by morning. I remember with pleasure the little bubbles of sound from many cowbells which came up from the dark below us. Things began to get difficult when, after a long climb, we had to file along narrow paths beside precipitous depths—something that a mountaineer would never even have noticed but which was more than enough for Alastair and me. We struggled on, complaining bitterly, but it has to be admitted that one sunrise over Mont Blanc was completely wasted on everyone except JB.

Once again my father accepted his children's feebleness with philosophy. We attempted no more mountains. What saddened me, on JB's account, was that Stanley Baldwin, whose soul was not romantic, was not available for the meeting to which JB had so much looked forward. We did go to Aix-les-Bains, but for a less exciting encounter with Professor Lindemann (later Lord Cherwell; scientific adviser to Sir Winston Churchill, 1939–45), of whom, one way and another, we saw quite enough at home.

7

THE LURE OF POLITICS

John Buchan was adopted in 1911 as Conservative candidate for the counties of Peebles and Selkirk.

> My motives were mixed. I had always felt that it was a citizen's duty to find some form of public service, but I had no strong parliamentary ambitions. While I believed in party government and party loyalty, I never attained to the happy partisan zeal of many of my friends, being painfully aware of my own and my party's defects, and uneasily conscious of the merits of my opponent. . . .

It would be hard to imagine a sentiment more likely to turn a party whip's hair white than that one.

> I came of a Liberal family, most of my friends were Liberals, I agreed with nine-tenths of the Party's creed. . . . Now that the once omnipotent Liberal party has so declined it is hard to realise how formidable it was in 1911—especially in Scotland. Its dogmas were so completely taken for granted that their presentation partook less of argument than of a tribal incantation. Mr Gladstone had given it an aura of earnest morality, so that its platforms were also pulpits and its harangues had the weight of sermons. Its members seemed to assume that their opponents must be lacking either in morals or mind.

My mother once summed up this attitude by quoting: 'Tories may think they are better born, but Liberals know that they are born better.' Substituting Socialists for Liberals that phrase would do very well today.

A quotation from Alexander Robb's 'Memorandum' for November 1879 well illustrates what JB called Mr Gladstone's 'Sinaitic authority'.

November

24th—Mr Gladstone's arrival in Edinburgh as candidate for the county of Midlothian attended by extraordinary demonstrations both in town and country.

29th—During the last few days Mr Gladstone has given several addresses in Edinburgh, Dalkeith and West Calder; his reception has been beyond anything that has taken place since the first Reform Bill; the enormous crowds of people that attended his meetings have been unprecedented. All Scotland is stirred to the very *core* by his wonderful eloquence. He has ten addresses to give in Glasgow before leaving for England. The weather on the whole has not been unfavourable for the great campaign against *Tory misrule*.

My father must have known that he had little chance of beating his Liberal opponent, Mr (later Sir) Donald Maclean, but thought the campaign good experience. It was to be fought among his own people, the Border countrymen whom he loved and admired more than anyone in the world, even though one or another of them frequently said to him, 'I'd dae onything for ye but vote for ye.'

As at everything that he put his hand to, JB worked hard at his constituency, quartering the large territory which stretched from within a dozen miles of Edinburgh to within twenty miles of the Border. My mother accompanied him on many of his canvassing trips and speaking engagements. They had taken Harehope, an old house in the Meldon Hills, four miles from Peebles. My mother was expecting her second child and so, I imagine, was excused the more strenuous undertakings. She always spoke of her time at Harehope with glowing affection: she had loved the place for its remoteness, lost as it was in rolling moorland at the end of a long farm road. Three-year-old Alice was well and happy, and John obviously enjoying himself greatly. Trouble was in the wind, but that summer of 1911 must have been golden, and thus my mother remembered it.

Fighting an election evidently brought out qualities in JB which I was never to see. His politics were an odd mixture. He had modified somewhat his imperial beliefs of six years before. His perception of the self-determining needs of the Dominions had caused him to change his mind about Imperial Federation, although he still believed passionately in 'the possibilities of the Empire as a guardian of world peace, and as a factor in the solution of all our domestic problems'.

I cannot think that JB was cut out to be a politician, certainly not 'a good party man', a blindly loyal specimen of lobby-fodder. He too easily—and, for party-political purposes, fatally—saw the other side's point of view, detected good in opposing doctrines, and refused to see things, in his own phrase, 'in terms of ink and snow'. He adopted for his own use political concepts which were anathema to his own party. He was at once too honest, too unprejudiced, too romantic and, in a sense, too innocent for the party-political game. Nevertheless he had much pleasure, and some useful experience, from his candidature, and he greatly enjoyed the rough-and-tumble of political meetings, the lively heckling as much as the serious questioning. He enjoyed bringing in national figures, such as F. E. Smith and Lord Robert Cecil, to adorn his platforms. Even though he knew he was pretty sure to lose the contest, and did in fact lose it, he enjoyed imparting a 'fairly thorough political education' to people who had not heard both sides of the question so scintil-latingly argued before.

JB's habit of seeing all around questions, his unwillingness to come down firmly on one side or another, was the cause of some anxiety, and probably irritation, to his political friends, several of whom genuinely wanted to see him in Parliament. The habit would persist with him throughout his life. It was certainly a cause of re-sentment to some of his compatriots, who no doubt disliked one or two coldly accurate appraisals of the Scottish character which came from his pen. Nevertheless it enabled him to draw sympathetic portraits, in his books, of conscientious objectors (at a time when these were being hounded), of rabid Socialists, even of the hated Kaiser himself. Because of it, his villains, albeit loathly, are never without one redeeming feature, except perhaps Moxon Ivery in *Mr Standfast* who is a physical coward. His despatches from the front, when he was *Times* correspondent at the beginning of the 1914 war, were models of objectivity, in marked contrast to the heat and hysteria of most war reporting; and, as Director of Information, from 1917 on, he set his face against the use of false and inflam-matory propaganda at home or abroad. Finally, when he came to his last and greatest work, as Governor-General of Canada, it was precisely his clear, instructed, all-round view of that country's place in the world, together with his embracing human sympathy, that guaranteed the success of his office.

At the time of his first adventures into politics, however, he aroused a certain amount of mystification, even of suspicion, among the orthodox. Those who wished him well were impatient to set his feet on the road to a political career. In a letter dated in January 1909, my mother wrote to him describing a dinner-party of political people which she had just attended: 'Mr Amery [the Rt. Hon. L. S. Amery] kept on saying at intervals throughout the evening: "John *must* stand for Parliament and he must belong to one side or the other!"'

On 19 November 1911 the Rev. John Buchan died at Peebles. Six days later my brother John was born, at the house in Bryanston Street to which my parents had moved from Hyde Park Square.

My grandmother was once again very ill, and JB had not only the sorrow of losing his father, but serious anxiety about his mother and concern for his wife as well, and all on top of constituency work and publishing and writing. (*Prester John* had appeared the year before. *The Moon Endureth* would be out in 1912, and the first *Montrose*, with all the research it needed, must have been in the making.)

It was in 1911, as my mother has recorded, that 'a small cloud had appeared on the horizon about John's health. He began to be troubled with indigestion which at first yielded easily to treatment, but the hastily eaten meals before meetings did him no good, and that year a deep sorrow came to us.'

JB had always been particularly close to his brother Willie, and had watched over his career when, as a boy, he had first idled at school and then suddenly taken to working very hard, having decided to aim for the Indian Civil Service. JB helped and advised him, and finally had the pleasure of seeing him follow his own footsteps to Brasenose, where he played football for his college, the only one of us ever to be any good at that game. Willie passed high into the Indian Civil, and was evidently going to be extremely successful in it when, home on leave in 1912, he became ill. He died on 11 November of that year.

Of all the sorrows and tragedies I have seen, this was one of the most poignant. We watched the worsening of his condition and the complete helplessness of the doctors in the face of his mysterious illness, and tried to gather fortitude from his stark courage. He was one of the finest looking young men I have ever seen, and his outstanding work in the Indian Civil Service was admired and recognised.

Willie went out to India in 1903 and his first job was as Assistant Magistrate and Collector in a remote district of Bengal. (Thereafter he was always known as 'Bogley' to his family, after the Collector of Bogley Wallah in *Vanity Fair*.) By 1907 he was Under-Secretary to the Government of Bengal and in 1908 he became Registrar of Co-operative Credit Societies in that province. These, known generally as Land Banks, were designed to help the Hindu peasants who, for centuries, had been enmeshed in debt to moneylenders, usually Muslims. The Land Banks were a detail of an agricultural policy which was one of the more lasting contributions to India of British rule. It was better for the peasants to be in debt to a bank than to a burly Punjabi whose method of enforcement was a bamboo stick. Willie, who as a boy seems to have shown his family's usual mixture of singular pugnacity with great sweetness of character had, like his father, a powerful sympathy for the underdog.

I have been in India, and have seen some of the places that Willie knew. I too have lived in Calcutta and so can imagine the life of this handsome and delightful young man, fond of polo and dancing and shikar, yet hard-working, determined, generous and just. Of such was the true excellence of the Raj. For Willie's epitaph I would quote the words of his bearer, Mohammed Zahur, in a heart-rending letter written to my Aunt Anna after Willie's death: 'Further I beg to pray that there will not be found in the world such a master as my master was.'

I have so often mentioned health, its presence or absence, as a crucial factor in John Buchan's life that I think it worth showing where it began to go wrong. I have suggested that his South African experiences were probably the efficient cause of the internal trouble which was to beset him all his life, but it was not until 1911 and 1912, with their private anxieties added to a very full schedule of work, that what he was later to call 'the viper' began to attack him in earnest.

All this had the worst possible effect on his health, and after Willie died at a Glasgow nursing home John had to have a long spell in bed. The discomfort and pain did go away for months at a time, and we always hoped that it would go for good, but it always returned. John never let it make any difference to the work he was doing, and he went on with business and politics as hard as ever.★

A distinguished surgeon has remarked that 'duodenal trouble is the complaint of the best people'. By these he did not mean, of course, the denizens of Debrett but simply the people whose thought and action, energy and talent are best for their fellow-men. It does not need much study of the lives of celebrated people, and particularly those of writers and artists, to see that a high degree of talent almost invariably has to be paid for by some kind of physical disability.

It is difficult to see the medical profession as coming very well out of this story, but then it must be admitted that JB was not a good patient. Again and again his doctors must have told him to cut down his commitments, stay still, diet, go to bed early, refuse all requests for help in writing, speaking or administration—in short, relax. He would accept portions of this advice—diet perhaps, and going early to bed—but nothing could contain his energy, his ardent wish to go out and get things done, frequently for no more reward than the satisfaction of seeing them done well. It is possible that he could have made enough money, later on, to maintain Elsfield and his family simply by sitting at home and writing: but, for JB, this could never have been enough. The truth is that he needed the world, needed it positively, to keep his mind and his imagination fed, and would not relinquish it until he had found and met all the challenges, special to his own needs, which he believed it to contain.

John Buchan sometimes said that life had to be lived according to the terms on which it was given. He therefore accepted the physical disabilities under which he suffered, and carried on, in the main, as though they did not exist. It was rarely that anyone heard him complain, and when he did it was with a particular wry humour, self-mocking but never self-pitying.

We talk glibly, nowadays, about psychological compulsions, compulsive neuroses, psychosomatic illness, and much else besides, all equally poorly understood and richly misapplied. I should think more than twice before ascribing any particular compulsions to my father, beyond those of a Scottish Calvinist upbringing and

★ Susan Tweedsmuir in *John Buchan by his Wife and Friends*.

the needs of his own temperament. His was a daemon that urged him forward continually, and he would not, I think, have had things otherwise. Nevertheless, I have always been puzzled by a remark made by a celebrated German specialist, Dr Marten, to whose clinic in the Black Forest JB went in the early nineteen-twenties. Dr Marten was a physician and a psychologist, who specialised in identifying psychological causes for physical illness. His comment on John Buchan was: 'Never in my experience have I met anybody less frustrated or less crippled by inhibitions. He is free from neuroses. His trouble must be wholly of physical origin.'

I have worried over this statement for years. Certainly JB was not frustrated, unless his refusal to accept frustration concealed an admission of it. In all the time that I knew him, if he came up against any kind of brick wall, he either fetched a ladder, or walked on until he found a door. He never wasted a moment trying to scale the unscalable. As to inhibitions, he had, of course, plenty, as do we all, but they were rather the kind of inhibitions (in the sense that they inhibited futile or dangerous courses of action) which he would have welcomed as liberating him to forge ahead in pursuit of what he thought desirable. Yet there remains still something a little odd about Dr Marten's comment. He was a scientist and a German: he cannot have made many such expansive pronouncements in all his professional life. I think it just possible that, in JB, the doctor had met his match, someone who could see many moves ahead, and who had not just an answer ready, but the answer which was most likely to be acceptable.

John Buchan's war service has been so well documented that I shall not go into it again, except as it affected his health and his literary output. In July 1914 the family went to Broadstairs in Kent. Alice had had an operation for mastoid, and had been prescribed sea air for her convalescence. JB, who had spoken with Sir Edward Grey, the Foreign Secretary, before leaving London knew what was coming in Europe. On 4 August war was declared and, from the beginning, things went badly; first Liège fell, then Namur; Belgium was overrun.

JB had a bad attack of his internal pain and had to go to bed. He had applied to join the army but 'was told that in his present state of health it was useless to think of it, and that he might be used in other ways later on'. So, faced with a temporarily unscalable wall, bored and restless in the seaside lodgings, he settled down to write a book.

He had once said to my mother, after reading some detective stories: 'I should like to write a story of this sort and take real pains with it. Most detective story writers don't take half enough trouble with their characters, and no one cares what becomes of either the corpse or the murderer.' He had probably had an idea in his head for a long time; now he wrote it down. It was *The Thirty-Nine Steps*; by no means his first book, but the one which was to make him famous all over the world.

That book was not, of course, a detective story of the conventional kind. To outwit the enemy, the hero, Richard Hannay, had to do some detective work on Scudder's coded diary, but the true originality of the book lies in its widespread and swift-moving action. Two favourite Buchan themes are developed: that of the amateur, thrown into bizarre circumstances, who reacts correctly and bests the professionals at their own game; and that of the permanent presence of crime and violence beneath the placid surface of what is called civilisation. The latter theme had been treated before, in *The Power-House* which, although written earlier, was published later (1916) than *The Thirty-Nine Steps* (1915).

Altogether JB was in bed for three months at the beginning of the war. He assuaged his despair at being so tied by the leg while the life of action called, and his friends were dying in France, not only by writing his novel but by beginning *Nelson's History of the War* which he was to continue with throughout the next four years. This venture was planned by Nelson's not only to provide a public service but also to ensure work for the machines and what was left of the work-force at Parkside. It was to appear in 50,000-word parts, once every four months, and JB was to write it. All the profits of the work, together with JB's royalties, were to go to the families of Nelson people who had enlisted, and to war charities.

The Thirty-Nine Steps was sent to Blackwood's the publishers with a note saying, 'It has amused me to write, but whether it will amuse you to read is another matter.' The book was accepted at once. In his dedication to Tommy Nelson JB wrote: 'I should like to put your name on it, in memory of our long friendship, in these days when the wildest fictions are so much less improbable than the truth.'

John Buchan in 1915 was in his fortieth year, well beyond the age of enlistment and in any case medically unfit. He was ill again during the winter of 1914–15, and was once again enjoined to rest, to make a long convalescence. For his convalescence he got himself appointed in May as *Times* correspondent at the Front, and there remained until after the Battle of Loos in September 1915. He was home for a short while after that, doing work for the Foreign Office, and bearing a heavier load at Nelson's than ever before, since two of the partners and 67 per cent of the firm's male employees had joined up. He was then commissioned into the Intelligence Corps and, in late autumn, was back in France.

In June 1916 the Foreign Office again demanded his services, and in August of that year he was appointed to Haig's staff in France, and so had to shuttle between the two spheres of activity. In a letter to an old friend he said: 'I have as usual too much work to do, but I like it and I think I have got the most interesting job on the globe, for I live at the heart of things here and in France.'* He was always to like living at the heart of things. In his autobiography he wrote: 'The attitude of the detached observer was always difficult for me. To achieve any peace of mind I had to have some share, however small, in the business itself.'

Taken all in all, JB's share in the war was far from small. It might not have been possible for him to be a combatant, but his services in writing war commentaries and lecturing were greatly in demand by both the Foreign and War Offices. Meanwhile, his health grew worse. For all his reassuring letters, arriving on odd scraps of paper nearly every day, my mother was not deceived. She knew that endless moving about, unsuitable meals grabbed at odd hours, cold and wet and rough living were almost as dangerous for JB as anything the official enemy might be throwing at him. In October 1916, while at the Front, he had a really serious attack. He was alone at the time. In great pain, and very slowly, he managed to crawl to the door of his billet and attract the attention of a sentry. He was taken to a Casualty Clearing Station. He refused to go either to a hospital or home to England, and, when he had more or less recovered, carried on with his work.

By the end of 1916 his illness had been diagnosed, at any rate to the satisfaction of his doctors, as duodenal trouble. He was invalided back to England and, early in 1917, underwent the dangerous, and at that time near-experimental, operation of 'short-circuiting' at his home in Portland Place. For his convalescence he and my mother went down to Checkendon in Berkshire to the house of old friends, the F. S. Olivers. She wrote of their stay in *John Buchan by his Wife and Friends*.

* Quoted in Janet Adam Smith, *John Buchan*.

We read aloud in the evenings and John slept for most of the day. If he could have continued living a peaceful and placid existence he would have been saved from ill-health for the rest of his life, but when we returned to London he had to take up his work. Red leather boxes poured in on him even while we were at Checkendon, filled with official papers.

Just before his operation JB had anyway been recalled from France to take over, as Director, the new Department of Information, under the War Office. It was an inspired appointment and although he was to find it thorny in many ways—age-old quarrels between the Foreign Office and the War Office, disagreements with powerful editors over propaganda—JB was able to bring to it his fertile imagination and romantic ingenuity, his persistence in persuasion, as well as his proved talents for writing and speaking, and his skill as an expositor, as one who could make complicated matters plain.

He collected a strong team of associates from many different fields, some of them old friends whom he knew to be both clever and trusty, others whose work and intelligence he admired. He fought running battles for his department up and down the stuffy corridors of Whitehall. He was not universally popular, particularly with the more old-fashioned sections of the press, nor were his vision and grasp of propaganda needs and methods always appreciated. To many people the word propaganda was still suspect, being equated with the propagation of vainglorious lies. JB believed in telling the truth about Britain and her struggle, to America, to the Dominions, to the neutral countries, and to his own people. He employed every medium then available—indeed, he was the first to use cinema on the battlefield, recognising that films were an unsurpassable method of driving home the facts of conflict—and he commissioned war artists to work on the different fronts.

Beyond illness and overwork, 1917 was a miserable year for John Buchan. Tommy Nelson was killed in France in March, and Alastair, the much-loved Mhor, fell at Arras on 19 April. JB somehow managed to write to his mother every day, to try to comfort her. She was nearly out of her mind with grief, and distressed her family greatly by insisting that Alastair's death was in some way a judgement on herself, retribution for faults or errors which none but she could see.

Contemplating this period in my father's life, I am staggered by what he managed to achieve and endure. Because his department was only that, and not a ministry in its own right, he had to put up with continual crossfire from the established ministries, and suspicion and incomprehension at Cabinet level. He worked successfully to alter that state of affairs and, in February 1918, the Ministry of Information came into being, with Lord Beaverbrook as Minister, and JB as Director of Intelligence. They worked well together. Beaverbrook showed the same flair and determination in that war as he would, as Minister of Aircraft Production, in the next. He fought for the new ministry in the Cabinet, was a loyal chief, and was particularly effective in telling the story of Britain's war effort in America.

'I never knew how tired I was till the war stopped,' JB said when it was all over. He had done a remarkable job and had lived, as he would always most like to live, at the very centre of affairs. As Director of Intelligence he had seen something of the more cryptic side of war. Once, when I was lunching with him at the Café Royal, he stopped in mid-sentence to say: 'Something's just come back to me. I have some funny memories of this place. I used to interview people here, in an upstairs room, under the name of Captain Stewart!'

He ended the war a lieutenant-colonel and, although he went very thankfully back to civilian life, he continued to be addressed as that for a long time afterwards. I do not think that he ever used the title himself, but the press usually referred to him as Colonel, and 'soldier' was always in the list of his achievements as set out in the newspapers. I think it likely that, because of Richard Hannay, whose military career made him (rather rapidly) a major-general, some people thought that his creator must be a regular soldier as well.

In addition to the more or less punctual appearances of the parts of *Nelson's History of the War*, John Buchan published *Greenmantle* in 1916, *Poems, Scots and English* in 1917, and *Mr Standfast* in 1919.

The short-circuiting operation in 1917 had proved a failure. The duodenal pain returned at more or less regular intervals. No doctor seemed able to find a cure for it, nor even to determine exactly what might be its cause. Since I am myself unable even to think, let alone work, if I am suffering from any kind of internal upset, I consider with admiration and astonishment the way in which my father continued with his writing, continued to fulfil a variety of obligations, whilst always in what would be, for most people, the most demoralising kind of discomfort, if not in actual pain. The malady entailed a regime of dreary restrictions upon food and drink and would have been, to almost anyone else, extremely lowering. JB bore it with admirable fortitude, refusing to allow it to restrict his life. Very occasionally he would make a disgusted face, when he was plagued by nausea or flatulence, but in no general sense would he allow discomfort to distract him from working or thinking, nor to spoil his pleasure in walking, riding, fishing or the society of his family and friends. It is just possible that the remedy really did lie in his own hands, and that he knew this. Nothing, however, would make him take his doctors' and his family's advice and slacken his high-speed progress. He must simply have decided that a continual battle with his stomach was the price he had to pay for being the kind of person that he was: that the rewards achieved, both tangible and intangible, made it all worth while.

It might be thought, because JB never allowed his ailment to interfere with his plans, that therefore, it is of no great importance in his story. I think otherwise. It does not require any intensive study of his works to see how often he harks back to youth, to youthful vigour, even to a youthful appetite for food, to an existence untrammelled by defects of body or mind. In what was perhaps an exercise in sympathetic magic, JB gave duodenal trouble to Blenkiron in *Greenmantle*, and then allowed him to be cured of it in *Mr Standfast*. At the time of writing the latter book, which came out in 1919, JB was still able to hope that the short-circuiting operation might really be achieving its object.

He continued to move with speed and worked concentratedly all through the nineteen-twenties; but every so often his pain would make him call a halt, if only for a few days, and drive him back to the doctors for yet another examination. He could not put on weight, looked perpetually much too thin, and not infrequently downright ill. Inured as he had been from his earliest years to the idea of human life as a kind of obstacle race, he accepted that there was one obstacle which he would probably never clear. He took comfort, therefore, from any bit of good news that could be provided by the medical profession. There was more than a touch of pathos in his assertions, after some examination, that he, in his fifties, 'had the arteries of a man of twenty-five' or that 'there was nothing whatever wrong with his heart'. His muscular strength held up almost to the end of his life. On his sixtieth birthday, in August 1935, while we were having our last family holiday near Brecon, he did a walk with Johnnie of forty miles, on one of the hottest days of the year. Two years later, in Canada, he nearly gave a lot of people heart-failure by climbing the hitherto unclimbed Bear Rock above the Mackenzie River, without benefit of rope or guide.

★

The years between my birth in 1916 and the outbreak of the Second War in 1939 were years of bitterness for very many people. 'What is our task?' Lloyd George asked, after the Armistice in November 1918. 'To make Britain a fit country for heroes to live in.' It may be that a few of the heroes prospered; it is certain that the majority did not.

> The war, the vastest disordering since the breakdown of the Pax Romana, must be followed by decades of suffering and penury. Many familiar things had gone, and many more would go. Britain had lost for good her old security in the world, and, like other peoples, she would have to struggle to preserve stability at home.

John Buchan's view of the post-war world was by no means dewy-eyed. He took some comfort from the things that had survived, was glad to see certain landmarks reappear as the smoke of war cleared away. Above all, what he had seen of ordinary men under battle conditions gave him 'a new confidence in human nature, in the plain man who for four years had carried the globe on his shoulders, with no gift of expression, unperplexed by philosophies, but infinitely loyal, enduring and unconquerable.'

We have come to see those two decades between the First and Second World Wars as simply a lull, an interim period between two phases of the same conflict. The plain man, and woman too, since civilians were to be as much involved as soldiers, once more, in 1939, took the globe upon their shoulders, but when the smoke of that war cleared away, it was to be seen that much which had remained apparently intact after 1918 was by then in ruins.

JB has noted that many people who survived the 1914–18 war had no other wish than to return to private life, to repair and consolidate what was their own, and to turn their backs on the larger affairs of the world. This, he thought, would have as bad an effect on the quality of public life as the loss of nearly a whole generation would have on the quality of management in business and industry.

My father had no intention of burying himself in a totally private life. Once he had recovered from the fatigue of the war years, his optimism returned. There was manifestly a lot to be done, and he was not going to be left out of the doing. We moved to Elsfield from London in 1920, so JB had his new home to put in order; he had Nelson's to reconstruct and expand; he had a new field of activity, having recently been appointed a director of Reuter's—

then also coming into full expansion—by Sir Roderick Jones, who had worked with him during the war; he had a dozen books in his head, and he had a strong wish to take part in political life. The early years at Elsfield were heady with hope and activity.

As children we were privileged in that we shared the good fortune which John Buchan had the power to create. In the simplest terms, all through the years of slump and depression and mounting anxieties throughout the world, we were fed, housed, educated and amused; we were party to important occasions, lived much in the society of clever, effective and often famous people; were listened to and encouraged to express ourselves; and could watch at close quarters, sometimes with awe, sometimes with amusement, sometimes with anxiety, the workings of an extraordinary mind and spirit.

JB knew that, as long as his health lasted, and the world remained—however precariously—at peace, he would always be able to make money by writing. The world wanted his books, and he could not imagine that he would not always be able to supply its need. He also knew that, for many reasons concerned with other activities than a writer's, the style of life which he had created would always use up a large part of his income. He did not, therefore, expect to be able to leave much money to his children: and this he always made plain to them. What he could do was to provide them with a happy upbringing, care for their health, and what was then thought to be the best education that money could buy. Thus equipped, and with his advice and some help from his extraordinarily wide acquaintanceship, they should be able to find something useful to do in the world, apart from anything that they might themselves be able to originate. He also expected them to be ambitious. He did not much care what, within certain bounds, the object of their ambition might be: for him ambition was an essential quality of intelligent and healthy youth.

We should have had to be remarkably insensitive not to have noticed, early in life, that some of the intense light which fell upon our parents fell also upon us. If, at a very early age, I was aware of my father's 'importance', it cannot have been much later that I realised that I, too, partook of it to some extent.

People were principally, of course, interested in JB, but some of the interest would spill over to include his children. Kind things were done for us, special attentions were given, not out of any desire to put our parents under an obligation, but rather, I believe, as an expression of gratitude for the pleasure that they gave. Very special privileges stemmed from this. For example, my brothers and I were serious amateur ornithologists and, in those unrestricted days, keen collectors of birds' eggs. During my childhood there lived in Oxford a certain Mr Tickner. His job in life was that of porter at the Clarendon Buildings in Broad Street, but he was a noted authority on birds.

Mr Tickner was short and slight, with a wispy yellow beard, and very bright eyes. His manners were courtly (he always addressed my mother as 'Gracious Lady'), and he treated small boys as if they were as grown-up and as expert as he. One day he arrived on his bicycle and announced that he knew where a nightingale was to be found, at the bottom of Woodeaton Wood. He thought it likely that she would be nesting. Should we go together to see if we could find the nest?

What followed very closely paralleled John Clare's famous poem. We stole towards the little enclave of thorns at the edge of the wood. We froze for many long minutes until, suddenly, the bird began to sing. Mr Tickner had told us that, for those who knew, the nearness of a nest could be judged from particular notes in the song. Evidently what the nightingale was singing, or rather gurgling, that morning indicated quite clearly that her nest was near. We crept forward, stooped, searched with the utmost care and eventually, were rewarded with sight of the tucked-away nest.

The story of the nightingale's nest may stand for many occasions when we were shown secrets, allowed to investigate mysteries, by knowledgeable and enthusiastic elders. Some of them might not have been particularly fond of children, but for John Buchan's children prejudice was put aside. It is for this reason, as much as any, that we grew up with respect and affection for a number of people older than ourselves, and were never conscious of what is now called 'the generation gap'.

We were lucky as children in that it was never even hinted that we were not all, in our own ways, interesting, and with interesting futures before us. No one who lived close to JB could ever have thought him anything but unique, complete in his own terms, irreproducible. We were not expected to be like him, except where his example was obviously to be followed. Lantern-jawed old gentlemen who shook their heads sadly, after inspecting me, with: 'Aye, ye'll never be the mon your feyther is!' were absolutely right—but then nobody had ever led me to expect to be that.

Naturally we grew up knowing that many eyes were upon us: that, one way or another, unusual things were expected. This was going to cause me difficulties during adolescence, at the time when the young seek most desperately for a style of their own, try their best to shape a valid identity. When it came to ambition, it was going to be hard to see what to be ambitious for, when JB had been so resoundingly successful in so many fields. The usual spurs to ambition are, I suppose, the need to escape from deprivation by making money; to live among beautiful and famous people; to make a mark in the history of one's country either through science, politics or the arts; or any combination of these. Our surroundings were far from humdrum, our influences liberal and audacious; our circumstances were ample; the famous and beautiful had been all round us since the cradle; we had much history in our blood.

8

THE VISITORS' BOOK

Of the many friends whom he had lost in the war, perhaps the one most continually mourned was Tommy Nelson. Heir to the Nelson publishing firm and many other things besides, he had captained Oxford at rugby football and later played for Scotland, and shot, fished and hunted with great skill and enthusiasm; yet, he was no ordinary sporting tough. Evidently he was one of those men exceptionally endowed with qualities of brains, heart, and attraction for others who seem now to have been bred for no other purpose than to be snuffed out in the shambles of the 1914 war. Perhaps they did not live in vain. Perhaps they existed to point a moral, to underline a truth, but it was a truth which, for many people, scarcely needed underlining, and their deaths deprived their country of talent and integrity and vision which, in the world after 1918, were to be so badly needed and so sadly lacking.

Returning to Nelson's after the war, with Tommy gone, and his brother Ian in charge, JB found a state of affairs less promising and less exciting than the one he had left in 1914. Still, he had his new responsibilities and he needed work that paid well, so he decided to continue with Nelson's, grateful for the presence of colleagues with whom he had always worked well in the past. He went to Edinburgh once a month, and otherwise worked in the Nelson offices in Paternoster Row, delightful, dusty, old-fashioned offices as I remember them, later to be destroyed by bombs in the Second World War.

JB had always believed passionately in education. He could see nothing but good coming from the spread of serious literature at cheap prices, and this thinking had inspired him to invent the famous 'Nelson Sevenpennies' of the early nineteen-hundreds.

After the war he decided to concentrate a good deal of his firm's efforts on educational works. He had become a full director of

Nelson's in 1915, when the firm became a limited company, and was on a contract which would come to an end in 1929. He had power to influence Nelson's publishing policy, which obviously came first with him, but he also gave a lot of his time and thought to managing the business, to paper supply and labour problems and machinery, as well as to the running of the overseas offices. To help with the editorial side he had brought in Sir Henry Newbolt, with whom he had worked closely at the Ministry of Information. Together they projected several series of books. The first, 'The Teaching of English', was followed by 'The Teaching of History', and a distinguished team of specialists was put together to write the separate volumes.

Sir Henry Newbolt's name is on the very first page of the Elsfield Visitors' Book, which begins in February 1920. The names on that page give an indication of the balance of the guests whom my parents entertained: my grandmother, Caroline Grosvenor; Gerard Craig-Sellar, a kindly man of enormous wealth who was my sister's godfather, and who had been at Oxford and on Milner's staff with my father; Harold Baker, one of JB's special circle at Oxford, later to be Warden of Winchester; and Henry Newbolt. These were the first to whom JB had chosen to exhibit his Elsfield improvements. His own family—mother, sister Anna and brother Walter—would come later, in the second week of April, as they would continue to do punctually for fourteen years, until the year my father and mother left for Canada and the house was shut up.

The Henry Newbolts came often in the first few years. It is strange how, from a shifting population impinging on my childhood, so few people—for all their celebrity, attitudes, mannerisms, courtesies (or lack of them), not to mention, in the case of some, the evident high opinion of their own value—managed to leave on me any lasting impression. But I remember Henry Newbolt for his fine, thin face, his gentle voice, his beautiful manners and the way in which he could give any child the sense of conferring a privilege by conversing with him.

John Masefield, who lived on Boar's Hill, an intellectual eminence on the south side of Oxford, used sometimes to come over; and, once again, speaking of memorable personality and fine manners, the impression he left is indelible. Years after I first met him, I took a journalist down from London to see him. Masefield had moved to a house on the Thames near Clifton Hampden. He was old by then, and rather fragile, but he gave us what some might call an 'old-world' welcome. Unfortunately my journalist was particularly thick-witted and, moreover, did not appear to have read any work by the man whom he had wanted to interview. Poor Masefield, struggling with a mind and method of expression with which he simply could not come to terms, looked increasingly unhappy—and unhappy, I am sure, not for himself but because he felt he was not, so to speak, giving value for money.

Kicking myself mentally for having let him in for such discomfort, I got the interview over as quickly as I could. My last recollection is of John Masefield waving to us from his front door, not (as might have been expected) with a look of acute relief, but rather with what I think was one of regret that he had not acquitted himself better.

Such manners as we acquire we learn from our elders. If the elders have bad manners or none, it will not be remarkable if their children have none either. Formal good manners, for the present, are out of fashion. What are called natural good manners are simply the expression of a naturally agreeable personality, and are happily not as rare as is sometimes proclaimed.

My father had the kind of manners which, without ever achieving them, I have always greatly admired. To begin with, when he greeted someone he greeted that person as a person, and not as an anonymous biped to be swiftly relegated in favour of something more exciting. When he talked to a person, at some gathering, he talked *to* him exclusively, did not allow his gaze to lift past his ear to see if someone more distinguished was coming into the room.

'He was enormously interested in people—interested, appreciative, receptive. . . . He would stand and face you and discuss endlessly—thin-haired, wedge-nosed, his head forward and to one side, his lips parted, eager to speak, eager to listen. I do not remember that he ever broke off a conversation.' Thus the Rt Hon. Walter Elliot—another Scot who had made a successful career in England—speaking in a broadcast to America two years after JB's death (published in a collection of broadcasts under the title *Long Distance*).

Marcel Proust began his great work of research into his past with the taste of a *madeleine* dipped in tea. I could consume half a hundredweight of *madeleines* and drink gallons of tea without producing a masterpiece. But to reinforce or galvanise my recollections of people the Elsfield Visitors' Book is certainly a great help.

In July 1921, Violet Markham (Mrs James Carruthers, CH) came to stay for three nights. I am surprised that more than a year should have passed before this visit, since Violet was one of my parents' oldest friends, and one who had a special influence on JB's career. To us children she was always Aunt Violet, although in fact she was no relation. She was also Alastair's godmother.

John Buchan, then aged twenty-eight, had first met the thirty-one-year-old Violet Markham in London in 1903. She was deeply interested in South African affairs, had enjoyed his book, *The African Colony*, and was a warm admirer of Lord Milner. The two had much in common, both in their reading of books and their political sympathies, although Violet was a passionate Liberal and JB his own special brand of Conservative.

Violet Markham came from a family of rich coal-owners in Derbyshire. Her mother was the daughter of Sir Joseph Paxton, gardener to the 6th Duke of Devonshire and architect of the Crystal Palace. The whole family was imbued with the sincerest humanitarian ideals; all were brisk, impatient and immensely hard-working. Violet's brother, Sir Arthur Markham, was a man of immense energy, a philanthropic colliery proprietor who spent as much time down the mine as he did in the board-room; who built model villages for his miners in Yorkshire and South Wales, and was a highly individualistic Liberal Member of Parliament.

His sister shared his liberal instincts, profound disquiet about the effects of unplanned industrialisation and passionate wish to improve matters by sensible, practical means. She travelled all over the world looking at industrial problems, and it was on a visit to Ottawa in 1905 that she met William Lyon Mackenzie King, then one of Canada's brightest young civil servants. They immediately became, and remained for all his life, firm friends who corresponded continually. Violet's knowledge of Canada and its leading personalities was considerable, and JB, in all his thinking about the Dominion—part of a life-long attraction to North America—must have found her a source of help and information.

It is interesting to follow the thread of JB's interest in Canada from the beginning of the century to his final apotheosis as its Governor-General. That interest had its first expression in the early nineteen-hundreds—before he knew Violet Markham—in articles for the *Spectator* and the *Scottish Review*. In those JB's tone is friendly, but inclined to be severe and a trifle patronising—he was still an avowed Imperialist—about the Canadians' wish to have their own navy and their own diplomatic service. 'The demand is, of course, impossible, but it is a healthy sign that Canada should make it. It is a proof of an advance in national stature.' In the end, Canada had both a navy and a foreign service, and there was to be no firmer defender of Dominion independence than John Buchan.

My parents met Violet Markham's friend Mackenzie King—by that time turned politician and, indeed, leader of the long-established ruling Liberal Party—with other Dominion Prime Ministers at Chatsworth in the autumn of 1923; the following year, on their first visit to Canada, they were invited by the Prime Minister to stay with him in Ottawa. It was a great success. Not only did JB and my mother enjoy it immensely, but he, by his speeches and his personality, made an excellent impression; so much so that Violet, knowing that Mackenzie King had greatly taken to JB, set about proposing him for the Governor-Generalship, to succeed Lord Byng in 1926.

Miss Markham, through her work for the once all powerful Liberal Party, her wide connexions in politics, her local influence in Derbyshire (she was at one time Mayor of Chesterfield), was a person of considerable importance—someone to be listened to attentively by such men as Baldwin, Devonshire and L. S. Amery. Since Lord Byng was very much on his side, it is possible, even probable, that JB would have become Canada's Governor-General ten years sooner than he did had there not been a constitutional crisis in 1926 involving Byng and Mackenzie King.

The idea remained; as did Violet Markham's determination that JB should once again have the chance of what she thought an ideal appointment. Mackenzie King never wavered in his wish to see John Buchan at Government House. He agreed with Miss Markham that JB as Governor-General would make an excellent change from 'the correct and conventional peer usually selected for these posts'. He had a somewhat ambivalent attitude to titles and honours, and wanted my father to come to Canada as plain John Buchan.

It would be otiose to look for romance in JB's relations with Violet Markham. At their warmest they might have been what the French call an *amitié amoureuse*, a close and loving friendship; and this was shared by my mother. Aunt Violet was short and brisk and definite, with a rather deep voice and a manner lightly reminiscent of the committee room. She had very shrewd bright eyes, and an air of great kindness tinged with impatience to get on and get things done. She had little time for trifles and, in her presence, it was impossible to think life anything but real and earnest. Nevertheless she had read widely, was an experienced mountain-climber, much-travelled, and deeply knowledgeable about food and wine. Her pretty Georgian house in Gower Street (next to Lady Ottoline Morrell's) was a centre for good talk and distinguished entertainment.

I am quite sure that it was Violet Markham who arranged the visit to Elsfield in October 1926 of William Lyon Mackenzie King and the Vincent Masseys. The latter my parents had also already met, two years before in Toronto.

The threads were being spun. All would, one day, turn out according to plan. John Buchan would be Governor-General of Canada and years later, as the first Canadian to hold that office, Vincent Massey would follow him.

In October 1920 I find the name of Charles M. Gere. He was, then, a comparatively unknown painter whom someone must have suggested to my mother as a likely person to paint portraits of her three sons. At that time I was four years old, Johnnie nine and Alastair just turned two. I think that he painted Johnnie's and my portraits then, and decided to wait for Alastair until he should be a little older. Alastair's portrait must have been done on Charles Gere's second visit when Alastair was six years old.

Charles Gere had a personality especially agreeable to children. He was very tall and thin and wore clothes of hand-spun, rough cloth which had, for me, a fascinating texture. He worked very fast, never made us sit for too long at a time, and would let us have samples of his paints, even such expensive items as Alizarin Orange, to use ourselves. The portraits are still in the family, and (although done in watercolour) seem to lose none of their freshness with the years.

Charles Gere was to become well-known, in academic circles at least. He was made ARA in the nineteen-thirties and his calm, profound landscapes of Gloucestershire have been collected and, I should think, treasured; they never seem to come on the market. He lived at Painswick in Gloucestershire in an old house full (but not too full) of the modernism of the Arts-and-Crafts movement: much hand-weaving, light woods, plain colours, beautifully made furniture by Gimson and Barnsley. As a very young man he had been secretary to William Morris. Once, much later on, when I was trying my hand at calligraphy, using a quill pen, he taught me how to choose and cut a quill correctly, as Morris had taught him.

Another painter in the Visitors' Book: William Nicholson. He really belonged to the family, having married Edie, widow of my mother's beloved first cousin, Jack Stuart-Wortley, killed in the 1914 war. It would be impossible to forget Nicholson if only for his delightful appearance. He was small and apple-cheeked, wore large-checked suits, their jackets cut long like riding coats, bright blue and white spotted bow ties, and generally looked as if he belonged on Newmarket Heath. He had a large but gentle Alasatian dog called Gipsy, who used to roam the house giving terrible frights to the maids. A photograph of his portrait of Miss Jekyll, the great gardener—the head and shoulders this time, not the famous boots—stood always on my father's pipe-table. It is an abiding regret to those of us who are left that William Nicholson was never commissioned to do a portrait of JB.

My parents had scarcely a note of music between them so that it is no use looking for professional musicians in the Visitors' Book. This lack of music was odd, at least where my mother was concerned, since her father had been an excellent pianist and a serious composer, and her Aunt Margaret (the Hon. Lady Talbot), her mother's sister, was the subject of one of Elgar's 'Enigma Variations', and a talented pianist: indeed, Elgar said he would rather hear her play Chopin than anyone else. My sister, my younger brother and I were all devoted listeners to music, if no more than that. As for my father, when he went to Canada as Governor-General, he was naturally the target of many national anthems. His was not quite a case of not being able to tell 'God Save the Weasel' from 'Pop goes the Queen' but he did have considerable difficulty in recognising 'O Canada' when it was struck up.

I have therefore leafed through the book looking first for literary or scholarly names. I think of Geoffrey Dawson, editor of *The Times*, as a political rather than a literary figure, but he is there, on only the second page, with his wife Cecilia, who was a relation of my mother.

For their great contribution to the arts in Scotland I would mention Alec and Rosalind Maitland who, in their house in Herriot Row, had the fine collection of modern pictures which is now in the National Gallery of Scotland, and who there held some of the most exciting concerts I have ever attended. They were responsible, too, for providing JB and Johnnie with much fishing and stalking on their Highland property at Letterewe.

Very early on in the book I find the historian and author, Professor George Trevelyan (later Sir George Trevelyan, OM) who was to be a frequent visitor, someone whose company JB particularly relished, and upon whose advice and criticism he greatly relied. J. St Loe Strachey, then owner–editor of the *Spectator* appears in 1921, and Enid Jones in the same year and often thereafter—this was Enid Bagnold, novelist and playwright, and author of the internationally famous *National Velvet*; she had married Sir Roderick Jones, Chairman of Reuter's, who had made my father a director of that company in 1919. In 1923 Jones invited JB to become Deputy Chairman of Reuter's, while retaining his directorship of Nelson's. This post my father accepted, somehow managing to do the new job to everyone's satisfaction without taking his eye, for one moment, off the old.

Hilaire Belloc came for a night in 1922, I imagine to speak at one of the Oxford clubs: many of our overnight visitors came for this purpose. Since my father was president of some Oxford clubs, and in touch with most of them, he was continually being asked to get one or another famous person to come down and speak. I expect that the famous persons took the equally famous 4.45 from Paddington, were met at Oxford by Webb, conveyed to Elsfield, where they bathed and changed, and if necessary were fed, and then sent off with JB to Oxford for the evening.

My father had no appetite for literary coteries. The writers he liked, he liked as people; many whose work he may have respected he would have found uncomfortable guests in his house.

The Robert Graveses were often at Elsfield. Graves and his young family lived for a while in Islip, five miles away, where he was a stalwart member of the village football team. We used to go to tea with them when I was about six years old, and I remember being fascinated by the freedom and liveliness and happy disorder of their household, as compared with the regulated tenor of life in my own home. That was my first taste of what was still called a Bohemian way of living, and I found it most attractive. JB thought highly of Robert Graves as a writer, liked him as a man, and helped him in one or two useful ways. Graves was later to write: 'It is impossible to do justice to John Buchan's warmth, modesty and generosity.'

I do not know why I remember Gordon Bottomley so clearly. He was an admired poet in his day, who is still remembered, at least by anthologists, for his 'To Iron-Founders and Others'. He came to Elsfield once or twice and I also remember him appearing in

Peeblesshire, on an extended motoring tour, and sitting down to a vast, traditional Scottish tea. He was a heavy, rather silent man, given to somewhat oracular remarks when he felt like talking. He had a solid brown beard and a thick moustache which came down to meet it, so that you could not see his mouth. During tea Johnnie and I watched him fascinated, as he steered a piece of cake through that hairy barrier. It was rather like seeing an animal being driven into a cavern concealed by creepers. One day my father, who was little given to that sort of joke, surprised me by suggesting that the poet's surname should be spelt Bolmondeley, to rhyme with Cholmondeley (pronounced Chumley).

Walter de la Mare I can scarcely remember from childhood, although I came to know him later in life. He had been a friend of my parents for many years, and his verses, particularly *Peacock Pie*, are woven into the stuff of my early years. At all events, he was another visitor to Elsfield, and a regular correspondent with my father on things to do with books, when he was doing some work for Nelson's

I have often been rebuked in my life, especially when young, but never so gently yet effectively as by Walter de la Mare. Once, not long after the war, I had gone down to see him at Twickenham. After we had talked for a while about something he was doing, he enquired, 'And now, what about you? Are you writing?'

I suppose that I assumed a harassed expression, as of one bearing excessive burdens, and said that I had no longer any time. De la Mare reflected for a little, looked up at me with a detectable gleam of irony in his eye, and said: 'I shall see if I can find you a piece of time . . . I imagine it dark, and green, like glass . . . to keep on your dressing-table.' A nicer way of being told not to be an ass I have never heard.

JB's attitude to contemporary novelists was idiosyncratic. For Hardy he had real reverence: 'I knew Thomas Hardy fairly well and revered his wonderful old age "like a Lapland night", and what T. E. Lawrence called his unbelievable dignity and ripeness of spirit.' He had always admired Kipling who, of course, by that time was no longer a novelist, having settled on short stories as his best mode of expression. 'I was fascinated by Rudyard Kipling's devouring interest in the human comedy, the way in which in conversation he used to raven the heart out of a subject.'

Of Henry James, who died in 1916, he had this to say:

Of the greatest figures, I saw most of Henry James. Would that I had seen more of him, for I loved the man and revelled in the idioms of his wonderful talk, which Mr Percy Lubbock has admirably described—'his grandiose courtesy, his luxuriant phraseology, his relish for some extravagantly colloquial term embedded in a Ciceronian period, his humour at once so majestic and so burly.'

It can be seen that JB would not have been at home with the kind of 'twenties' intellectuals so sharply described and parodied in Aldous Huxley's *Antic Hay*. It is strange, all the same, in view of JB's own considerable intellectual capacity, to find him so often pillorying intellectuals in his novels. I think that what he most objected to was pose—the pose of intellectual superiority, and the spectacle of a mind, of however high quality, 'bombinating in a vacuum'. He believed seriously in the importance of a well-trained and enquiring intellect, but did not believe its possession to be enough in itself. 'A first-class mind, but nothing much behind it?' somebody queries of the evil Barralty in *The Island of Sheep*. A good mind, in John Buchan's view, was a gift of God, and one which must be trained and tempered to a worthy purpose, not allowed to run free in idle speculation or serve its owner as a means of self-flattery. Hence, I am sure, this literary man's intense dislike of literary society.

Intolerance, however, is not a word I can associate with my father, for reasons of temperament that I have tried to show. He was never rigid in outlook, but I think that he saw in the post-war world of letters so much that he knew he would not like—so much, indeed, that might seem a betrayal of the youthful dead he unremittingly mourned—that he preferred to turn his eyes away from the scene.

We might regret that he did not adventure into the world of the younger European writers for, if some might have infuriated, others would surely have rewarded him. But he had settled his life to his preferred pattern: he was seldom well and always overworked; he was not looking for the shock of combat, or violent challenges to his most deeply cherished ideas. He preferred to pursue the lines of thought which he had developed over the years, in the company of minds as fastidious, highly trained, and idealistically inclined as his own.

W. H. Auden, in the early thirties, wrote some highly minatory poems about what catastrophes would come to all of us if we did not pull up our social socks. He was whistling, I sometimes thought, to keep his courage up, because I could not believe that, in his heart, he really desired a Communist state any more than I did. But we were all terrified of Fascism to the point of not being able to see Communism as its mirror-image. At some point Auden spoke of 'private joking in a panelled room' as something that was going to have to come to an end very shortly. 'Private' was beginning to be a dirty word among the mass-conscious left-inclined young. 'Joking' was out, naturally, because the whole thing was too deadly serious. And 'panelled room' was simply a symbol of privilege. I think, all the same, that, if put to it, my father would have thought serious private conversation (with some relieving jokes) in any room, panelled or otherwise, a worthy and civilising occupation; and so, indeed would I. (And what about private joking in the gilded salons of the Kremlin, I should have liked to ask.)

As with people, so with literature. JB was far too professional, far too good a critic, not to see gold when it was under his nose: simply, sometimes, one had to go on patiently putting it there until he agreed to pay it attention. He had no special admiration for D. H. Lawrence, but thought 'The Rocking-Horse Winner' one of the best short stories of the century. Similarly with Aldous Huxley, who did not appeal to him either: he thought the story of the dwarf Sir Hector Lapith and that of the greedy Lapith ladies, which are sandwiched into *Chrome Yellow*, as nearly perfect as could be.

Nevertheless, as he grew older, and more preoccupied with his own affairs, he had less time and mental energy to spare for new movements except in historical research and, oddly enough, physics. He read Whitehead, Jeans and Eddington with real excitement, and had a long correspondence with J. W. Dunne (author of *An Experiment with Time*) after the publication of *The Gap in the Curtain* (1932). It is interesting to note that some French critics regard JB as one of the fathers of science fiction, chiefly on the strength of this book, which describes the actions and reactions of a number of people after they have been given, by a physicist, an induced preview of their own death-notices in *The Times* of a year thence.

When it came to writers in his own genre, I think that JB enjoyed A. E. W. Mason as much as any. I do not think that he had any time for 'Sapper'—bracketed with JB, I think wrongly, by Richard Usborne in *Clubland Heroes*. He always claimed, with his tongue in his cheek, to have been set on the road to writing what he thought of as 'shockers' by E. Phillips Oppenheim, whom he once called 'the greatest Jewish writer since Isaiah'.

Certainly he liked an eventful story to be plainly but well told; he thought there should be no dereliction of the rules of style, even for lightweight stuff. Although their aims were so completely different, he had respect as well as affection for P. G. Wodehouse who, more perhaps than any other writer, could send him into helpless laughter. Him he regarded, quite seriously, as one of the best living writers of English prose. It seems as though a sound classical education, which was common to them both, may still, whatever nonsense is talked about dead languages, be the best foundation for good, flexible, plain English.

JB could seldom be got to read contemporary novels, however much they might be hailed as works of genius in the two leading Sunday papers by those noted genius-diviners, Gerald Gould and Ralph Straus. He had, as the Scots say, taken a scunner to the country-life school of novelists—A. G. Street, Ethel Mannin, and company—possibly because, in a reversed sense, they reminded him of the 'Kailyard School' in his own country against which he had once waged war. He was correspondingly delighted by Stella Gibbons's *Cold Comfort Farm* when it came out in the nineteen-thirties. I remember him convulsed with silent laughter as he read this book, chuckling away, sometimes putting it down to announce: 'Really, this lady goes too far!' and then joyfully going on reading. No doubt but that this book was the perfect, and well-deserved, 'send-up' of a school of writing which was totally humourless as well as wholly one-sided in its view of country life. (I believe that if *Lady Chatterley's Lover* had been available at that time, and if I could have persuaded him to read it, he might have enjoyed *Cold Comfort Farm* even more.)

John Buchan's own gentle, somewhat elliptical sense of humour usually had a literary tinge. Discussing the functions of a Governor-General, some writer said disparagingly that they mainly consisted in opening bazaars and laying foundation-stones, or words to that effect. JB retorted with a quotation from Gray's 'Elegy': 'Let not ambition mock their useful toil.' He also had a taste—which he shared with me—for really deplorable puns, enjoying, for instance, my reply when, on his remarking one day that the dog looked more like a fox than a terrier, I came up with 'Fox magna, terrier nihil.'

John Galsworthy—another name I find in the Visitors' Book—was, I regret to say, always known to JB as 'Bilgeworthy'. He conceded Galsworthy's gifts as a novelist, his strength of construction, his grip on his plot and characters. Simply, my father, the romantic, found long chronicles of the *haute bourgeoisie* stupefyingly dull. It would be many years before Galsworthy, through the medium of television, would be seen as the inspired chronicler of a vanished and by no means insignificant world.

We had visits from publishers, too. Once a year Ferris Greenslet would come over from America, where he looked after JB's publications for Houghton, Mifflin at Cambridge, Massachusetts; while from Cambridge, England, came Humphrey Milford, head of the University Press. I also find the name of Ralph Hodder-Williams, the Chairman of Hodder & Stoughton, the firm which published most of JB's later work.

Of politicians in the Visitors' Book there is a fairly rich variety, from Neville Chamberlain at one end, by way of Sir Stafford Cripps, to Stanley Baldwin at the other. Although he and JB were friends for years, and at one time worked very closely together, Baldwin seems only to have stayed once, and that in 1948, after JB's death. Rationing was still in force, the gardens had reverted to primeval meadow, there was no upstairs staff in the house, and John and my mother were managing as best they could when Baldwin asked to be put up for the night. My brother welcomed him, and showed him to the library, whereupon Baldwin turned to him and said, 'Tell them not to unpack anything but what I shall need for the night.' Johnnie silently acquiesced, toted his guest's leather bag up the back stairs and then, for the occasion, became 'them'.

Looking through the Visitors' Book I have been struck by the consistency of achievement among people, unknown or scarcely known when they first came to us, who went on to have careers of considerable worldly importance. I wish I could say the same of the youngest generation represented, school friends of my brothers' and mine. They were, almost without exception, killed in the last war.

I suppose that it was only natural for ambitious young men, clever and full of ideas, to gravitate towards John Buchan, a man who had so evidently made a success of nearly all that he had touched. Also, his extreme patience with, and positive interest in, the rising generation must have become known from the dozens of undergraduates who came to seek his advice and, almost always, receive his help.

How tall they seemed to me, those undergraduates, when I was a small boy. How tall, in fact, a great many of them were. Lord Longford has told me how he used to walk out to Elsfield from Oxford for tea on Sunday, in the company of Roger Makins and

Jim Scrimgeour-Wedderburn (now Lord Sherfield and the Earl of Dundee). Lord Longford is a tall man, but the other two were taller than he by several inches. Small wonder that I concluded that the great world must be largely peopled by giants. By contrast, my father seemed short; he was about five feet eight inches—of medium height, in fact. Both my brothers achieved more than six feet. I ended up perhaps half an inch taller than my father.

When he was in the company of tall people my father would have to stretch and crane a little to converse with them, and they would stoop to listen to him. But he had none of the short man's aggressiveness and, although I saw him often in very large gatherings of, on the whole, much taller people, I never knew him fail to dominate his surroundings. This was done, as I have said, not by aggression but by a kind of collectedness, poise, concentration coupled with his unique appearance, the bright blue flash of his eyes, a look of expectant eagerness, which marked him out inescapably as somebody to be noticed, a personality in his own right.

Like a highland stream, the flow of guests recorded in the Visitors' Book runs in still pools and sudden cascades. For two or three months together all is peace, with only a few names, generally members of my mother's family, or occasional speakers down for a night. Then, suddenly, there is great activity, with a house overflowing for days at a time. This begins to show itself when my sister Alice is rising eighteen, and there are dances in the county, or Commemoration Balls in Oxford, to which she must go with a party. So, every so often, there is a list of young men and women all staying together between the same dates.

Elsfield was a house which overflowed rather easily. The Victorian wing contained, on its first floor, one very large spare room, one slightly smaller one communicating with it, two smaller bedrooms, a linen-cupboard, a bathroom and a lavatory: so little in so apparently large a space. On the top floor were the night nursery, Alice's and Alastair's bedrooms and mine. Other rooms at that level belonged to Mrs Charlett, Annie Cox who doubled as housekeeper and my mother's maid; and there was the long slope-ceilinged room shared by the younger housemaids. Accommodating a house party, therefore was by no means easy.

Fortunately, in those days, visiting bachelors did not expect elegant quarters. (I once stayed in a house in the West Country where a tin bowl, placed beside my bed, collected drips from the ceiling.) But for them to have anywhere at all to sleep Alastair and I had to go elsewhere. I do not record this fact as any kind of hardship: we greatly enjoyed our nights away, either in Miss Parsons' house, much spoiled by two elderly maids who still wore mob caps, or farther afield, at Old Marston, in the house of Mrs Honour. There, in an interior perfectly preserved from the previous century, with good food and the additional interest of an outside privy, we settled down to our brief exiles with complete good temper.

From the last year's entries in the Visitors' Book, before my parents left for Canada, I have two vivid recollections. Virginia Woolf came to us on 2 July 1935 for two or three days and we took her on an expedition into Gloucestershire to visit the Necromancer of Snowshill. I so clearly remember my father's manner with Mrs Woolf. Always courteous with women, and deeply interested by what they had to say, he seemed, for her benefit, to deploy an extra delicacy, a more pointed attention even than usual. Although by no means an unqualified admirer of her work, he had yet the greatest respect for Virginia Woolf's qualities as an essayist and critic. He knew also that she had suffered from melancholia, and that social gatherings could sometimes be torture for her. So he laid himself out to reassure and please her, as though she were an angelic visitant, someone from another world. Other-worldly she certainly looked, with her long, thin, almost luminously pale face, the ivory hoods of her eyelids over eyes which were sometimes absent-looking, often disconcertingly alert. Her clothes belonged to no period, to no order of fashion, were simply, in their quiet colours and flowing lines, entirely right for her.

The Necromancer of Snowshill was not a Necromancer at all, and I think that this label had been pinned to him on account of a stuffed crocodile and other magical looking implements to be found in the workshop-studio-laboratory which was part of his fascinating domain. His name was Mr Wade; he had retired from business in London where he was 'in' something like sugar or tea, and had bought the manor house of Snowshill, a tiny village then lost in the wolds to the south-east of Cheltenham. It was a house of an extraordinary romantic quality which could have belonged to one of Walter de la Mare's most cryptic, most allusive, stories. You went through a blue-painted door in a high grey wall into a grassy court, to be faced by a small but perfect William and Mary house of Cotswold stone, fronting a taller, grimmer Jacobean structure, built into the side of a hill. Over the garden door, in fine gold lettering were the words *Pax in intrantibus, salus in exeuntibus* (Peace to those entering, health to those departing).

Mr Wade had done more than leave London; he had almost left the century as well, or rather he had taken all centuries as his province, to roam at will. He had a calm, rather craggy face, framed in what, if he had been a woman, would have been called bobbed hair: a common enough sight nowadays, but then decidedly unusual. He wore clothes which gave a general impression of the eighteenth century—long coats, breeches, stockings and buckled shoes.

His house inside was truly amazing, for Mr Wade was a collector in the widest sense of the word. There were ancient looms and spinning wheels, and the tools of a dozen different crafts, sharing space with suits of Japanese armour. There was a fine collection of glass of all periods scattered about, and of course there was the crocodile. Wonders did not cease with the house. The outbuildings contained as astonishingly heterogeneous an assortment of objects, from flowered silk waistcoats to astrolabes; and where a small stream ran below the house, a miniature harbour had been built with ships to scale and a complicated model railway system around. It was to this house, then, that we took Virginia Woolf, feeling that nothing stranger or more surprising could be found for an excursion.

I claim the distinction of having made Virginia Woolf laugh, not by anything said, although I was at an age to exhaust myself trying to be witty, but by something that happened to me. I was sitting on my usual seat, the strapontin, as we bowled, rather fast, along the Cheltenham road, when the door of the car suddenly burst open. I was leaning against it at the time, with quite a lot of my weight, half turned as I was to talk to the people on the back seat. I managed, by grabbing something, to save myself. Webb, aware of a commotion, brought the car to a halt. There were expressions of dismay, anxious enquiries, but not from Mrs Woolf who had gone off into a fit of delighted laughter.

On 10 September 1935 a definitely exotic note is struck. There in, thick black ink, and in beautiful handwriting which could belong to the seventeenth century, are the names of Justinian Seredi, Prince Primate of Hungary, and of his suite, Dom Ildebrando Vannuci, Abbot-designate of San Paolo at Rome, and Dom Placid Turner, Prior of Downside Abbey. This cardinalatial visit was promoted by

Count Roberto Weiss, who had been given the job of showing Oxford to Cardinal Seredi. Roberto, who had been a friend of Johnnie's at Oxford, did a lot of research work for JB, most particularly in connexion with *Augustus*, and went on to become a distinguished historian himself.

As I have mentioned in Chapter 1, my mother had never been happy about the passage which was the only way of getting to the dining-room. So, with my help she had elaborated a plan to pierce a door through to the dining-room directly from the library. She was going to pay for this undertaking herself, and it was to be a surprise for my father, who was to know nothing about it until he saw it for the first time. We both knew, without actually admitting it to each other, that my father, if he had been told about the plan in advance, would have vetoed it out of hand, since it involved the abolition of a certain amount of shelf-space, and would break up the wall of books on the northern side of the library. I advised that the door should be as narrow as possible, so as not to displace too many books, and that a new set of shelving should be constructed to take the place of the tall blue screen which hitherto had done duty between the door and the fireplace as a not very efficient draught-excluder. This, we felt, would meet any objections about loss of book-space.

This hideous plot had to be carried out during my father's absence, I cannot now remember where, and sure enough, when he came home to find our improvements he was very far from pleased. My mother, however, was considerably happier with the new arrangement until the day of the Prince Primate's visit. Cardinal Seredi was a very large and impressive man, rendered larger and even more impressive by the clothes of his office. When he came to go into luncheon he stuck in the door—only momentarily, of course, because with a neat backing and turning movement he managed to get in sideways, but for my mother it was a moment of heart-stopping anxiety, not least because she could feel rising in her the beginning of a fit of giggles which she feared she would be unable to control.

I have often wondered whether my Scottish grandmother was ever told about my mother's having had a Cardinal to luncheon. I think that it must have been kept from her or old suspicions, long dormant, might have come strongly back to life.

9

'THE GENTLE TWEED'

Now that I have come to write a memoir of my father, I cannot help regretting the times with him, the special unrepeatable occasions, which I missed through being away at school. No doubt because of what I have called his magician's gift for making our life at home both comfortable and exciting: because my brothers and I loved Elsfield so dearly; because most of the time that we were away we seemed to be missing so much fun, we were not particularly successful as schoolboys. I intend the word schoolboys rather than scholars for, occasionally, we did give and receive some satisfaction in our work. It was simply that being neither remarkably good nor noticeably bad at games, and lacking anything much in the way of team spirit, we never succeeded in throwing ourselves completely and joyously into our school environment, as many undoubtedly could and did. And we found that the principal effect of being sent away to school was to make the holidays a time of almost painfully heightened excitement and pleasure, all the more poignant for the knowledge that they must come to an end, and that much too soon.

Before I went off to school, I had lessons for about four years with my sister's governess, Miss Smeaton. These lessons, although I regarded them as little less than slavery, not only taught me a lot but used up only my mornings. When Miss Smeaton went away for a holiday, my holidays began, and I am sure that I felt almost as bounding a sense of release from that gentle durance as I was to feel later from the severer discipline of school.

As young children we spent several summers at Broughton. Once or twice we went as a family: those must, I think, have been the earliest years because, as Johnnie grew older, he and JB, and sometimes my mother as well, took to going to the Highlands for fishing and stalking.

Moving the whole family to Broughton must have needed some

careful planning. My father took charge of the travel arrangements while, for many days before the journey, Alastair and I would be in conference with Elsie Charlett or my mother about what we could or could not take with us. My father had an irreducible minimum of books as part of his luggage; no small item, in fact, since these were works which he had to read for something he himself was writing, some he had to review, and books which he had promised himself to read as soon as he had a minute's leisure. Left to ourselves, each of us would probably have taken as many as he, and so, day by day, the piles of things we were sure we should need had to be slowly reduced.

When the day of departure came we would leave in something of a flurry, and with plenty of time to spare. (One of the few qualities I have inherited from JB is a compulsion to punctuality, which leads me often to catch trains and aeroplanes with an hour or so in hand.) Trunks and bags would be strapped on to a steel rack let down from the back of the car. Small luggage, known to my mother as 'kittens', would be piled all over us inside. Everyone would be squashed to breathlessness when we finally set off for Oxford and the LMS (London, Midland and Scottish) station.

In those fine days of competition, before nationalisation was anything but an item on Labour Party agendas, there were two railway stations at Oxford. Generally, the line we took was the Great Western with its chocolate and cream livery, because this carried us to London for visits to my English grandmother. The line for Scotland, which ran parallel, for some distance, to that of the GWR, belonged to the London, Midland and Scottish, and the trains had a livery of dark crimson. The train from Oxford would not take us all the way to Scotland. We should have to get off, or as railway authorities put it, 'alight', at Bletchley and there wait for the Scotch express which would halt, panting majestically, for just long enough to let its passengers scramble on. Bletchley station had a small dining-room and there, ravenous after an early start, we would be given breakfast, before going out to watch other great expresses thunder by.

We travelled third class, in a reserved compartment, where we were well supplied with games and books for the dull part of the journey through the Midlands. My father had a seat to himself somewhere nearby, where he could smoke without upsetting those wretched travellers, his children, and read, and annotate his reading, in peace.

Once we were clear of the Black Country—which in those days

before smoke-abatement schemes really was black, as often as not pressed on by a low, dark ceiling of what was politely called industrial haze, its grass more grubby viridian than emerald green—the countryside began to hump itself increasingly into hills. It could be seen that my father, as the land steepened to the Westmorland fells, was beginning to give signs of an eager pleasure. He would drop his reading to gaze out at drystone dykes, flocks of sheep, farms isolated on low hills, rivers and streams that ran and tumbled where, until then, we had seen only the sluggish waters of Midland rivers and canals. He would talk to us with animation and erudition, pointing out the shape of the country; giving us the names of hills and ranges to which they belonged, telling us where each river rose, what it was called, and where it ran to in the end.

The country was becoming perceptibly like his own Scottish Borders and as the train, with the help of an extra engine, ground its way up Shap Fell and Beattock Summit, we would be infected by his high spirits, his sense of coming home. The journey had been long and in parts tedious. Coal-burning trains could never be clean and by then we children had black hands and smuts in our eyes, and a great wish to be done with the express train and get on to the next, and best, part of the journey.

From his earliest days John Buchan had enjoyed long summer holidays on Tweedside in the house of his maternal grandparents, the Mastertons of Broughton Green. Until he was thirteen his home was in Fife at Pathhead, within the sound of the sea and the smell of the linoleum works. Each summer there came release from dull and unattractive surroundings into a world not only beautiful in itself, but ever more fascinating the more it was explored; for, besides its physical beauty, the variety of its landscapes, its glens and hills and waters, it possessed history of a marvellous complexity—blood and treachery, ballad and legend, magic and simple comedy. It was sheep country, and the Mastertons had been sheep-farmers for generations on the confines of three shires, Lanark, Midlothian and Tweeddale. There JB had his first introduction to an old and happy world:

I helped to drive sheep to the local market and sat, heavily responsible, in a corner of the auction ring. I became learned in the talk of the trade, and no bad judge of sheep stock. Those Border shepherds, the men of the long stride and the clear eye, were a great race—I have never known a greater. The narrower kinds of fanaticism, which have run riot elsewhere in Scotland, rarely affected the Borders. . . . As the source of the greatest ballads in any literature they had fire and imagination, and some aptitude for the graces of life. They lacked the dourness of the conventional Scot, having a quick eye for comedy, and, being in themselves wholly secure, they were aristocrats with the fine manners of an aristocracy. By them I was admitted into the secrets of a whole lost world of pastoral. I acquired a reverence and affection for the 'plain people', who to Walter Scott and Abraham Lincoln were what mattered most in the world.

It could be thought that JB, writing the passage just quoted after a lapse of more than fifty years, might have been viewing the places and people of his childhood through a flattering mist. Writing this forty years later, and having known unaltered the places he loved, as well as another generation of the same shepherds, I can say that I would underline every word.

It was not to be wondered at that my father, as we draw near to the place which had given him so much joy, should seem to shed a burden of pain and care and fatigue and become almost as excited and happy as we were ourselves.

The final stage of our journey to Broughton was in the small train belonging to the Caledonian Railway, which we would find waiting for the Scotch express at Symington. Two things were all that we needed to know that our Scottish holiday had really begun: the great wash of moorland air, thrilling as spring-water, which met us at Symington, and the little train of four carriages with its smart, tall-funnelled engine which was going to take us on what I still think was the most satisfactory, even if not the most spectacular, railway journey in the world. The Symington–Broughton line, with stations at Culter and Biggar, was opened in 1860. Its continuation, through Stobo and Lyne to Peebles, was achieved in 1864. Another line, from Peebles to Edinburgh, was opened by the North British Railway Company in 1855. So the local railways were already in existence in 1875, when my father was born, and we, as children, could feel that, in spite of our southern upbringing, here was one set of pleasures which we could share with the child that he had been. Another set which he loved to display to us was the whole beauty and fantasy of the Tweed Valley, which had so shaped his mind and his tastes, and so richly fed his imagination, when he was our age.

At the Broughton station, smart as a new toy and bright with flowers, the family party would divide, the children setting off for Broughton Green and Maggie Lorimer's warm welcome, the grown-ups in the opposite direction for Gala Lodge.

Gala Lodge would not have been thought a large house in those days, although today it looks larger than it did then. Somehow the senior members of the family fitted themselves in. Somehow, when my father was with us, it seemed unusually small. Although by no means a big man, nor in the least unaccommodating, it was a little like installing a powerful motor in a living-room to have him in any house. His personality was vibrant; he gave off energy; you could almost hear things hum. At Elsfield, when long days of holiday had induced a pleasant lethargy in all of us, the mere sound of his step, of his umbrella dropping into the hall-stand, was enough to galvanise us into giving at least the appearance of doing something useful.

Fortunately for family life, and for his own comfort, there was seldom reason for staying in Gala Lodge for anything much but meals, some quiet evening talk, and sleep. The weather had to be quite overwhelmingly bad for any of us to stay indoors. If expeditions had to be cancelled because rain or mist had come down and there was no hope of seeing whatever might have been their object, there were always the hills and glens for walks, and fishing could be pursued in any weather.

A friend, recollecting visits to Elsfield as a schoolboy of ten or so, once remarked that the protection put up around my father by his family and servants was the chief thing he remembered. 'You practically had to sign a form in triplicate to get to see him,' he said: an exaggeration, certainly, but I can see what he meant. The protection stemmed, I am sure, from my mother's perpetual anxiety about JB's health. If he would insist upon doing more than mortal strength, even in a strong man, could really be expected to stand, she must see to it that he should work without distraction. JB's staff abetted my mother in this, knowing as well as any of us how important it was that he should keep to his almost incredible self-set schedule without interruption and without annoyance. No person from Porlock, arriving inopportunely, would have got within a hundred feet of JB on any occasion when he had asked not to be disturbed.

For the time of our holidays at Broughton my mother's vigilance could be relaxed. Rather thankfully, I imagine, she could leave JB to be fussed over by his mother, herself free to enjoy the country which she, too, had come to love, and to see something of her children. No doubt she had to parry a number of sharp thrusts from Gran about our manners, our appearance, perhaps even our English voices, most probably our ignorance of any but the most obvious Biblical texts. No doubt she had to listen, as we had, to stories of wonderfully brilliant and pious children, already at early ages doing remarkably well and being a comfort and inspiration to everyone. If anyone worshipped success, it was my grandmother, provided it took place within certain confines, and carried a powerful moral message with it. We could not blame her for remembering the days when her own clever children had taken themselves to school and university by diligent hard work resulting in scholarships and bursaries. What it was not in our power to do was to make her see the contrast between the relatively carefree and ample life which JB had created for us and the severe restrictions which he himself had known; nor to explain that, however you looked at it, our lives were not subject to the same absolute necessities. We were happy where we were, at that time, seeing no world more desirable into which to escape. Tales of deprivation and duty, moral eagerness and worthy achievement, fell dully on our half-Sassenach ears.

My grandmother, however, had an extremely high boredom-threshold and this, coupled with a truly bountiful instinct for hospitality, and a natural wish to show off her famous son, did let JB in for one or two social occasions, even on holiday, which, out of affection for his mother, he endured with his usual good nature.

Casual visitors were another matter. It did not take long for word to get about in the valley that John Buchan was holidaying at Broughton, and one or two determined people—there being no telephone at Gala Lodge—would set out to visit the family, on the chance of finding him at home. The house stood high above the road; there was no drive; a car stopping at the gate could be heard and recognised in time for evasive action to be taken. The Hill O'Men rose abruptly behind: the garden above the house was precipitous and well out of sight of the road. In no more time than it took to snatch cap and stick my father could be out of the house and striding upwards to safety, before the first of the invaders had got through the garden gate. This technique he would use again when, later, we went as a family to the Island of Mull, for not even islands were safe from time-devouring admirers, so mystifyingly certain of their welcome. He was a most sociable man but one who reasonably enough preferred, whenever possible, to choose his company: and a family holiday, and that alone, was what he planned to enjoy.

Now that we had joined the Scottish migration, I found myself seeing more of my father, in one season, than I had seen in all my short years before. Since, when he was working, he worked so concentratedly, when he took a holiday he enjoyed it with gusto. It was not in his nature to do nothing at all with his time, and he tended to organise his pleasures as carefully as he organised his work. 'Relaxing', in the sense of lying back and staring at the sky, he would have found not merely hateful but quite impossible. So, on holiday, he took with him as well as all the books he wanted to read, his fishing rods, and the kind of clothes appropriate to very long walks in every kind of weather. For much of the time, at Broughton, he and Johnnie, and often Uncle Walter (his only surviving brother) were out fishing together, either in Tweed or in one of the tributary burns—Holms Water, Kilbucho, Megget, Lyne. Alastair was still too young for the sport, but, when I was allowed to, I followed Johnnie like a dog as he carefully explored the possibilities of Biggar Water where it ran beside the railway line below the house. I think it gave my father pleasure to see his sons fishing where he had fished with his father, and he with his: as it gives me pleasure, today, to see my own sons doggedly at work after trout in precisely the same places.

It says much for the intelligence, sensitivity and quick-wittedness of our grown-ups that recollection of those holidays, even allowing for memory's censoring tendencies, is so consistently happy. We were living at pretty close quarters much of the time, and there could be days on end of unremitting rain which severely reduced outdoor possibilities at least for the youngest of us. Yet, somehow, we were kept amused. If things became dull or difficult, my aunt would arrange a trip to Peebles, something which could always raise our spirits because there we could visit Bank House, with all its space and peacefulness and interesting treasures, and the town with its magnificent sweet-shops, its shopkeepers who always seemed pleased to see us, and perhaps we would have luncheon in one or other of the quiet old-fashioned restaurants.

Bank House in summer holiday time was the domain of Uncle Walter, whose official holiday had been taken in the spring. He would come up to Broughton by train at weekends, and sometimes on weekdays as well, following a pattern set by those who had built the substantial houses which flanked Gala Lodge. One of the pleasures of a visit to Bank House was a brief sight of that brisk, twinkling man.

He was always busy, or else the law business, the bank and the town itself would probably not have achieved their notable order and efficiency; but he would always come out of his office to have a look at us before bustling back again. He was more stockily built than my father and so, where JB darted, his brother Walter bustled. He was of an independent nature, pursuing his own interests, and overseeing the affairs of Peebles with the same kindliness, vision and good sense as his Uncle Willie from whom he had, so to speak, inherited the positions of Town Clerk and Procurator Fiscal. He played golf, and was a good fisherman and nearly as great a walker as his brother John.

Uncle Walter was deeply interested in Napoleon and his wars, had a good collection of Napoleonic relics, and had written a life of the Duke of Wellington (JB very much disliked Napoleon, which may partly have influenced his brother in his choice of a hero). It was respectfully treated by the critics of its time, but his literary monument was, and remains, the three-volume *History of Peeblesshire* which he edited, and indeed largely wrote.

It is possible that John Buchan could only stand family life, as lived on holidays, in small and varied doses. His presence was a real, if rather anxiety-creating delight for his Peeblesshire family. My grandmother's view of life was as I have described, and if she thought that much of what engaged her eldest son was rash, excessive and unsafe, his brother and sister, I think, shared her feelings to some extent. They were as enormously proud of him as they were deeply fond, but they could not have helped feeling that he had grown far away from them. With his English marriage, his English home, and very English-seeming children, together with a life lived largely amongst a crowd of 'southern' notables, they probably felt that their own concerns, however vitally interesting to themselves, must seem to him provincial, trivial and dull.

If they thought in this way, they were certainly wrong. His love for them, and his interest in their lives, can never have waned. It was more a question of divergence of aim. He could appreciate their pleasures or anxieties with his mind and heart; he could probably not have helped being glad that he did not have to share them. They in turn found what he had to tell them (of vital interest to himself) so remote from life as they knew it, perhaps so alarming-sounding, that they could almost have wished not to be told of it at all.

Even as a child, however, I was aware of the strong bond of family affection uniting my father and what was left to him of his family. They were at their best together when recalling incidents of childhood and early youth, and my grandmother lost all her power to irritate when she joined in such reminiscences. She, too, was at her best in those, just as she was when she told us the fairy stories with which, once, her husband had delighted his own children. Sometimes the four of them would seem to shed years under my eyes, to become young again, happy in one another's company, momentarily free of care as, for instance, when we were out to tea at the end of some expedition, they would fight among themselves to decide who should have the privilege of paying the bill.

In the main I think that my father, as time went on and he became ever more engrossed in great affairs, in politics and his dreams of an ideal Empire, and ever more preoccupied with writing and his career, found too intimate a family reunion less and less desirable. It is my recollection that he never stayed with us at Broughton for very long, although he characteristically made the very most of his stay. He would have a Highland visit planned and with John and Alice (in the early days), and often with my mother, would go to stay with friends at some place where he could fish and stalk to his heart's content. None the less, when at Broughton, JB did not neglect certain duties which were also, I think, pleasures. He liked to visit his uncles at their farms and hear their news, and be taken back again to boyhood by their strong Border idiom, the unchanging nature of their concerns. He, in his turn, would give them news of politics, or at least of those politics which had to do with farming—for all consideration of affairs, whether home or foreign, eventually came back to that.

Somewhere about my sixth or seventh year my father must have thought, or someone must have suggested to him, that he should try to see more of his two younger children. In those early days the gap in ages between the elder and the younger two must have been as evident to him as it was to them. Indeed he used to speak of Alice and Johnnie as 'the Greeks', and of myself and Alastair as 'the Barbarians', implying not just that we had arrived late on the scene, but that we were different, although not necessarily worse. In fact, this was a joke with a rather sharper point than was perhaps intended. My arrival five years after Johnnie's, and Alastair's three years after mine, must indeed have brought back into prominence the needs and demands of very small children at a time when life might have been easier without them.

In any event, I have two recollections of expeditions alone with my father both of which, for very different reasons, remain perfectly clear. The first is of a hill walk on a day of uncertain weather. It cannot have been a very long walk, for even JB would have thought twice about taking a six-year-old on anything but what he would have considered an easy stroll. We certainly climbed for a while, most likely on Ratchill or Trehenna, the nearest hills of any size to Broughton. Eating our sandwiches on the top of a hill we were suddenly enveloped in the kind of cold drenching mist which is a speciality of the Border hills. My father was protected by thick tweed, but I had set out in jersey and shorts, with bare legs and plimsolls. Within minutes I was soaking wet and shivering, my teeth chattering uncontrollably.

JB always had a flask of whisky with him when out on the hill. It was a silver flask, the base of which made an oblong cup which could be detached for drinking. (If you offered a stalker a 'dram' he got a much more satisfactory one from this than he ever could get from the mouth of the flask.) My father half-filled this cup and gave it to me. I downed the whisky, disliking intensely its taste (so unlike what I had imagined) but grateful for its effect. Whatever my grandmother might have said about so early an introduction to a strong drink, that prompt action of my father's certainly saved me from a severe chill, if not actually from pneumonia.

The other expedition, which took place when I was seven, was a much more serious affair, prepared for a long time ahead. I was to accompany JB on a whole day's fishing expedition, down the River Tweed at Dawyck. We were to start early, travel in the postman's cart and picnic by the river, just the two of us.

This plan was enunciated with such impressiveness, and I was given so many injunctions about behaviour, and so often reminded of my luck and privilege in being offered such a treat, that I must have come near to wishing that something would happen to prevent it. I must have gone to bed on the evening before the great day troubled by mixed emotions of excitement, anticipation and anxiety.

Whatever misgivings I might have had the previous night, I was in no way to be disappointed. The day dawned brightly, with a touch of mist and no wind at all. My Aunt Anna, as usual, was up and about before anyone else, and our lunches—square grease-proofed parcels, were ready in the hall. My portion, together with a bottle of milk—that is to say a large, corked medicine bottle into which milk had been poured from the metal can in which it had come from the farm—was packed, with apples and chocolate, into my small satchel. My father's wicker creel stood ready and into it went his lunch, to join the leather fly-book which had been his father's, his reel and line and boxes of casts. He stood ready too, or rather (since he rarely simply stood) moved with precision to collect his rods, adjust his cap, look at the sky, glance at the barometer, and take from the hall stand the crook which was so much part, always, of his holiday equipment.

He must have been wearing a variant of the holiday rig I remember from every holiday: a knickerbocker suit of tweed, checked in grey or brown, stout shoes, thick stockings, and sometimes a spotted bow tie. He might well have been wearing a flannel shirt, even on a day like that one which promised to be a scorcher. He was too thin—as he would have said himself, 'too poorly fleshed'—ever to feel heat. Often I spent long summer days in the open with him, when he would wear an unwilting starched collar all day.

Promptly at seven the post-cart jingled up. My father and I gathered our belongings and made off down the steps to the steep path of river pebbles which slipped and chattered under our feet. The green iron gate gave its familiar singing click behind us, and we climbed into the cart. It was a beautifully spick and span vehicle, with its four wheels, a high box for the postman, and a long rectangular open body, made to take parcels and other gear of all shapes. Mr Lawson, the postman, wore the official cap of his day, tall and tapering in black and red, with a shiny peak and a badge in front. His uniform and the trim of his cart were all in black and red, and the sun dazzled on the speckless paint. With a shake of the whip we were off, heading up the valley, making an impressive clatter. Wedged between the two men, who were exchanging measured pleasantries over my head, I could contemplate, with excitement but not without awe, the prospect of a whole day in the company of that mysterious and important man, my father.

> . . . for sheltered places, bosoms, nooks and bays,
> And the pure mountains, and the gentle Tweed,
> And the green silent pastures yet remain.

William Wordsworth, reproving the Duke of Queensberry for cutting down some of the woods around Neidpath Castle, thus comforted himself that all was not yet vandalised.

The Tweed was gentle enough that morning, and the pastures beside it, variously known as 'haughs' or parks, exquisitely green. We turned off the southward-going Moffat road (the old main road to England) at Rachan Mill and headed eastwards for Drumelzier and Dawyck.

Grown-up conversation—the weather, crops, sheep, the political scene, news of farms and families—went on above my head. I am sure that I would not have noticed this at the time, would simply have taken it for granted, but my father's ability for getting on with pretty nearly anybody must have been evident that morning. From a later awareness I know that he would have broadened his speaking voice a little to accommodate it to Mr Lawson's deep-throated Lowland tones, and allowed a quantity of Scottish words and phrases into his conversation. I know also that he would have answered his companion's questions about political doings in that faraway London, which probably seemed as remote to Mr Lawson as Kamchatka, in homely terms, never talking down, but also never introducing facts or ideas which could not be immediately appreciated by a shrewd and sensible man.

I was travelling with my father a road which he had known since earliest childhood, a road which he had tramped a hundred times, or ridden along on his first bicycle, the old kind with solid tyres. He had the faculty, in any place, of studying and absorbing very rapidly, not only local history and associations, but physical geography as well. My mother used to say despairingly that he kept a compass in his head and confused her dreadfully with north and south, when the cardinal points meant nothing to her whatever. He confused me, too, travelling by train through hill country—for instance Westmorland—by his talk of watersheds. I wonder why I never asked him straight out what a watershed was instead of carrying for a long time in my mind the picture of a small wooden building clinging to the side of a mountain in torrential rain. This not asking of questions has often puzzled me, since no one was gentler or more painstaking with any questioner than JB. It was an effect, I think, of my father's peculiarly spellbinding way of talking. He never chattered or left a sentence unfinished, or asked unanswerable questions of himself. When he talked he discoursed, not pompously, but in a measured manner, his remarkably lucid and orderly mind having set each thought in place before he came to utter it. The effect of this was, precisely, that one sat spellbound, waiting for more, deeply unwilling to interrupt. He never talked down to children any more than he did to supposedly less well-educated people like Mr Lawson.

As we drove down the Tweed Valley, haunt and playground of his happiest childhood years, he would modulate his talk with Mr Lawson, to drop me remarks from time to time about the landscape through which we were passing. Here had been fights and skir-mishes. The woods in front of us had once been part of a great forest. That hill and the one beyond were called so-and-so—strange names like Scrape and Dollar Law. At that farm across the valley there was a large stone with the mark on it, deep-set, of a hare's foot, left by a witch who, being pursued, had changed herself into a hare to leap the Tweed.

We got off the cart at the Dawyck lodge and crossed the bridge with the road, taking, as we went, a good look at the water on both sides; then we walked through a little pine wood, down to the meadows at the river's edge.

About fishing, and preparations for it, my father was later to write in the fragment *Pilgrim's Rest*: 'I have few theories, and I want only a modest equipment. For trout, wet-fly or dry-fly, I do not use more than a dozen patterns, though I believe in varying the size; for salmon about the same. I like old and well-tried rods and reels—everything old except the gut.'

The August day settled round us, hot and peaceful. The strong sun glittered on open water and lit the shallows where I played so that each smallest floating particle or minute insect, translucent pebbles and the bright green weed which streamed with the current, were clear and distinct.

My father fished, and I made dams and moles and fortifications in the small backwaters where the river had eaten away its bank. The sounds of cattle lowing, the continual conversation of sheep on the hillside above the railway, birds calling, the occasional barking of a dog all went, with the river's constant splash and gurgle, to make up that rural concert which, in retrospect, we tend to think of as silence.

Having doubtless received many injunctions to look after me, see that I did not drown or even get too wet, my father kept me in sight all morning. Sometimes he would take a rest from his fishing which, I rather think, was not productive that day, and come to sit near me on the bank and smoke a cigarette.

I was never to be either so good or so devoted a fisherman as my father and elder brother, although I have had much pleasure from fishing at different times in my life. My father was a real master, my brother is also. Both have written about angling, and the passion that it can be for some people, as well as anyone since Walton.

Here is Johnnie, in *Always a Countryman*, on JB as a fisherman:

My father, for all his slight figure, could throw a salmon-fly thirty yards, and use a heavy Greenheart rod all day. He was one of the finest salmon fishers I have ever watched. The rod appeared to do his work for him. The perfect curve of his back-cast seemed to follow forward with the fly drawing out the long, straight line ahead, independent of his agency. It is the hallmark of all experts that the instrument appears to do its own work.

Salmon, of course, were hardly in question that August day at Dawyck: but I can clearly see that 'slight figure' fishing dry fly upstream from a spit of shingle into the dark golden water of the pools under the farther bank. I would pause in my game for minutes on end to watch this seemingly effortless exhibition of skill, and the strange and magical person giving it. I use the word strange purposely because, as I have tried to show, for a number of reasons my father was a stranger: an impressive and welcome stranger, but one who had his being on the outskirts of my life. It was an awesome pleasure to me to be off with him on this special jaunt. I have often wondered who had suggested that I might benefit from a day in his company. It may have been himself, but I rather think not.

Shortly he would come and sit with me—and not a moment too soon, since I must by midday have been dying of hunger—while we opened our lunch-packets together on a level piece of sheep-cropped turf. From then onwards I know I would have had all his attention. He would have bent on me that curiously compelling face with its pointed chin, long nose and broad forehead slashed down the left temple by a scar like a sabre cut. With his dark brown hair, never in my recollection even to be touched with grey, his tanned complexion and what someone has called his 'frosty blue eyes', his look was wholly original, entirely his own. Nothing of this shows up in any picture of him, save one or two amateur snapshots. Posed for a portrait he appears serious, burdened, even gloomy; it is impossible to divine the kindness of his expression, his particular way of smiling with his eyes, or to guess how easily the rather long, thin mouth, so severe-looking in pictures, could lose all severity in laughter.

Below the ugly concrete road-bridge the river flows shallow, wide and calm. Twenty-five years before, in 1898, my father had published his second novel *John Burnet of Barns*; the house of Barns stands some two miles downstream from Dawyck on the same side. For most of the way there are tall trees and drystone walls, standing back from the water, leaving a broad strip of green turf dotted with thorns and wild roses. The young John Burnet escapes from his tutor one June day, to go fishing.

> I took my way up the river past the green slopes of Haswellskyes to the wood of Dawyck, for I knew well that there, if anywhere, the fish would take in the shady, black pools. . . . A stretch of green turf, shaded on all sides by high beeches, sloped down to the stream-side. The sun made a shining pathway down the middle, but the edges were in blackest shadow.

Nearly sixty years later, that scene, imagined for the seventeenth century, but recorded in the nineteenth, has scarcely changed. Someone no doubt brought the seven-year-old JB to the very places we were visiting in my seventh year—that little boy who was to love this river and its landscape more dearly, and write of it more eloquently, than anywhere else he found in his travels.

In those days, and for all the years that I knew them, up until the early thirties when we forsook Scotland temporarily for Wales, the banks of Tweed were not much trodden except by sheep. The fishermen who came to those shores mostly came singly and sometimes from far away. They were quiet and tidy people, many of whom, in those hungry days, fished to get food. JB wrote of an earlier generation of these.

> In my youth I formed a deep attachment to the democracy of the waterside. There was the ragged weaver out of work, with his ancient home-made rod, who was out to catch his dinner and kept the smallest fingerlings. . . . But the commonest objects of the waterside were miners from the Lothian and Lanarkshire

178

coalfields. They would come by train on a summer evening to some wayside station on Tweed or Clyde, fish all night, and get back to their work in the early morning. Somehow or other they never left with an empty creel. . . .

I know that my father had his share of 'fingerlings' on that day at Dawyck, because I remember my excitement at seeing the rod-point bend, and the line tighten, and my disappointment that the spinning copper-gold fish had to be thrown back. Even then, and although indulgent grown-ups would sometimes let me keep, and cook for my breakfast, fish that were scarcely big enough to eat, I knew that there was a limit below which they simply must not be kept.

The shadows were lengthening when my father looked at his watch and began to reel in. I was, I am sure, very tired as I dragged my wet boots back through the pine wood and over the bridge to where Mr Lawson was waiting.

Tired yet exhilarated, my face burning from the sun, I heard the gate to Gala Lodge click and climbed the steps for the familiar welcome, which could scarcely have been warmer if we had just got back from Greenland: 'Come away in,' and my grandmother's persistent, and to me most annoying question: 'Are you none none the worse?' Far from being any the worse, I was very much the better—for sunshine, for birds and beasts and small fish, for an extended horizon, for the quietly smiling, thoughtful presence, the day-long company of my father.

IO

THE PERFECT SPARE MAN

I went to Eton in the summer of 1929, at about the time of the great
Wall Street crash which presaged our own slump. JB had always
had romantic feelings about Eton, bred, I imagine, at Oxford by
friendship with one or two Etonians. There are Etonians for all
tastes, and I think that his were probably delightful for their
manners, their elegance, their skill at games and unstressed excellence in work, their air of worldly ease. I cannot see JB getting on
with another kind of Etonian that he might have met at Bullingdon
Club dinners: drunk and 'baying', in Evelyn Waugh's words, 'for
broken glass'. However it may have been, he had a particular
admiration for Eton. (One of the protagonists in *John Macnab* is
spotted in disguise because he wears on his watch-chain a small gold
shield, 'badge of athletic prowess at a famous school'.) This sentiment of his was not the only reason for our being sent to that school.
My mother's father had been there, her uncles, her favourite cousin,
and a number of other relations as well. Also, and most important,
it was only fifty miles from Elsfield by road, so that we could be
visited easily and spend the least possible time in getting home for
Long Leave.

Eton College, which now stands as a fortress on the very front
line of the class war, is an extraordinary institution, a medieval
foundation with eighteenth-century trimmings which had in my
day many powerful influences from the Victorian age. To say that I
was not entirely happy there is merely a note about myself; it is no
reflection whatever on the school. I should not have been entirely
happy in any school. Between the ages of thirteen and seventeen I
should probably have been unhappy in the Kingdom of Heaven. I
arrived at school, in my thirteenth year, a compact, rather sunny
child. I had done well in my Common Entrance, and found my new
work easy and agreeable. Apart from its size and strangeness, and

Above left: At the age of five, 'fishing' with John Buchan: I was never to be either so good or so devoted a fisherman as my father.

Above right: John Buchan with his mother at Elsfield. A past mistress at creating physical comfort, she was adept at creating moral discomfort over almost any matter, however small.

Left to right: Alice, William, JB with Alastair, and Johnnie, in the garden at Elsfield. He used to speak of Alice and Johnnie as 'the Greeks' and of myself and Alastair as 'the Barbarians'.

Familiars. *Above left:* Spider, the Woolworth of *Castle Gay*; *above right:* with my father and Mrs Brock, all looking apprehensive.

JB with a kestrel and Johnnie with his goshawk Jezebel. 'I never liked [Jezebel], for she was as big as an eagle and had a most malevolent eye, but she was the joy of his soul.' (Mary Hannay in *The Island of Sheep*.)

Lord High Commissioner to the General Assembly of the Church of Scotland (1934 and 1935)—JB and Susan visiting a children's hospital in Edinburgh.

'An office thickly encrusted with history'—the Lord High Commissioner with his entourage. Front row: Alice (third from left) with our grandmother on her left; JB and my mother sixth and seventh from left. Back row, far right, Brian Fairfax-Lucy, Alice's fiancé, in the dress uniform of his regiment. JB's uniform is that of a Deputy Lieutenant of both Oxford and Peeblesshire.

His ten days of quasi-regal glory were judged a thorough success—JB and my mother leaving the Palace of Holyroodhouse, with an escort found by the Royal Scots Greys.

JB was a beneficent magician in his ability to create a safe and often magical world for his family. My father, in string armour, goes through his part with Alice for a pageant at Elsfield in the 1930s.

By contrast—Their Excellencies the Governor-General of Canada and Lady Tweedsmuir, a signed official photograph.

Left to right: John Buchan, Mackenzie King and Franklin Roosevelt on the arm of his son, James, Quebec, 1936. This was the first official visit to Canada of an American President, and a matter for interested comment all over the world.

Reading papers outside Rideau Hall in February 1939, a year before he died. He was already working on *Sick Heart River*—'His Excellency is writing a very odd book . . . so unlike him, so introspective.'

The Commander-in-Chief of the Armed Forces of the Dominion of Canada with his newly joined-up sons, Johnnie (*left*) and Alastair. JB had signed Canada's declaration of war on 9 September 1940. *Inset:* In his last letter to me, my father wrote: 'If I were a young man, nothing should keep me from the air!' By the time my letter telling him of my entry into the RAF arrived in Ottawa, he was dead.

'Teller of Tales'

the truly terrifying mass of traditional rules and customs needing to be learned quickly on pain of beating, and in spite of my feeling extremely small and newly hatched, Eton during my first half was fascinating rather than frightening. My elder brother had so put the wind up me about penalties for failure in terminal exams that I worked very hard, distinguished myself, and thus earned some good opinions which I was later to falsify sadly.

After my rather too enthusiastic start at school, the worst effects of adolescence set in. All the screws came loose. From being what I have described, a compact and sunny small boy, I lost all my positive qualities and, most particularly the power to work. I received school reports which were almost uniformly awful. My father regarded these with semi-humorous despair. I can see now that it must have been extraordinarily hard for him to understand how anyone, confronted with a challenge, could fail to respond whole-heartedly.

I can only marvel at the patience of those set over me, the constant attention and anxiety that was spent on my rather dismal career. Eton does not care to fail with her pupils, believing that no case should ever be considered hopeless. I won the English Literature prize a couple of times, which slightly raised the spirits of my masters and parents. I was writing a lot of verse in those days and when, in my sixteenth year, with a poem of quite staggering banality, I won the Harvey English Verse Prize, things took a decided turn for the better. Eton, with five hundred years' experience of the anfractuosities of the human temperament, made a decision. Evidently I was a poet, and must be treated as such. A great deal of the heat was taken off me and, for my last year, I pursued my rather languid way with more ease and pleasure than had ever been possible before.

Do children appreciate good manners in grown-ups? I think they do. I remember that while at Eton I was twice given the awesome honour of breakfast alone with the Provost, Dr M. R. James (author of *Ghost Stories of an Antiquary*, etc.). Punctual to the second I would arrive, to be bowed into the great dining-hall by the Provost's butler, there to be greeted with the gravest courtesy by his master.

Dr James—'Monty' to almost everybody, but not to me—was a mountainous man with round gold-rimmed spectacles and a face of benign good sense. After indicating to me a laden sideboard, with a variety of things sizzling quietly over spirit-flames, under silver domes, he would hand me a copy of *The Times*, throw open another and leave me to feed in peace. If I had been an elderly Professor of

Greek, of international reputation, I could not have been treated with greater care or respect, except that I was spared any questions more searching than those about the health of my parents and what interested me most at school.

Chiefly I remember Eton's oddities, its originality, its almost total lack of resemblance to anything else in life. Never having got on with the game of cricket, I took to the water and, being small, acquired a modest distinction as a cox. I recall with nothing but pleasure long summer afternoons on the river; the very smell of 'Rafts' where boats of all kinds were kept and serviced by old watermen in straw hats; rowing with a friend in a small boat called a 'dodger' a long way up-river to Queen's Eyot for a feast of ducks' eggs, bread and butter, and beer.

Then there were all the great events, the Fourth of June, the match against Harrow at Lord's, Henley Regatta, occasions when it was absolutely essential to have parents, or at least relations, to escort. In my early days, my parents came regularly to the Fourth of June when, although I know that the weather could sometimes be brutal, I remember it as invariably fine. I think that my father enjoyed those occasions. Knowing him, I can believe that he learned as much about Eton in a few hours as many ever learned in five years.

If privilege means the enjoyment of good fortune not given to others, we, as a family, were certainly privileged. Thanks to John Buchan's abilities we rode smoothly over the rough ground of the inter-war years. That ground, we were later to feel, was quaking under our feet, but nothing happened in my time to alter the stately round of events in the Eton calendar. The massed hydrangeas bloomed punctually round the luncheon and tea tents at Lord's, at Henley, on the Fourth of June. Cold salmon, lobster salad, strawberries and cream, were eaten in a golden half-light smelling of crushed grass and hot canvas. Eton beat Harrow at cricket. At Henley Eton won the Ladies' Plate. Squiring my sister Alice, I happily took my part in the scene.

There were few of my fellow-pupils, at either of my schools, who were not devoted readers of John Buchan's books, particularly the first four of those which feature Richard Hannay. This gave me a certain cachet among both boys and masters but could also work against me. Because I had JB for a father I was expected to be good at English, expected to know how to write. When I made some small success in English, say in essay writing, it tended to be discounted, as though I had started with an unfair advantage.

I early became used to answering questions about JB; interested, sympathetic questions when I was young, not always so sympathetic in later years. I very soon became accustomed to acting as a sort of spokesman, and it may have done me no harm to realise that my interlocutors' interest was in JB rather than in myself. Nevertheless, it could sometimes be irritating: sometimes I should have been glad to have been spared. Even now, and since the questions keep on coming, I am aware of my face stiffening into a kind of attentive simper when somebody says: 'Buchan . . . mmmm . . . you aren't by any chance related to—you know?—*John* Buchan?' This has had its comical side. Once, during the war, a North Country colleague in the RAF began, in a manner familiar to me, to feel his way towards a personal question. 'Are you,' he asked, 'by any chance related to the *great* Buchan?' I said yes, I supposed I was. His eyes lit up. 'Not *Charles* Buchan?' he said. (Charles Buchan, who played for Sunderland, was a celebrated footballer, who wrote several books on the game.)

Schoolboys continue to read John Buchan, as well as the gamier offerings of the late Ian Fleming and others. Journalists continue to talk about 'the Buchan touch', to compare him favourably or otherwise with new writers in the same vein. Forty years after his death he remains very much alive.

From 1921 to 1937 JB produced a book a year in his popular style—distinct, that is, from histories or biographies—several of which came into the category which he insisted on calling 'shockers'. This was a real misnomer since, in the terms with which we are now familiar, there was nothing shocking about those books, nothing to insult, distress or revolt the reader. Shocker, as a description, was a survival from the days pre-1914 when detective stories, full of murders, were sold on bookstalls for one shilling, and known as 'shilling shockers'. JB's use of it represents the kind of meiosis of which he was rather fond.

Reading references to John Buchan by other writers, I can see that what might be taken for modesty—as I believe it genuinely was—about his popular books can be a source of irritation to those who have not found success to come easily. When he spoke of himself as 'a copious romancer', and implied that writing fiction came so fluently, so pleasantly to him, that he scarcely deserved credit for producing it, I have no reason to doubt that he meant what he said. Writing novels was truly, for him, relaxation. He worked them out in his head, almost down the last detail of dialogue, before he ever took up his pen. To examine his manuscripts is to be astonished by the rarity of corrections, of scratchings-out, of any of the stops and starts, false trails and confusions which mark most writers' work. What sticks in some throats, I fancy, is that JB not only enjoyed writing his novels, easily, professionally and punctually, but that he also made a good deal of money out of them. Even that might be forgiven, were it not that he acquired a vast and devoted public which did not desert him at his death. The books, therefore, cannot seriously be dismissed as popular trash, dug out of a lucky vein at some remove from the true mines of literature. They are too consistently good in their own terms and they continue to be read.

Like the majority of people who try to write I find the process painful and laborious. When, in my teens, I began to struggle to get some things down on paper, the sight of my father working through his orderly and productive day drove me nearly to despair. There is a delicious passage in the *Goncourt Journal* about the Dumas, father and son. Someone asks after the son.

'And how's Dumas *fils*? Still ill?'
    'Oh, terribly unhappy. You know what he does these days? He sits down in front of a sheet of paper and stays there for four hours. He writes three lines. He goes off to have a cold bath or do some exercises. .... Then he comes back and decides that his three lines are damn stupid. . . . And he crosses out everything except three words. Every now and then his father arrives from Naples and says: "Get me a cutlet and I'll finish your play for you."'

Dumas *père*'s further activities, on such an occasion, would not have been in character with JB; but the little scene nicely illustrates two extremes among the approaches to writing.

The ten years between 1925, when I went to my first school, and 1935, when my parents left for Canada, were years of intense interest and high productivity for my father. Three times after the war he had been asked to stand for Parliament, but only at the third proposal did he accept. He had concluded, probably with some reluctance, that he no longer dared to subject his health to the rigours of the hustings, such as he had known in Peeblesshire in 1911. When, however, the Unionist Association of the Scottish

Universities asked him, in early 1927, to contest one of the three Scottish university seats which had just fallen vacant, he was happy to accept. In those days there were twelve seats for the English, Welsh and Northern Irish universities. Although regarded by some as anomalous, these seats had a usefulness for those represented in that their candidates were likely to have a really good knowledge of the special problems of universities. From the candidate's point of view, they were nearly ideal since they involved no expenses, no campaigning and only one election address. Voting was by post, so that there was no exhaustingly climactic polling day. Best of all, the candidate was not required to be a rigid party man.

Such a candidature might have been tailor-made for John Buchan, who duly beat his opponent by 16,903 to 2,378, and had majorities in all four Scottish universities. On 3 May 1927 he took his seat in the House of Commons, which he was to hold until, at three o'clock in the afternoon of 28 March 1935, his appointment as Governor-General of Canada was officially announced from the Palace, and he ceased automatically to be a Member of Parliament.

When John Buchan entered Parliament his party had a majority of more than two hundred over the others. The Prime Minister, Stanley Baldwin, was already an old friend. He and JB saw eye to eye on many things, and particularly on the need for a revitalised, more generous, more intellectual and more socially conscious Conservative Party.

The wounds of the General Strike of 1926 were still open, and the right wing of the government party had succeeded in persuading Baldwin, against his real inclination, to table the Trades Disputes Act which would effectively prevent them from healing. If the Conservatives were to be seen as a party of progress anxious, in their best tradition, to 'clear away lumber' while retaining what was still good and useful in accumulated practices, there was much to be done—and much, John Buchan must have felt, that lay along the lines which he had himself been recommending since his earliest days as a journalist.

It was not on industrial matters, however, that JB chose to make his maiden speech. The Government, that year, was putting forward proposals for reform of the House of Lords, which would have restored to it some powers lost through the drastic curtailments of the 1911 Parliament Act. Ramsay MacDonald and the Labour Party moved a vote of censure, and it was on this that JB spoke in Parliament for the first time. True to himself he attacked both the opposition and his own party, in a speech which won him

high praise from his colleagues and from the press. In her biography
Janet Adam Smith quotes the Liberal *Daily News* as reporting that
JB demonstrated to the satisfaction of the House 'that the Government are a pack of fools, that the Peers are out of date but
exceedingly useful, and that the mission of the Tory Party is to use
them.' The vote of censure was lost, but the Government's proposals sank without trace.

John Buchan soon came to love the House of Commons, and to
spend many hours in it, conferring on a variety of matters or
attending debates. The House is a curious, rather cagey body. Skill
and ability are not enough for it; other, more arcane, qualities are
required as well, if a member is to gain a reputation as 'a good
House of Commons man'. This, I think, JB never quite achieved.
Some quality of his, something which occasionally made people
impervious to his charm, his openness, militated against complete
acceptance by an organism which can sometimes seem as childish
and ill-disciplined as a kindergarten, for all its pretensions as an
august and exclusive club. While I believe that I know what that
quality was, I should find it difficult to define. The nearest I can
come to it is a French word: *insaisissable*. This does not properly
translate as 'unseizable', since that word in English is rare and used
only with a legal connotation. The French word can be used to
describe something (or someone) that cannot quite be grasped,
possessed of a certain elusiveness which, in JB's case, was not only a
trait of character, but a function of his extraordinarily swift movements from place to place. Since his mind also moved at great
speed, it is understandable that slower minds, more lymphatic
temperaments, might have found his personality disquieting. No
doubt but that some people took his ability to express himself
lucidly for glibness, his declaration of high aims—*non inferiora
secutus*—for preaching, and thought his protean abilities, his success
in so many fields, 'unsound'.

Men to whom I have spoken about JB's Parliamentary days, who
were young Members at the time, have told me of his great kindness
to them, his concentrated attention to their problems, his unstinting
willingness to help. As always throughout his life, he was at his best
with the young. That those young men, now elderly, remember
him with so much grateful affection, is among the pleasantest of his
memorials.

I have heard it said that JB was 'a bad committee man'. Myself, I should be inclined to take that as a compliment, having suffered much from the contemporary tendency to use committees as a means of avoiding decisive action. Nevertheless I can see the force of the criticism.

JB's first experience of practical politics had been with Lord Milner in South Africa where, in complex yet swiftly changing situations, decisions needed to be made quickly, and as quickly acted upon. Parliamentary committee-work is a very different matter, requiring patience, cunning, an ability to adhere closely to a pre-considered line of argument, and a degree of more or less genial brutality in putting it over. It also tends to drag on and on. My father had patience and any amount of goodwill, but I fear that he may sometimes have been undermined by his fatal propensity for seeing both sides of a question, and his equally fatal belief in the good intentions of others.

Whatever John Buchan's feelings about committees may have been, he certainly sat on a great many of them at different times. In addition to his ten-year stint on the Oxford University Chest, he was to be concerned with several educational bodies, with re-vivifying Conservative politics in the universities, with fulfilling plans—inspired by disgust with the feebleness of the Conservative Central Office at the time of his Peeblesshire campaign—to revise and improve his party's education system. He helped to start the Conservative Educational Institute, and became Chairman of its executive committee. When money was forthcoming to found a Conservative college, JB was instrumental in setting it up, at Ashridge, the former home of Lord Brownlow.

Of his almost innumerable unpaid jobs the one which gave him the greatest pleasure was his trusteeship of the Pilgrim Trust. I suspect that this charity particularly appealed to JB because its founder, Edward Harkness, an American of British descent, fell squarely into that category of benevolent millionaires which I have called one of his most romantic inventions.

In 1930 Harkness gave two million pounds of his own money (an enormous sum even at present-day rates) for use as a picked body of trustees should see fit. There were five members of the Trust, of which Baldwin was Chairman, and the elusive but influential Tom Jones Secretary. Harkness wanted his money to be used to save, or preserve, items of the British heritage, but he allowed the Trustees to interpret that word very widely. They decided that the country's heritage was not merely in the stones of its past, but in the people of its present who, at that time, were suffering badly from unemployment and other hardships of the slump. Their aim was to awaken in the distressed areas a 'sense that life might still be worth living where all seemed so bleak and hopeless'. Among other activities they set up and assisted community centres, educational and infant welfare institutions, clubs and hostels, craft industries and holiday camps.

Where Britain's architectural and aesthetic heritage was concerned, the Trust cast its net widely. I remember driving to Suffolk with my father to look at the noble church of Blythburgh, whose fabric, especially the magnificent flight of carved wooden angels below its roof, was in a state of near-dereliction. Money was found for its repair, as it was for Durham Cathedral, the first rescue operation of this kind to be undertaken by the Pilgrim Trust.

The Trust's work continues, on exactly the terms originally devised by JB and his colleagues. Just such a happy conjunction of a generous donor with men of vision, goodwill and practical sense had been foreshadowed long before by JB, not once but several times.

Those few years between entering Parliament and leaving for Canada were a time of intense busyness for JB. In 1929 the Conservative party lost the General Election to Labour, and Ramsay MacDonald became Prime Minister. JB's own constituency of four universities imposed no strain upon him beyond the writing of an election address, and returned him with a handsome majority; but he threw himself into campaigning for various Conservative candidates in England and Scotland and, once again, made himself ill.

His contract with Nelson's was due to end in that year. JB could probably have renewed it, but decided not to do so. He must have realised that, somewhere, he must cut down on his commitments. To repair the loss of income from Nelson's he again took up regular journalism, writing for the *Graphic* and contributing, for five years, the 'Atticus' column in the *Sunday Times*. He went on with his work for Reuter's, but left London on Friday mornings, so as to have three days at home for his writing, at which he worked harder than ever.

JB's productivity as a writer over the years 1929 to 1935 is almost alarming. 1929: *The Courts of the Morning*; 1930: *Castle Gay, The Kirk in Scotland* (with Sir George Adam Smith); 1931: *The Blanket of the Dark*; 1932: *Sir Walter Scott, The Gap in the Curtain, Julius Caesar,*

The Magic Walking Stick (for children); 1933: *The Massacre of Glencoe, A Prince of the Captivity*; 1934: *The Free Fishers, Gordon at Khartoum, Oliver Cromwell*; 1935: *The King's Grace* (for King George V's Jubilee), *The House of the Four Winds*. Of these, *Scott* and *Cromwell* are serious full-length biographies; *Caesar, Gordon* and *Glencoe* shorter studies; but all required considerable reading and research. *The Kirk in Scotland*, written to commemorate the reunion of most of the elements of the Presbyterian Church into one Church of Scotland, is a beautifully balanced short study of a long and often anguished historical process, written with great sympathy, clarity and erudition.

His accession to Parliament had considerably altered the routines of John Buchan's life. In the early days at Elsfield, while he was working for Nelson's, he used to go to London on the 8.40 from Oxford and return in the evening by the 6.05 from Paddington, occasionally by the 4.45. Once in Parliament he found the whole business of the House so absorbing and there was so much to be done outside it, during the Parliamentary Session; there were so many people to be seen, so many invitations to lunch or dine, so many meetings to attend, that he took to staying in London from Monday until Friday, usually with my grandmother in Upper Grosvenor Street. So it fell out that I quite often saw him in London, during those parts of my holidays from school which coincided with the Session. Once in a while he would find time to take me out to luncheon. He always asked me where I would like to go and, remembering his stories of the days when much of London life centred on and near the Strand, I would ask to go to Gatti's, then still in being, or the Cheshire Cheese. Once, after the theatre, he fulfilled a pledge by taking me to supper at the Savoy Grill and introducing me to his favourite devilled kidneys—surely contra-indicated, as doctors say, for such an ailment as his. If he was pressed for time we lunched at the St Stephen's Club, a singularly gloomy haunt, smelling of soup and stale cigar smoke, which he used because it was handy for the House, being literally just across the street, and also next door to his private office.

Sometimes he would take me with him to an afternoon reception at somebody's house. Cocktail party would be quite the wrong words for what I have in mind, which was something altogether more stately. With my head full of Henry James, Marcel Proust and Ronald Firbank, I enjoyed those occasions enormously since, like my mother at her Drums, I was not required to do anything but smile and listen and observe my surroundings.

On the whole I took great pleasure in my outings with JB. Naturally, I hoped that conversation would remain general, and that neither my current performance at school, nor the question of what I meant to do with my life, would loom too large. With his habitual stoicism JB had evidently decided to take his children as he found them, and not to expend too much anxiety on their very obvious differences from himself and his brothers and sister at their ages. He held himself always ready to help, to answer any question, to make any introduction, to suggest or supplement any line of enquiry. Mostly, I think, we talked about books, and about writers, and I tried to interest him in the poets who were having so great an influence at that time.

Satire and parody are often the refuge of the insecure. Sometimes I had sent him specimens of these from Eton, and he had responded immediately, and with real amusement. One he had called 'argute and facele', being fond of seventeenth-century words and phrases. At the same time he had warned me seriously about remaining content to parody the work of others, rather than produce something original of my own.

When we came to the uncomfortable subject of my future, and I perhaps said that I wanted only to be a writer, he would briskly quote Sir Walter Scott's dictum about writing being a good stick but a bad crutch. By all means I should write, but there must be something else, less hazardous, for bread and butter. Once he said to me, rather wistfully, 'I wish ambition would wake in you.' Alas, I could think of no one career to be ambitious about. Later he was to say to me; 'I don't think I really mind what you do in life, so long as you are not an Interior Decorator!' I perfectly saw what he meant.

After the 1914–18 war social life in London still retained a pattern similar to that of pre-war days. Much had cracked or crumbled. Many once solidly established families, through human losses in war, and economic losses thereafter, had dropped out of the social scene. New people with new money had taken their places. But the pattern of the 'London Season', of public occasions and private entertaining, continued until the first days of September 1939, and then, like a cobweb, was blown clean away. Private patronage and private charity, now largely withered away, were real forces in the social life of the time. Society was still small enough—although more heterogeneous and far less exclusive than in my mother's youth—for anyone with a cool head and a sense of relationships to chart the interconnecting channels of influence, to know who 'counted' and who did not, when it came to promoting a political career, a symphony or a play.

Decidedly, John Buchan counted. He was living his preferred kind of life, 'at the heart of things'. He had powerful connexions and an exact knowledge of the movements of power. More important perhaps, he was perfectly approachable and evidently neither greedy nor self-seeking. From a hostess's point of view he had several other virtues. He was genuinely charming, punctual as well as punctilious; he never asked favours for himself, although he did so often enough for others: when he gave a promise he kept it. His presence was stimulating, his conversation always entertaining, and often brilliant. He was attractive to most women, chiefly, no doubt, because of that elusive quality which I have mentioned. All in all, since he was alone in London during the week, except for a short time in the summer when my mother joined him, he must have been a nearly perfect 'spare man' for any luncheon or dinner party.

One of the leading political hostesses of the nineteen-thirties was Lady Londonderry, wife of Charles, 7th Marquess of Londonderry. JB had known her for some years, and had helped her with a biography of her father, Lord Chaplin, the famous sportsman. She and her husband entertained at Londonderry House on a really lavish scale. The house, which stood at the southern end of Park Lane, has since been rebuilt as an hotel, and is still called by its old name. It was a rather ugly early nineteenth-century building, too broad for its height, but inside it had what was needed for political entertaining—many high rooms communicating with one another from either side of a grand staircase.

One hot afternoon, when I was eighteen, I remember treading that staircase behind my father, dressed in my best, excited, ready to be impressed. I was impressed. The scene was splendid. We went from room to room slowly, since JB was accosted at almost every step, and we had to halt, as in some stately dance, for introductions and a word or two, before moving on.

The political importance was probably lost on me; but the pictures were not, nor the furniture, nor the feeling of Ruritanian splendour, the gilding and the crystal, the wigged footmen moving so dexterously. By that date such entertainments were becoming rare; possibly, in the middle of a serious economic recession, they were inappropriate; but such social conscience as I possessed could not nag me out of my pleasure in something which, I perhaps half knew, I might not often see again.

Lady Londonderry, supported by so much grandeur, was a powerful figure: solid, plethoric, somewhat domineering. I have always supposed her the model for the great lady who pockets the Labour politician in Howard Spring's *Fame is the Spur*. Certainly she had a powerful attraction for Ramsay MacDonald, that solitary Scottish romantic whose followers so often thought that he had betrayed his own ideals and the principles of his party. When, in 1931, beset by financial and industrial difficulties, the Labour Government resigned, King George V proposed a coalition to Ramsay MacDonald, and the National Government came into being, with Cabinet Ministers from all three parties, and Mac-Donald again as Prime Minister.

In those days JB was often at Londonderry House, chiefly to keep an eye on the Prime Minister, who was a regular guest at Lady Londonderry's intimate small dinners at which, many believed, important political strings were pulled. The importance of that string-pulling was probably exaggerated but, as can be imagined, it gave no pleasure to the Prime Minister's party to see him apparently at the beck and call of what some would certainly have seen as arch-enemies of the Labour movement.

Ramsay MacDonald's was an enigmatic character, poetical, erratic, at times almost tragic. If Londonderry House cast a spell over him, it was very likely because he had grown out of all sympathy with the self-conscious cloth-cappery of his own followers. They were naturally disgusted when, for instance, he insisted upon court dress for his colleagues at certain functions; but then the majority of them were not romantic Highland Scots. JB was a Lowlander and moreover had seen very much more of the sort of thing Londonderry House had to offer than had the Labour leader. He was amused by it but never, I think, enthralled.

Some wit, observing that Lady Londonderry had taken to calling the inner circle of her guests by the names of animals, christened her Circe, and her circle the Ark. JB was, of course, the Buck, and Ramsay the Ram. Mention of the Londonderrys caused my mother a delicate wrinkling of the nose. She thought the Ark business silly and vulgar, and was not pleased to see JB mixed up in it. An innate political wisdom probably told her that what the Londonderrys were doing was politically unsafe as well as socially bad style.

John Buchan has sometimes been reproved by critics for setting his stories in scenes of extreme grandeur—London ballrooms, large country houses, distinguished clubs. I think such criticism naïve, given the dates at which those stories were first written. When the young JB came to England, to London, that very world of grand families, grand establishments, grand clubs was precisely, as the young might now say, 'where it was at'. All political and social manoeuvring of any immediate significance went on inside that very close-knit and seemingly self-perpetuating society, and still continued to do so even between the wars.

With a different temperament JB might have taken a very different road. He might have joined Blatchford's *Clarion* rather than the *Spectator*, the Fabian Society rather than 'The Club'.* He might have frequented the rich radical bourgeoisie of the Sidney Webbs, or the plain-livers and high-thinkers of Letchworth and Welwyn Garden City. The truth is that he very much enjoyed the Disraelian world into which he sometimes leads his readers; and I must insist, once again, that those readers (his sales prove it) were perfectly happy to be led. If, in the end, his particular settings lost their original magic, even became stereotyped, these were effects of social changes among JB's public, and of a certain fatigue in himself. Most of his critics, never having known the world of which he speaks with such easy authority, find that world stuffy and unreal, and cannot get over a feeling that, in some way, they are being patronised.

There is no doubt whatever that my father liked what used to be called 'high life': stately functions, glittering occasions, the whole pomp and splendour of a formal, orderly, traditionally constituted society. But, as I saw for myself, he never wanted to be wholly integrated into it. For all his disclaimers about detached attitudes, he liked to keep his freedom of action.

In a London ballroom he was a benevolent observer, in, but not entirely of, the social scene. He liked to look in on such affairs, to reassure himself that all was still well, that the crust was still holding over the fires of disorder, of the existence of which he was always so acutely aware. He never cared to stay long at any gathering. He did not wish to dance, nor to join the elderly card-players in the farther rooms. If he found no one he especially wanted to talk to, no one whom he had perhaps purposely come to find, he would quite early take his leave. It is worth noting, when he describes a ballroom

*Founded in 1764 by Dr Johnson.

scene in a London house, that JB has brought his character there for the express purpose of meeting someone else, an explorer perhaps, or a soldier just back from the North-West Frontier—in any case another detached observer who counterpoints, by his unconventional experience, the conventionality of the others present. He also uses such occasions to criticise, quite sharply, the manners and appearance of the young. Such scenes are never used simply to dazzle the unsophisticated, but to underline the fact that, to preserve civilisation there are some who must keep alert, remain active and unsleeping in their watch over its citadel.

One thing is certain: John Buchan would never have given five minutes of his time to the society he describes had he not found it to contain, with all its fools and fribbles, its brutes and bores, some very acute minds, a high level of culture, a serious philanthropy, and particular graces of outlook and manners only possible upon a basis of purposeful selection and secular ease. JB was the last person to wish to throw babies out with the bathwater. He wanted social changes, some of them radical, but not at the expense of certain resolutions about living which had been arrived at after centuries of experiment and which he thought valid.

Lowering skies and swimming streets added to the depression which was settling upon Birkpool as thick as its customary coronal of smoke.

On one such day Adam was passing down a side-street, where dingy tram-cars screamed on the metals, and foul torrents roared in the gutters, and the lash of the rain washed the grease from the cobbles. There was a shabby post office, for in that quarter of Birkpool even the banks and post offices looked shabby, from the swing-doors of which men and women were emerging. They had been drawing their old-age pensions, the women were clutching their purses in their lean, blue-veined hands, and all had that look of desperate anxiety which the poor wear when they carry with them the money that alone stands between them and want. A miserable tramp on the kerb was singing 'Annie Laurie' in a cracked voice, and from a neighbouring alley, which led to a factory, there poured a crowd of grimy workmen released at the dinner-hour, turning up the collars of their thin jackets against the sleet. The place smelt of straw, filth, stale food and damp— damp above everything.*

* *A Prince of the Captivity* (1933).

194

Clubs, ballrooms and high-powered political dealings were one set of things. John Buchan's pleasure in the world's splendours did not blind him to its miseries. He had spent eighteen years of his life in close contact with the poor of Fife and Glasgow, had seen from near at hand the struggle for existence in an industrial city where the extremes of wealth and poverty were glaringly obvious, and there was little but the charity of such as his parents, themselves far from rich, to keep the weakest from going to the wall. He believed that poverty was a disease which, like all diseases, must one day be susceptible of cure. He distrusted 'philanthropic sensibility in the face of poverty and sickness; a minister's family had little time for such a luxury. . . . I lived close to working-class life and knew that it had its own humours and compensations, and that it nourished many major virtues like fortitude and charity.' What he had not known, or had known perhaps only in one or two instances, was the creeping despair felt by so many in the twenties and thirties, when it became apparent that unemployment was not going to be temporary, a brief if disagreeable interruption in a working life, but permanent; that strong hands would be idle for a lifetime, that skills which were a source of pride and a joy to use would waste unwanted, because the market for them had fallen away.

My mother, being in close touch with Oxford, was fully informed of what was being done there to try to alleviate the misery of what were then called 'the Distressed Areas'. She joined the committee which set up and ran Oxford House, at Risca in Monmouthshire. Two leading spirits of that committee were Alan Cameron, then Director of Education for Oxfordshire, and his wife, the novelist Elizabeth Bowen. The morning-room at Elsfield became a depot for boxes of clothes and other necessities collected for the people of Risca. My mother went down to the Welsh valleys to see what could possibly be done, what immediately supplied, to make life a shade more bearable for the Welsh people she came so soon to like and admire. A drop in the ocean of course: no amount of kindness and compassion could affect the root causes of so widespread an industrial disaster; but perhaps better than nothing. In his Communist–prophetic days W. H. Auden spoke scathingly of 'our metaphysical distress, our kindness to ten persons'. His 'metaphysical distress' perhaps parallels JB's 'philanthropic sensibility'.

There was nothing metaphysical about the Risca Committee's thinking, which was wholly practical, even pragmatic. Many people would have thought it better to be kind to only ten persons than to hang about waiting for a revolution which might or might not produce perfect conditions for the toiling masses of the world.

The ill winds of the thirties blew me one wonderful piece of good: my friendship with Elizabeth Bowen, which lasted from my sixteenth year until her tragic death in 1973. Elizabeth and Alan Cameron had not long come to Oxford when my mother first met them. They lived in what I think was a converted stable in a quiet backwater of Headington, and their small house very soon became the rallying-point of all that was most brilliant and amusing in the Oxford colleges. Elizabeth had the luminous look of a Holbein portrait, a slight stammer, and the same gift as my father's for making people feel original, clever and interesting.

One is never so avant-garde as in adolescence, when what is said to be new really seems new, and one lacks the experience to recognise old hat refreshed with new trimmings. I was desperately keen to be in all the movements that were going, although not always able to detect which of them were moving in circles. By the time of my sixteenth year the age gap between my sister Alice and myself had narrowed.

Alice was not yet married. Rather than tread the expected path of a girl from her background—a path not much less circumscribed than in her mother's day—she found kindred spirits among contemporaries more amusing and less conventional than the Guards officers and dull, decorous young men whom she generally met at dances. She would delight me with stories of strange parties, and tell me about people she knew whose names were beginning to be known in the world of writing: John Betjeman, Anthony Powell, Roger Fulford, Robert Byron. She it was who brought home Eugene Jolas's *transition*, Waugh's *Vile Bodies*, and Betjeman's *Mount Zion*, printed on different-coloured papers by the private press of Edward James. Alice introduced me to the work of Jean Cocteau, through the medium of *La Voix Humaine* which she translated herself and performed at one of the Easter entertainments which we produced every year for the visit of our Scottish relations. For her as for me, the advent in our lives of Elizabeth Bowen was a great delight.

Elizabeth was extraordinarily kind to a spotty boy who found in her company something not to be found at school, nor always at home—a tranquil acceptance. I desperately wanted to be thought clever by someone: with her I felt clever. She encouraged my researches into various movements, lending me copies of the French magazine *Surréalisme* which had its name printed in luminous ink so that it could (how usefully!) be seen in the dark. She invited me to meals and to sherry parties where the conversation of the other guests seemed to me wonderfully revealing, exhilarating, exactly what I had always hoped that intellectual conversation might be. I devoured every line that Elizabeth wrote, from her astonishing first novel, *The Last September*, to the collection of stories *The Cat Jumps* which contains not only the haunting horror story of the title but also 'The Disinherited', perhaps the best short study ever made of a kind of social disintegration very much in evidence in the years between the wars.

Elizabeth Bowen was not only a brilliant and wholly original writer; she was also an Anglo-Irish lady of substance, last of a family of landowners in County Cork. Thus, although she shone in literary society and derived much pleasure from it, she was perfectly at home in other spheres. She and my parents became friends, and after my mother had introduced her to the Women's Institutes, she started a successful branch of her own in Headington. She came often to Elsfield, where my father admired her penetrating intelligence as much as he loved her turn of phrase, the delicious sense of humour which was hers alone. Elizabeth was one of the few contemporary novelists whom JB would willingly read. Once, when he thought her style, delving down through layer after layer of feeling, was becoming a trifle too involuted, he announced that he was going to speak to her like a Dutch uncle.

11

THE PALACE OF HOLYROODHOUSE

For two years running, in the early thirties, my parents leased a house in London for the Season. This was partly to provide my sister with a place to return hospitality and entertain her friends, and partly for them to do the same thing.

Why, in a country where the climate is so perpetual a subject of aggrieved comment, where the weather can never be counted on to do the desired thing at the right time, I should remember those summers of the nineteen-thirties as golden, I cannot tell. Perhaps there was a series of fine summer weeks occurring at times of high social activity. Certainly that last, fatal, summer of 1939 was of an unforgettable beauty.

When I was sixteen my parents, for a couple of months, took a small and attractive house in Gayfere Street, Westminster, just behind the school. That quarter was, and still is, pretty and quiet, with a lot of moderate-sized late-Georgian houses. It has a cachet of its own, largely political, since it is handy for Parliament, is much lived in by such Members as can afford it, and is within range of the Division bell system, so that they can attempt some sort of home life while awaiting a summons to vote.

For a few weeks that little house hummed with life. Outside, the hot sunshine lay on the pavements like golden syrup. The striped sun-blinds were lowered all day and the rooms were full of a warm dusk. Caterers' vans came and went. In the late afternoon waiters appeared; glasses were laid out; the air began to smell of wine and gin. People arrived: aunts, cousins and old friends anxious for a glimpse of my mother, serious young men hoping for a word with my father; my sister's friends, insouciant, far from serious, bringing in a sense of gaiety, a breath of different air; pretty women, beautifully dressed. This was almost my first experience of London entertaining. I found the atmosphere heady, not least because I kept finding before me faces which, until then, I had only seen in picture papers.

During those years JB was at the height of his celebrity as plain John Buchan, admired, sought after, influential, the subject of continual publicity in the press. He worked much behind the scenes of politics, particularly in helping to support the Prime Minister, who suffered from crises of decision and whose spirits needed keeping up. JB often described to me those early morning walks, when, with a detective clumping behind, he would accompany Ramsay MacDonald round St James's Park, reassuring, counselling, suggesting, trying to set him on course for the day. He had much affection for MacDonald, and great sympathy for a man who, he believed, had knowingly made himself bitterly unpopular with his own party by accepting a coalition out of a sense of his duty to the nation.

JB was at the heart of affairs, but the public recognition which he would have liked to have, and felt he deserved, was not forthcoming. Baldwin, for all his admiration and affection for JB, did not think him right for the Cabinet. The balance of the three parties was anyway delicate and the appointment of another Tory would have been difficult. Even so, JB might have been offered a Ministry without Portfolio, but even to that Baldwin would not agree. Perhaps the words which JB used of F. E. Smith might be applied to himself: 'He was too much the brilliant individualist for our queer synthetic polity.'

There is no doubt that JB was disappointed, his mother vociferously so. With advancing years Mrs Buchan senior had become more worldly. She saw her splendid son working himself to death for a pack of southern politicians; she heard him widely praised; she had always believed strongly in official rewards, and yet her son received none. She thought little of the Order of Companion of Honour which he received in 1932.

If political office eluded JB, something significant was nevertheless coming his way. In March 1933 he was asked by Ramsay MacDonald if he would accept the appointment of Lord High Commissioner to the General Assembly of the Church of Scotland.

I gladly accepted the office, for the Scottish Church had always been a principal part of my background. I was born and brought up in a manse. I was an elder of the Kirk,* my historical studies had lain to some extent in Scottish Church history, and I had had a small part in bringing about the union of the United Free Church (of which my father had been a minister) with the Church of Scotland. . . . The Lord High Commissioner is the sole subject in Great Britain who on occasion represents His Majesty, and he must therefore conduct himself high and disposedly.

The Kirk in Scotland has always claimed the right to be self-governing, and many words, much ink and even some blood have been poured out over this claim. After the Union of the Church of Scotland, in 1929, with the United Free Church—itself a union of the original Free Church and the United Presbyterians—the Kirk had settled down to being governed by its General Assembly.

The Assembly sits for ten days in May. The High Commissioner takes up residence in the Palace of Holyroodhouse as representative of the Crown. JB wrote:

It is an office thickly encrusted with history. In the seventeenth century the Lord High Commissioner presided over the Scottish Parliament, and a stormy time he had of it. . . . Since the Union of 1707 he presides at the Assembly alone.

Edinburgh since 1947 has become used to the annual excitement of the Festival, but at the time of JB's appointment the brief appearance of the Lord High Commissioner was a high moment of its year. There were luncheon and dinner parties, receptions, morning levees, and, for my parents, a thick schedule of visits to hospitals, schools, boys' clubs and exhibitions. JB went alone sometimes to deliver addresses to church societies, clubs and committees, while my mother visited children's nurseries and nurses' homes. He had a large amount of speaking to do, in addition to his opening and closing addresses to the Assembly itself. He and my mother drove out to inaugurate the proceedings in an open landau with a cavalry escort of the Scots Greys. There was a guard of honour at the Palace which turned out whenever my father left the building or returned to it. Each of my parents was addressed as 'Your Grace', and my mother had two ladies-in-waiting and five maids-of-honour, one of whom was my sister Alice. My father had a Purse-bearer, a Mace-bearer and four aides-de-camp.

*St Columba's, Pont Street, London SW1, the chief Scottish church in London.

John Buchan's military career was many years past, but it was felt that he needed some sort of uniform, something more impressive than a tail-coat and top hat, in which to perform his duties 'high and disposedly'. Accordingly he was sworn in as a Deputy Lieutenant for both Oxfordshire and Peeblesshire and it was in the uniform of that office—scarlet tunic, narrow trousers, cocked hat with white plumes, ceremonial sword—that he made his first public appearance in Edinburgh. Upon his thin and wiry figure clothes always sat well; the DL's uniform became him extremely.

Every man who has to perform stately and traditional functions in public should have a touch of the actor in his make-up; that is, he should be able to assume and sustain a role, to play the part 'as written'. It is essential also that he should believe in his role and think it well worth the playing. JB's historical sense, his accurate knowledge of the past and present significance of his duties as High Commissioner, enabled him to act with exemplary dignity, and to answer more than adequately the various calls they made upon him. His ten days of quasi-regal glory were judged a thorough success: so much so that he was asked to undertake the same duties again in the following year.

A number of political figures were guests at Holyrood during those two Assemblies of 1933 and 1934, and among them was Stanley Baldwin. Being, in his apparently sleepy way, very shrewd, he took note of John Buchan's bearing, the quality of his speeches, and the effect he created at the Assembly and among the many guests from all over Scotland who came to the Receptions. If he had ever doubted JB's suitability for a high office such as Governor-General of Canada, his doubts must have been quickly dispelled.

I was at Holyrood with my parents for part of the time in both 1933 and 1934. For the first time Alastair came with me, leave from Eton having been granted for so special an occasion. Having no official duties we enjoyed ourselves greatly, exploring the Palace and its wonderfully elaborate royal plumbing. Holyroodhouse had been taken in hand in, I think, King Edward's reign, and made both comfortable and elegant. No longer had the High Commissioner 'to bring his own plate and linen and other accessories, and bivouac in windy chambers where the rats scampered'.

Alastair and I had no sartorial problems, since our school clothes and hats were perfectly correct for all the daytime occasions. It was on my second visit that I was made to wear 'levee dress'. This was a sort of poor relation of proper court dress (velvet tail-coat and breeches, cut steel buttons and buckles, cocked hat and rapier), being the top half of evening tails worn with black stuff breeches, black silk stockings and patent leather pumps. Rigged out in these I was required to stand for two hours, without moving, as part of the furniture for an evening reception.

It intrigued me to see my father, for the first time, as the central figure in a long, complicated and occasionally exciting pageant. He attacked his part with all the concentration, intelligence and sense of occasion that I had come to expect of him. He was grave without being pompous, dignified without being stiff. Whenever a chance came to relax, he relaxed. Setting out for some important event he never assumed the blank glare usual in those who are constipated with their own importance. Without relaxing decorum, he would pass by me with a slight change of expression, not quite a smile nor yet a wink, the merest hint that we were in a conspiracy together, and both—surely?—enjoying it.

I could never be quite sure how my grandmother took the High Commissionership; naturally she was fêted and deferred to wherever she went; and she sat sternly throughout all the proceedings of the Assembly, as once she had done with her husband. But that her son should have come in the end to the Assembly—somewhere where she must have always longed to see him—in a secular rather than a religious role—this might have caused mixed feelings.

In spite of the burdens which they put upon him, I believe that JB enjoyed his Holyrood days intensely, and most of all because there, for a while, he was back in the heart of Scottish history.

I shall not soon forget those dinners in the great gallery of the Palace, where sometimes a hundred sat at table—the lingering spring sunshine competing with the candles, the dark walls covered with the portraits of the Kings of Scotland (daubs two hundred years old, but impressive in the twilight), the toast of the King, followed by the National Anthem, and that of the Church of Scotland, followed by Old Hundred, the four pipers of the Argylls, who strutted round the table and then played a pibroch for my special delectation. On those nights old ghosts came out of secret places.

On the last night of the first visit, my sister Alice announced her engagement to Brian Fairfax-Lucy (the late Major Sir Brian Fairfax-Lucy, Bt of Charlecote) one of the ADCs. Everyone was delighted;

no one saw any reason why the young couple should not be married as soon as they liked. Looking back, it seems to me that their wedding must have required some high-powered organisation. Engaged in May, they were to be married in the first week of August, just after the end of the Season. The rooms at Elsfield began again to fill up with boxes and parcels, but this time they contained wedding presents, of which, in spite of the times, there seemed to be a great number, all, with the names of their donors, later to be listed in the Oxford and Peebles papers. Home from school I enjoyed taking part in the arrangements, inspecting the presents, helping with the invitations. Alice and Brian were married in the old, red, perpendicular St Columba's in Pont Street, which was later to be gutted by bombs and replaced by something more in the Scottish tradition.

Brian Fairfax-Lucy was a most welcome addition to the family, much loved by my parents, as indeed by all of us, from the very beginning. Finding that he had joined a family most of the members of which went in for writing, Brian decided to take a hand himself and sat down to write a book for children. The book found a publisher immediately and was an instant success, as were the others which followed it.

In the early autumn of 1934 my parents went once again to the United States. The founder of the Pilgrim Trust, Edward Harkness, had added to his benefactions by presenting a library to Columbia University in New York, and JB was invited to give the dedication address. He and my mother were much fêted both in New York and Washington, where JB met Franklin D. Roosevelt for the first time; a highly significant meeting as things turned out.

By this time John Buchan was fifty-nine years old. He had already had an astonishing career which had delighted many people and infuriated some. He had kept his buoyant optimism, and neither his several real disappointments nor his continuing ill-health had dimmed his hopeful and romantic view of the world. His boyish enthusiasm for adventure, his own or other people's, had never diminished. He still thought that there were great things to be done, and that youth had still an infinity of possibilities before it.

It was perhaps a fault of his optimism that he seemed unable to take seriously, as even my own contemporaries did, the rapid rise and spread of dictatorship throughout Europe. What Hitler and Mussolini wanted, and the forces they represented, simply did not fit into his settled, classical view of human nature. He thought the dictators ridiculous rather than deadly, and believed that their very vulgarity would one day defeat them. But it was their vulgarity, the fact that they could influence people who were obscure, embittered, deprived and power-hungry, and unlikely to be moved by classical or humanist considerations, which was their strongest weapon of all. Had he studied Napoleon as carefully as he had studied Cromwell, JB might have drawn comparisons between that dictator's army of upstarts shattering old conceptions and almost invincibly imposing new ones, and what was then taking shape in the Europe of his time.

He must have found his trip to America refreshing. Nothing had happened to cloud his admiration for that country, nor his belief in its majestic possibilities. Eastern countries had never appealed to him; Europe was in a mess; America was just emerging from a bad time, but dealing with her difficulties and facing her future, in ways that he understood and approved.

That year's Christmas was to be John Buchan's last at Elsfield. All his family were present, except for Johnnie, who was still in Uganda. Although the possibility of Canada had been in the air for some time, the offer of the Governor-Generalship had not yet been made. Nevertheless, something prompted my father to heighten the festivities of that particular Christmas season. He never normally paid much attention to the commissariat, being obliged to be a mere spectator at other people's meals. This time he went shopping in London by himself—something that he seldom found time to do—and arrived home one evening with a large selection of delicacies. He had always been a benevolent but slightly remote presence at Christmas; this time he threw himself into all the plans and preparations. The occasion began to take on a tinge of pleasant solemnity.

Although nothing had been settled, I think that JB knew that he would be offered the Canadian appointment, and knew in his heart that he would accept it; hence, I am sure, the somewhat ceremonial nature of our family Christmas that year, which JB thought would almost certainly be his last at Elsfield for at least five years.

Our family Christmas had always been so exciting, so much looked forward to and so deeply enjoyed that none of us, in later life, could ever join the chorus of those who professed to find Christmas a bore. We were, in any case, by nature given to festivals of all kinds. One of the pleasures of India, for me, lay in the fact that there was a festival going on—Hindu, Muslim or Christian—in almost every month of the year.

As children we had certain Christmas rituals and duties which were almost as pleasant to look forward to, and to perform, as our own part in the festival. For many years, for instance, Mrs Charlett not only made the puddings for the house but a couple of dozen more for distribution round about. On Christmas Eve, Johnnie and I would set off in a horse-drawn milk float full of puddings and go to all the cottages in the village, and then on to others more remote, hidden away at the end of long narrow lanes. Christmas Eve, too, was the occasion when the children from the village came to their Christmas tree. The tree, a tall one, was put up in the morning-room, and we were busy for hours decorating it and setting out the presents. Our job, on the day, was to see the children fed, make sure that each boy or girl received the designated present, and try to prevent the tree, which was lit by coloured wax candles, from catching fire.

On Christmas morning, waking much too early to the promising weight of JB's shooting stockings filled with small presents on our feet, we would fume and fidget our way through breakfast until the time came for present-opening. This took place in the drawing-room, and the scene as I so vividly see it makes one of the most characteristic memory-pictures that I have of JB.

There was a small ceremony connected with the giving of presents to the staff. Before we could get to our own the servants must have theirs, and so we went in procession to the drawing-room, JB leading, to find everybody, headed by Mrs Charlett and the butler of the day, lined up and waiting. One of us came behind with the bulkier offerings—rolls of dress material chosen by my mother—while JB went down the row proffering envelopes, his personal presents. The envelopes contained treasury notes. As he stopped before each person, he would cock his head, smile shyly, say a word or two, and diffidently tender his gift. One felt that if somebody had refused it he would not have been at all surprised.

Christmas, as a family festival, was not universally observed in the Scotland of my father's youth; some of the more strictly orthodox thought it Popish. The pattern of our Christmas must, I think, have been set by my mother from recollections of the country Christmases of her own childhood.

★

Not long before JB's departure for Canada, there were weeks of bitter, brilliant cold. Our pond froze almost solid, ridges of plough-land hardened like concrete, all manner of birds normally too shy to approach a dwelling came to our bird-table.

My father and I were invited to skate at Shotover House, where ice on the lake was bearing well. Shotover, a fine eighteenth-century house, lies in its park to the south of the Oxford-to-London road, beside the village of Wheatley, and is the home of the Miller family.

JB had done a lot of skating as a young man. There can be no doubt that winters were consistently colder then, since skating was so often mentioned, and there were no indoor rinks. Apart from the deep and noticeable scar from his childhood accident, he had another, scarcely visible, a small triangular mark where, playing ice-hockey at Oxford, he had hit his forehead on the heel of another player's skate.

Some scholar, some day, should write a learned thesis on John Buchan's head and the things that happened to it in the course of his life. On that winter day at Shotover, it was going to be in trouble again.

We were hospitably made free of the lake, which stretches a long way from the terrace of the house to a stone pavilion on its farthest shore. We skated happily for a long time, crossing and re-crossing each other's tracks. At some point, skating towards the house, I shouted a question to JB who, I thought, was close behind me. There was no answer. I turned to see him stretched flat on his back on the ice, motionless. Naturally I thought he was dead. After reassuring myself on that point I rushed to find Amos Webb, and he and General Miller's man improvised a stretcher and bore my father into the house. A doctor was sent for, concussion was diagnosed, and presently we were able to take a still muddled JB home to Elsfield and a couple of days in bed. I have always felt sorry for our host and hostess on that occasion. They were kindness itself, but it must have been trying to have a distinguished person so knock himself about on their lake, when all they had done was to offer a pleasant morning's skating.

A very few years later my father was to die of a cerebral thrombosis, and I have sometimes wondered whether, that morning in Oxfordshire, he did not give his head just the one blow too many, the one that would begin the dislodgement of a clot which perhaps had been lurking there all his life, legacy of the fearful accident he had suffered when he was five years old.

I2

THE GOVERNOR-GENERAL

John Buchan's appointment as Governor-General was duly announced in March 1935, and was greeted by a journalistic deluge on both sides of the Atlantic. Mackenzie King had lost his battle to have John Buchan come to Canada as a commoner; King George V preferred to be represented by a peer. For other reasons than Mackenzie King's we all rather regretted JB's change of name. As John Buchan he had become so extremely distinguished—would people recognise him under his new name, under the (to most people) impenetrable guise of a peerage? There was nothing to be done about it, however, so we sat down to earnest discussions about possible titles—one of his own 'creations', perhaps, Lamancha or Manorwater?—but came back every time to Tweedsmuir, the title for which, as I have shown, there were the most valid grounds.

It has been borne in on me since those days that a large number of people never managed to make the connexion between John Buchan and Lord Tweedsmuir. The English may love a lord, but the majority of them are extremely hazy about the principles of the peerage, hazier still about functions like that of Governor-General. I have sometimes been surprised to be asked whether or not I was born in Canada.

Life in 1935 took on an accelerated tempo. My parents were due to leave for Canada in the autumn. There would be only seven months in which to make an extremely complicated mass of preparations. JB had to wind up various affairs in London and say farewell to the many committees and other bodies with which he had been occupied. Arrangements had to be made to shut up Elsfield Manor and to provide for its staff. My parents had decided to shut it up, at least for a while, thinking that this would save some money, although in the end it turned out to be a mistaken economy.

The Webb family—with the exception of Amos—Jack Allam and Frank Newall would all continue in their cottages and generally look after the property and keep an eye on the house.

Amos Webb and James Cast, the butler, were to accompany JB to Canada, the latter to act as his personal valet throughout his tour of duty. The Wolseley would be shipped across the Atlantic for Webb to drive, and another, more imposing, car would have to be acquired, as it were 'for best'.

Many people were anxious to do honour to the new Lord Tweedsmuir, and so there would be luncheons and dinners and many speeches for him to make and hear. On 10 June JB received the Freedom of the City of Edinburgh, along with J. A. Lyons, Prime Minister of Australia, and the Maharajah of Patiala. Other distinguished occasions were arranged for him in London, but it was good to see that Scotland honoured him first.

Even JB's remarkable powers of organisation must have been strained to the limit during those months. There was so much to be learned, so much to be seen to, there were so many people to consult. First, he had to choose his staff. Lieutenant-Colonel Eric Mackenzie, who had been with JB's predecessors, Lord and Lady Bessborough, was to stay on as Comptroller of the Household. He came to Elsfield early in August for consultations, as did Shuldham Redfern (later Sir Shuldham Redfern, KCVO) who had been appointed Private Secretary. Shuldham had been strongly recommended for this post, which was one of crucial importance in a Governor-General's life, since the Private Secretary acted as liaison with the Dominion cabinet, and had control of all his employer's official engagements. He belonged to that élite of the old Imperial services, the Sudan Civil, and although quite young, was already Governor of the Province of Kassala.

Fortunately, for every eventuality there was a precedent; otherwise it would have been quite impossible to get everything done in the time. Tailors, uniform-makers, jewellers, knew exactly what was required, and did their work with smooth efficiency. Court officials, the Dominions Office, Canada House, all contributed essential information and guidance. JB went from one urgent conference to another, from Buckingham Palace to the uniform-makers, to the College of Heralds, to the premises of Messrs Mappin and Webb. The latter's contribution interested me most, and I enjoyed examining the samples of things which a Governor-General was obliged to take with him for bestowing in the Dominion. There were photograph frames for presentation to every sort of dignitary from the Prime Minister and the heads of foreign missions to provincial governors, headmasters, station-masters and many others. They were made in solid silver, in shagreen, in leather, and each was surmounted by the initial T and a baron's coronet. There were gold cuff-links with the same cipher for very personal presents; there were cigarette cases and silver salvers, and other items that I cannot now remember.

My mother was almost as much beset with problems and the need for decisions as was JB. She had to have dresses, dresses of all kinds, including some very regal ones, with trains, for high cere-monial occasions, not to mention large quantities of hats, gloves, and shoes. She would take Annie Cox, the housekeeper, with her, as her personal maid, and Annie, like everybody else, had many new things to learn.

Then came the question of the motor-car. Our Wolseley would have to be demoted because the official car must comply with certain specifications, the same that applied to the royal cars at home. It must have large enough windows for its occupants to be clearly seen by members of the public as it passed in procession, and its doors must be high enough to allow people in tall hats to enter or descend without any undignified bending or crouching.

In the end JB had talks with the Armstrong-Siddeley company about a car called a Siddeley Special, which had to be made to order. Its design answered the requirements mentioned, its appearance was sufficiently impressive, it could be produced and shipped to Canada in time, and so it became the Governor-General's principal motor-car.

The Governor-General's uniform,* a handsome affair of blue and scarlet, with gold epaulettes and much gold braid, was worn with the accompaniment of a cocked hat like a field-marshal's, crowned with a cascade of white feathers, and an ivory-handled ceremonial sword. So swordmaker, hatter and the makers of those glistening black half-boots known as dress Wellingtons, all had to be fitted in to an ever-contracting time-scheme. There was a caped overcoat for use in cold weather, and JB, too, needed a large number of pairs of white kid gloves.

Amos Webb and James Cast had also to be instructed by experts, the one about winter driving in Canada and the right-hand rule of the road; the other about the dozen different kinds of dress into

* The post of Governor-General is not wholly a political one, but military: he holds the rank of full general with its attendant honours, uniforms and duties; in addition his post is also that of King *in absentia*.

which he would have to put his employer, and the proper management of decorations, sashes and stars.

In this year JB was created Knight Grand Cross of the Order of St Michael and St George (GCMG); he was already a Companion of Honour. (Two years later he was to be made Privy Councillor; and in 1939 he would be invested with the Grand Cross of the Victorian Order.) Fortunately—since he was to be Canada's thirty-fifth Governor-General—there was a precedent for every conceivable kind of occasion, and so there was no real danger of the Governor-General ever turning out improperly dressed.

Once JB had made up his mind about Canada he threw himself with his usual gusto into all the preparations, and put to work the formidable absorptive mechanism of his mind and memory to learn and remember many things in a very short time. Already certain possibilities of his new job were beginning to suggest themselves. Once the traditional ceremonies were over—and he must have appreciated the value of these for placing him firmly in an historical context—the world would see what could be done with a conventional appointment without any infraction of the rules.

There was to be no holiday that year in Wales or Scotland. In the Elsfield Visitors' Book there are guests for every month, most of them relations or very old friends. The Warden of Winchester, Harold Baker, one of the few survivors from JB's Oxford days, came for two nights early in the year, as he had done when we first settled at Elsfield. The Peebles family made their last visit in April, this time for a whole fortnight. After 8 October there were no more visitors. My Grosvenor grandmother's signature and Violet Markham's are on the last page.

The summer, with all its publicity, congratulations, farewell dinners, its piles of letters from all over the world, its comedies and anxieties, wore on towards autumn and the moment of departure. My father was already miles ahead of the game, planning and thinking: in a sense he was already in Canada. For my mother things were different. She had so happily adapted to country living, knew both village and county so intimately, was so engrossed in her work for the Women's Institutes and the Risca settlement, and in her own writing, that the Canadian adventure for her meant a painful pulling-up of roots. She had never cared much for public life, nor for large social gatherings, preferring a limited circle in which true friendships could develop, significant exchanges be made. If my father was to set off for Canada with a high heart, my mother was not to go without some misgivings.

As the weeks went by the pressure increased. My parents were bidden to stay with the King and Queen at Windsor; George V had always liked John Buchan. During the First War JB had often been summoned to the Palace for discussions with the King, and he had written a number of speeches for him. In that year, for the Silver Jubilee, JB had published *The King's Grace*, with which George V had been very pleased. In the library of the Queen's Doll House there is a tiny book with John Buchan's name on it, and his signature inside.

My father, who had felt a real sadness at leaving the House of Commons, had some rather melancholy hours of farewells. His close friends, however, although they regretted losing him, were delighted with his new appointment, believing that nothing but good could come to him from having to concentrate on one single aim. In their view (and in his family's) he had been doing altogether too much for his strength: and, worse, dissipating in work for various causes the talents and the single-mindedness needed for his best writing.

In 1935 there was no commercial flying of the Atlantic. Removing to Canada would mean a sea journey of five days, and a train journey of nearly two, between my parents, their children, and my father's own family. Weighing the pros and cons of the appointment, JB had noted that 'the boys could come out for all their holidays', and provided an immediate solace for my mother by deciding to let Alastair, then rising seventeen, leave Eton at the end of the summer half, and accompany his parents to Canada where, under his father's tutelage, he could study for Oxford.

A few days before the sailing date, in October, we all went up to London to help with the eleventh-hour preparations. On my parents' and Alastair's last evening we dined together in one of the rococo upstairs rooms of the Café Royal which had once made a meeting-place for 'Captain Stewart' (JB's occasional alter ego when Director of Intelligence).

On 25 October my sister, her husband and I were at Euston Station, to see the party off on the boat train for Liverpool. A drawing-room car was reserved for my parents, filled with flowers from well-wishers. A section of the platform was railed off so that official goodbyes might be said with dignity. The station-master wore a top hat and tail-coat. A Lord-in-Waiting represented the King; the Secretary of State for the Dominions and the High

Commissioner for Canada were there in person; senior representatives of the LMS railway and the Canadian Pacific Steamship Company added to the throng. It was all splendid, appropriate, even inspiring. As the train drew out of the station and my mother ceased to wave—she had always told us that it was unlucky to wave people out of sight—we turned away with the official party, feeling a little forlorn. None of us doubted, however, that we had just sped John Buchan away to yet another triumph.

One of the lighter moments of those months in 1935 was the visit I made with JB to the Gaumont British Studios at Lime Grove, Shepherd's Bush, to see *The Thirty-Nine Steps* being shot.

In 1934 John Buchan had sold the film rights to the Gaumont British company for what, in those days, was a rather modest sum. The film was to be directed by Alfred Hitchcock, then only just coming to fame.

JB, most mistakenly, particularly at that period of vast fees, regarded dramatic film-making as something rather quaint, something akin to raree-shows at a country fair, and taking money for it like taking pennies from a child. He felt little or no pride of authorship about his thrillers, and minded much less than most of his readers the liberties which Hitchcock was obliged to take with *The Thirty-Nine Steps*.

Many people objected to the various departures from the original novel which were made in that film. My mother, in particular, could never be got to understand why the book could not have been filmed exactly as it had been written. Artistic considerations apart, there were several good reasons: to begin with, JB's story was set in 1914. Twenty years later that date was too remote to be contemporary. That year Adolf Hitler had become President of Germany and the Foreign Office had let it be known to film-makers that hostile representations of Germany were, for the time being, highly undesirable. It was only sixteen years since the signing of the Armistice, and the majority of people had no wish to be reminded of the Great War. Finally, since this was the heyday of cinema-going, when there was a really enormous public for films, and one regularly swamped by Hollywood productions, no British film-maker would have risked producing a film, however thrilling, which contained no love interest.

This is where the genius of Alfred Hitchcock came into play. He kept the dramatic core of the book, but transposed the action into a

contemporary world, where the enemy was never actually iden-
tified and there was no explicit mention of war. And he added a
light and amusing love interest perfectly suited to the talents of
Robert Donat as Hannay, and the beautiful Madeleine Carroll as his
unwilling accomplice. The film was a triumphant success both in
Britain and in America, and one which may be said to have given
Hitchcock the real impetus to his great career.

We all accompanied JB to the première of the film at the New
Gallery Cinema in Regent Street. He was thoroughly amused by
Hitchcock's transformation of his book, declaring that he thought it
a great improvement on the original. Since that date the film has
been remade twice, the latest version, now that 1914 has become
'period', being rather nearer to the original than the first.

That excursion to Lime Grove studios was to have an effect on
my own life. For some time it had been apparent that my academic
performance at Oxford was not likely to be any more brilliant than
it had been at Eton. I had been a year at Oxford and had enjoyed
myself very much indeed but it was eventually put to me that that
was not really the whole point of a university career. It was very
nicely suggested that perhaps someone a shade more serious than I
might benefit by my place. I could only agree.

I was, besides, feeling particularly unsettled—and was not alone
among my contemporaries. One would have had to be either
exceedingly stupid or quite blinkered into some absorbing speciality not to be affected by the general anxiety of the mid-thirties. I
believe that we read the signs of our times correctly: I think, that we
all believed, deep down, that there would be war, in five years, in
ten, perhaps, but quite inevitably. It was useless to expose this
feeling to our elders who, naturally, regarded it as an excuse for
idleness; and so, in a sense, it was. Some of us, the wise ones, carried
on in a disciplined way, settled down to work for and to achieve
careers. Others more anguished became Communists, or at least
left-wing sympathisers, believing that to be the only possible
antidote to Fascism. Some, needing immediate action, ran off to the
grim fiasco of the Spanish Civil War. Others again, and I was one of
them, wanted to get as much experience of ordinary living, in as
many ways as possible, before the bell rang, and this made us
impatient of university life. Looking back on my contemporaries
and myself, I see us as children playing on the shore, touched by the
last light of a departing day, and trying not to notice the thunder-
clouds inexorably closing in from the sea.

My short visit to the set of *The Thirty-Nine Steps* had stirred something in me. I had always been interested in theatrical production, particularly in stage lighting. Now I thought that I should like to go into film-making, on the production side. When I mentioned this to my father he was distinctly relieved. Any wish, any ambition was better than none. He moved into action with his usual speed, and before long it was arranged that I should leave Oxford at the end of the summer term and go to work at Gaumont British in the autumn. Since I should then be alone in London, it was further arranged that I should go as a paying guest to the Alan Camerons who were leaving Headington for a house in Regent's Park, Alan having just been appointed Head of Schools Broadcasting at the BBC. So my immediate future appeared settled and this must have been a considerable weight off my father's mind.

When I joined the film company the team to which I was assigned was settling the preliminary shooting schedules for Hitchcock's *Secret Agent*, a thriller based on Maugham's *Ashenden*, which was to star John Gielgud and Peter Lorre. The company at that time ran an apprenticeship scheme, which I joined. I was given the handsome title of Third Assistant Director: Director's assistant would have been a better phrase, the person named being a fetcher and carrier and not likely to be consulted about anything to do with direction.

I knew myself privileged, once again, in living with Elizabeth and Alan Cameron, who had taken No. 2 Clarence Terrace, a house just inside the Clarence Gate of Regent's Park, in one of the most elegant of Nash's smaller creations. I was far from sharing my father's dislike of literary society. Life in Elizabeth Bowen's household, which was regularly visited by pretty well every English writer of significance at that time, was all, and more, than I had dreamed.

The Tweedsmuirs arrived in Quebec at sunset on 2 November 1935, to the sirens of all the shipping in the harbour and a nineteen-gun salute from the Citadel. Two days later they reached Ottawa, to another salute of guns, and were taken in procession to Government House, riding once again in a state landau with an escort of cavalry.

For a short while there was silence. I knew no more of my father's doings than could be read in the newspapers. Then letters began to arrive, by bag I think, via the Dominions Office, thick white envelopes with the Royal Crown on the flap.

JB, once installed at Ottawa, quickly found his own routines for living. These were not very different from his old working habits at Elsfield; that is, he would work in the morning and again, if he had no visitor to see or function to attend, in the early evening. The afternoons he tried to reserve for exercise—walking in the park, or farther afield; ski-ing on some easy slopes nearby; or skating on the private rink. Every so often, in spring and summer, he would take off for a few days' fishing on lake or river. Three times a week he would go down to the Parliament buildings where he kept an office, for a morning of talks with any MPs who wanted a word with him.

My father wrote to me of his engagements, of a visit to Toronto for the Winter Fair, of speaking at the Universities of Toronto and McGill; my mother of the snow, and the pleasure of driving in a sleigh, of the big rambling house with its park, where there was a skating rink with a pavilion and flood-lights and a broadcast system for music in case anyone should care to dance. But soon such jollities were shattered: on 26 January 1936 King George V died and the Governor-General's household was plunged into mourning. The vice-regal nature of JB's appointment meant, in those days, a very strict adherence to the etiquette and regulations of the British Court, which, of course, is what the words vice-regal imply. All public functions had to be cancelled, deep mourning worn, and my letters began to arrive with black borders a quarter of an inch wide. As the time of mourning went on a little relaxation was allowed, and at regular intervals the black borders narrowed until, at the end, they measured only a sixteenth of an inch, and not long afterwards disappeared completely.

Court mourning meant the cancellation of the State Banquet and Drawing-Room which were ordinarily held in February and, although my father was allowed to open Parliament, things were quiet at Government House. This gave JB a chance for private, informal meetings with politicians, journalists, university people, which might not otherwise have been possible, and he profited by these to learn as much as he could about his new country, and to plan the moves which he meant to make.

The Imperial Conference of 1926 had formally considered the question of Canada's Sovereignty, which had been coming increasingly to the fore since the Proclamation of Confederation by Queen Victoria in 1867. The result of the Conference was the establishment of complete sovereignty for Canada.

The 'Fathers of the Confederation', in the eighteen-sixties, were

Jack Allam at Elsfield could read 'reading' but not 'writing': we all had difficulty in reading my father's handwriting. JB wrote an enormous number of letters, which I believe was what turned his handwriting into the appalling cryptogram it became. It was a great relief when, during his last years in Canada, JB finally took to dictating his personal letters along with his official correspondence. This sample of his minuscule and indecipherable hand dates from shortly after George V's death: the black borders here were approximately ¼ inch wide, to be reduced at regular intervals, eventually disappearing as official mourning ceased.

unanimous that they wished to keep Canada as a monarchy. One of Canada's most revered statesmen, Sir John A. Macdonald, said:

> By adhering to the monarchical principle we avoid one defect inherent in the Constitution of the United States. By the election of the President by a majority, and for a short period, he never is the Sovereign and the chief of the nation. . . . During his first term of office he is employed in taking steps to secure his own re-election, and for his party a continuance of power. We avoid this by adhering to the monarchical principle. . . . I believe that it is of the utmost importance to have that principle recognised, so that we shall have a Sovereign who is placed above the region of party . . . who is the common head and Sovereign of all.★

Walter Bagehot, in *The English Constitution*, published in the same year as the Canadian Proclamation of Confederation, wrote: 'The Sovereign has three rights: the right to be consulted, the right to encourage, and the right to warn, and a King of great sense and sagacity would want no others.'

By the time that the new Lord Tweedsmuir came to be Governor-General of Canada the country was entirely self-governing. Certain questions continued to be discussed with that other independent government in London but, where the choice of his representative in Canada was concerned, the King acted solely on the advice of his Canadian ministers.

'The right to be consulted, the right to encourage, and the right to warn.' As the King's representative JB possessed all these rights, and it is clear that he used them to good effect. It must have been an effort for him, sometimes, to refrain from taking a hand in politics, which had never lost its fascination for him. He might not be allowed to have a say in political affairs but he made sure, none the less, that he was fully informed of all that was going on. For this he found time to talk to editors, scholars, economists, agricultural experts, as well as Canadian politicians, both English- and French-speaking.

He was seldom out of earshot of his Prime Minister, W. L. Mackenzie King. JB respected King as a remarkably astute politician, and one who had provided his country with stable government through difficult times, but sometimes found him tedious. He was an odd mixture of hard, political shrewdness and

★ Quoted in Professor Fr. Jacques Monet, *The Canadian Crown*.

an unappealing kind of sentimentality, and was given to fits of high enthusiasm punctuated by sulks. He was extremely touchy and inclined to imagine slights where none were intended. JB was patience itself with him and should be given full credit for the undoubted success of their working relationship.

Certain themes run all through John Buchan's literary work, certain beliefs and preoccupations which neither change nor lose their force throughout nearly fifty years of writing and public speaking. Those themes are youth, leadership, patriotism, courage, endeavour, achievement and duty. With the exception of the first it would be hard to imagine, at the moment of writing, a more generally unfashionable collection; yet they were the springs, the motives, the pre-occupations of his life. In his several biographies of great leaders—Montrose, Cromwell, Augustus, Julius Caesar—his faculty of empathy, of 'feeling' himself into historical characters works so well because the characters chosen exhibit some or all of the characteristics which he most admired.

He could not be a political leader in Canada, but he could and did use his right to 'encourage'. He had no need to be a warrior, although, ironically, since he was both Governor-General and Commander-in-Chief, he would once again wear a soldier's uniform when war was declared in 1939. He could, and would, see visions of Canada's possibilities, and he would use his powers of exposition, his ability to make complicated matters plain, to show how those visions might be made reality. He would display the Canadians to themselves, and gently urge them towards new horizons by reminding them of the achievements of their past.

To those who had perhaps settled too comfortably into the life of cities he would speak of the wonders of Canada, the variety and bounty of her natural resources, the need to be aware of the undiscovered greatness of their land. To the farmers who had suffered years of drought and had seen their rich wheat-land turn to dust he would go in person, to assure them that they were not forgotten, that the remote powers in Ottawa were working to help them. He would fulfil all the requirements of his vice-regal state, and perform his official duties with proper dignity; but would increasingly, as time went on, find his way out among 'the plain people', and take longer and more adventurous journeys throughout Canada than any of his predecessors had ever made.

Writing to a friend in Scotland JB said that he felt little homesickness, except perhaps for Oxfordshire. Scotland he did not miss, since he found Canada to be 'simply Scotland on an extended scale'.

Not only was much of the landscape of mountains and pine forests, lakes and fast-flowing rivers reminiscent of Scotland, even though on a vaster scale, but everywhere he went he met Scots men and women, an appreciable number of them from the Borders, some even from Peebles.

JB, as I mentioned earlier, had first met Roosevelt on a visit to America in 1934. Now, as Governor-General of Canada, he was involved in talks and exchanges of ideas with the American President and his Secretary of State Cordell Hull, and their friendship ripened fast. One result was an official visit by President Roosevelt to Quebec on 31 July 1936, with State functions, followed by a long talk between Roosevelt, JB and Mackenzie King. It was the first official visit from an American President to Canada, and a matter for interested comment all over the world.

Once the visit of the Roosevelts was over, JB set off in his train for a trip across Canada, first to the Northern Prairies, then to Vancouver, and then back through the Southern Prairies, the region worst damaged by six years of drought. This journey set the pattern of many others. 'There is not much I can do, but I can at least show the people of the Prairie Provinces that the King's representative is deeply interested in them. Half the trouble is that they feel cut off from the rest of the world.'

Before he could give to Canadians the clear message which was in his mind, JB had to get the measure of their enormous territory. Canada is larger than the USA, three and a half thousand miles at its broadest, and three thousand from the American border to the farthest north. JB was determined to visit as much of the country as possible, and to meet the farmers and miners, the engineers and lumbermen, to many of whom the Ottawa Government seemed as far off as the moon, and the Governor-General merely a glittering abstraction. Their first encounters with the seemingly frail, small, gently spoken man, dressed in ordinary clothes, who asked such telling questions and really appeared to take in the answers, must have caused a radical revision of ideas.

JB was in his element, consulting with experts, learning new things. He was fortified and delighted at every turn by evidence of courage and endurance, friendliness and good humour. In his travels he visited Northern and Western Ontario and French Canada, the Prairie Provinces, British Columbia (where he toured the 5,000 square miles of Tweedsmuir Park, recently designated as a reserve by the provincial government), the Maritime Provinces, the Arctic, Eastern Ontario and Hudson's Bay.

He was dismayed to find provincial chauvinism deeply ingrained and nowhere any real sense of Canada as one whole, sovereign, independent nation. The provinces, he found, knew little of one another, and what they knew tended to make them envious. Increasingly, as time went on, the Governor-General's speeches would contain calls for a greater national awareness, an enhanced appreciation of a common Canadian identity.

JB's interest in economics had never amounted to a passion. He had had to study close at hand, urgently and pragmatically, agricultural possibilities in South Africa, and the effects of a world war on his own country's industry. But he would never have made a professional economist, any more than he could have been a left-wing politician, since he saw people only as individuals and never as units in an economic calculation, nor as components of 'the masses' in a political one. What he had to write and say about Canada's economic future, however, was shrewd and far-sighted. In particular his visits to the far north when, as the first Governor-General ever to do so, he journeyed into the Arctic, heartened him enormously, after the depressing experience of the dehydrated Southern Prairies. He saw very clearly where Canada's future wealth might be found, and he fully appreciated the utility of light aircraft in the development of industrial activity in an immense and difficult terrain.

For the new Governor-General 1936 was to be a troubled year. The death of King George V had removed, for many people, the last comforting symbol of a more settled world. Dictators were on the rampage in Europe and, whatever we might have thought to the contrary, it was not only I and my contemporaries who were haunted by the prospect of another war. Then came the abdication of King Edward VIII.

Edward, Prince of Wales, as a young man had toured the Empire and had won many hearts. In Canada, where he possessed a ranch near Calgary, he was especially popular. When he became King upon his father's death, the more optimistic and romantic of his subjects were able to believe that this forty-two-year-old sovereign, once called 'Prince Charming', would inaugurate a new era of youthful enthusiasm, of imaginative action, and an end to the hesitations and compromises of tired old men.

Those of us who lived in London and were connected, however casually, with its social centre, had long been aware, to the point of being largely bored with it, of the story of the King's devotion to Mrs Simpson. Sometime early in 1935 the American press got hold of that story and, since Mrs Wallis Simpson was both an American and a married woman, gleefully ran away with it. Few American publications of the more sensational kind came to England in those days, but some form of crude censorship must have been imposed, because I remember my copy of the *New Yorker*, to which I had a subscription, arriving with several pages of a central story rather roughly torn out.

Trouble began for my father in the autumn of 1936. As Janet Adam Smith writes:

So far, out of a combined respect for the King's private life and for the laws of libel, the British press had kept silent on the subject. But it was splashed all over a section of the American press, and articles, with a modicum of fact carrying a lurid superstructure of rumour and speculation, had been published in papers with a big Canadian readership. So Canadians as a whole were more aware of the situation than Britons in the other Dominions—or, indeed, than most Britons in the United Kingdom.

In October the King's private secretary, Sir Alexander Hardinge, wrote to my father asking for his view of the effect that the American articles might be having on Canadian opinion. JB replied that his impressions had had to be gained at second hand since, in his position, he could not discuss the subject directly with any Canadian, but he made the observations which he was later to repeat to the British Prime Minister, Stanley Baldwin, and which Hardinge showed to the King:

Canada is the most puritanical part of the Empire and cherishes very much the Victorian standards in private life. . . .

She has a special affection of loyalty for the King, whom she regards as one of her own citizens. This is strongly felt particularly by the younger people, who are by no means straitlaced; and they are alarmed at anything which may take the gilt off their idol.

Canada's pride has been deeply wounded by the tattle in the American press, which she feels an intolerable impertinence. She is very friendly to America, but she has always at the back of her head an honest chauvinism.*

JB sincerely thought that if the King could really be made to understand Canadian feelings both about himself and the monarchy, he would abandon his intentions, at whatever cost to himself.

Naturally, JB had been kept well informed of the King's situation by friends at home long before Hardinge's letter forced him to take a hand. But it would be hard to imagine any idea more distasteful to my father than that of his Monarch even considering a dereliction of duty for emotional reasons, let alone actually proposing to marry a divorcee; and it is certain that the majority of Canadians would have felt the same.

In early October 1936 my mother left for England, and her letters to JB in Ottawa throughout the abdication crisis contain interesting sidelights on the state of affairs at home:

9th November
Everyone in London is seething with excitement about Mrs S. War is never mentioned at all. No one wants the job of going to remonstrate with HM, who shows them the door. The American papers are being laid before him, also all that comes in day by day from the British Isles to Alec Hardinge.

29th November
I went to B.P. [Buckingham Palace] and saw Tommy [Sir Alan Lascelles]. The burning subject has never once been mentioned to anyone there by the person most concerned.

4th December
Oh, my dear, you cannot imagine what London was like yesterday. The whole place placarded with 'The King and Mrs Simpson', literally everyone in the streets and in Selfridge's (where I lunched) reading papers and discussing it in under-tones. . . . I lunched with the Vincent Masseys [High Commissioner for Canada] on Wednesday. The Archbishop was there, but he never said a word about it though it all came out in the papers that evening. Whether what the Bishop of Bradford said about the King precipitated the thing, or whether it anyhow was coming out that day I don't know. . . . I am dreadfully sorry for you, my thoughts are with you the whole time, as I know

* Quoted in Janet Adam Smith, *John Buchan*.

in some ways Canada minds more than anyone, though Australia appears to be absolutely up on end. I feel a desperate sense of discomfort, misery and unhappiness, everything else is put in the background, nobody mentions the war or anything else.

6th December
There is a feeling of things slipping and crumbling everywhere, and that the King has given a blow to monarchy from which it won't easily recover. . . . It is an awful mess—I have seen no one who knows much. All the papers have come out with photographs of her which they must have bottled up for at least a year. There is a *little* danger, I think, of a pro-marriage movement— everyone is so sorry for the King. The firm stand of the Dominions is, of course, a tremendous help, in fact a real bulwark. . . . Apparently the country in general knew very little about it and it has come as a very great shock to heaps of people.

From my own recollection I can testify to the feelings of misery and disorientation felt by so many and, most of all, naturally, by those older than myself. I also learned for the first time how remote, in those pre-television days, the affairs of the capital were from the rest of the country. What had become, for my friends and myself, a pretty tedious and depressing topic, struck the bulk of our fellow-citizens, when the Bishop of Bradford gave his famous sermon, with the force of a thunderbolt.

When King Edward VIII abdicated on 11 December 1936 and his brother became King in his place, a sad and exasperating story came to an end. My mother had been right. There had been an attempt to form a 'King's party', led by Beaverbrook and Churchill; in the former's case largely out of a wish to embarrass Baldwin, in the latter's probably from a despairing sense of loyalty. My father signed the Order in Council regularising the new state of things, and the ship of state, so severely buffeted, rocked back on to a more or less even keel. As for JB, he was 'desperately sad about the whole business. I cannot bear to think of that poor little man with no purpose left in life except a shoddy kind of amusement.'

While all the excitements of the previous summer—1935—had been in progress Johnnie, in Uganda, had fallen seriously ill with amoebic dysentery. He had seemed to recover by autumn and had returned to work in his District. Soon, however, he fell ill again, and so severely that he had to be invalided out of the Colonial Service. This was a bad blow for him. He had loved Africa—a less turbulent and neurotic Africa then than now—and had greatly enjoyed his work. He returned to England early in 1936 and, after weeks in the Hospital for Tropical Diseases in London, he went to Canada in March.

Health went badly for me too in 1936. Early in the summer I began to have what I was later to know as 'laryngeal spasms', during which my throat and nose closed up almost completely, so that I had to fight for breath like someone drowning. The spasms occurred at more frequent intervals until, one weekend when I was staying with some friends in the country, they came so thick and fast that I was urgently carried off to a nursing-home in Windsor, where a tracheotomy was performed. When I had recovered my mother, who had come home in a state of considerable anxiety, took me back with her to Canada.

We sailed from Liverpool on Christmas Eve, 1936. Our ship was the *Duchess of Bedford*, one of the small sturdy Canadian Pacific liners which were known as 'Drunken Duchesses' for their lively performance in heavy seas. The December gales in the North Atlantic can be savage, and we had an exciting trip. Conditions were so rough that I had no time to be sick, being mainly occupied with trying not to break a limb. My mother was chased by a grand piano which had broken its moorings and came charging after her as the ship gave an extra big lurch. Luckily, before it could catch and crush her, all its four legs collapsed and its carcase slid away with the opposite roll.

The Governor-General's train had been sent to meet us at Halifax, and we settled thankfully into it, tired with our almost sleepless five-day voyage. The train, less impressive-looking than it sounds, was in fact two of those typical North American coaches which look so huge beside our own. They contained a drawing-room, a dining-room, kitchen, offices, bedrooms and bathrooms, and were air-conditioned. They did not run on their own but were attached for different journeys to scheduled trains of the many Canadian railway services.

Canadian trains did not rush and rock. They pounded steadily along, every so often giving a warning blast on their sirens. I remember those sirens blowing in the icy darkness of winter nights in Ottawa, the most haunting sound, at once melancholy and stirring, like the mourning of some strange, sad beast.

Travelling into the dusk, one began to get an idea of the

immensity of the land. Mile after mile of forest, broken by farmland cleared of trees not so very long ago; small farms, small townships, enormous barns, were only squares on a vast patchwork of wilderness and habitation stretching up into the Arctic and away to the Pacific shore. As night fell I had a bath, not very luxuriously as I had to sit hunched up in the short tub with my knees almost touching my chin, but it was something all the same, to have a bath in a moving train.

Ottawa is an official town, the seat of government, and had then an atmosphere quite different from Montreal with its French accent, or Toronto with its brisk hard-driving commerce. In Ottawa there were the Parliament buildings and government offices, stony and vast, and streets of old-fashioned frame houses which made me think of an earlier North America, out of Edith Wharton, perhaps, or Booth Tarkington.

Government House, most often known as Rideau Hall, lay out of the town a short way, next to the smart suburb of Rockcliffe. There were woods around it and a small park and, not far off, the bluffs above the Ottawa River. The river looked enormous to me although I assumed that, for Canada, it was nothing remarkable. Size, sheer size, is the first impression given by the country, but though the land is immense and much of it is wild, people, here and there, have tamed it delightfully to the human scale.

Rideau Hall was imposing enough, at first sight. On further acquaintance I found it peaceful, friendly and very comfortable. It was not an architectural masterpiece, having been given varied treatment by different hands since its adoption as Government House in 1864. The rather heavy stone pediment over the façade carries the Royal Arms, believed to be the largest stone coat-of-arms in the world. It was added to please Prince Arthur of Connaught who was Governor-General from 1911–16 and, I think, found the original front of the house insufficiently regal.

My father thought that Rideau Hall was 'like a very big comfortable English country house', and that was my own impression. It was a house which had been enlarged and adapted for all kinds of entertaining. On either side of the main block were lower wings, one containing a ballroom, and the other a badminton court. Once inside there was a big hall with a broad staircase and, thereafter suites of rooms of varying sizes, but none oppressively large. The stairs and corridors were laid with a dark mauve carpet, that colour having been the favourite of one of my mother's predecessors. Guests coming to meals had a long walk over the carpet and, in wintertime, in the dry heat of the house, generated a strong charge of static electricity. It was usual to receive a sharp shock when taking someone's hand. The Papal Legate, a man of great charm, must have been sad only ever to be greeted with low bows; but, clad in a silk soutane, he acquired so much electricity on his way over the carpet as to be very nearly lethal to the touch.

Royal protocol had to be observed down to the smallest detail. When I made my first visit to my parents in the morning I had to bow before greeting them and, in my father's case, retire from the room backwards, a process which he watched with some amusement and a touch of apprehension. On Sundays I went with him to church, the small Presbyterian church across the park which was so powerfully heated that it was known to some as 'the igloo'. Sometimes, to give an ADC time off, I took his duty, which meant riding in the front of the car and leaping down while it was still moving, to open the rear door. This manoeuvre, performed with top-hat and gloves, entailed landing on an icy pavement with every chance of turning a full somersault.

Snow in Canada comes in autumn and stays for most of six months. I have spoken of the dry heat of the houses, and the production of electric sparks. In more modern buildings there were up-to-date humidifying systems which took a lot of the dryness out of the air. At Rideau Hall the system was neither new nor efficient, wisps of steam coming up from small brass-ringed holes in some of the floors. Coherent thought became difficult, and sometimes people would go into or out of rooms with a look of remote vagueness, as though they had not expected to be where they found themselves, or, after a long silence, would come out with remarks of striking irrelevance. I began to appreciate some of Tchekhov's more whimsical dialogue as never before.

Ottawa society was lively and agreeable and I often found myself being hospitably entertained, and in ways less bound by protocol than were possible at Government House. One does not, nowadays, hear of legations, even the least considerable of countries having long since inflated theirs into embassies. At Ottawa, in 1936, the foreign countries represented all had legations, presided over by Ministers. There was also a British High Commission. The legations to which I went most frequently were the American, the French and the Belgian; I cannot remember ever going to either the German, or the Japanese or the Italian. The anxieties and animosities and setting to partners which were going to lead us all into war were already apparent in the polite diplomatic circles of Ottawa at that time.

My parents had let it be known that they did not intend to allow Rideau Hall to become a winning-post for social jockeying. Official entertaining apart, they did not wish to see created any kind of 'Government House set'. My mother had always found a fixed, limited social round boring if not distasteful. My father had his eyes only on performing his duties, and doing everything his mind or imagination could suggest for the Dominion which was to be his concern for five years. Nevertheless the big, expected events duly took place: the State Banquet, the Drawing-Room, the Levee, a ball at Government House, and many large luncheons and dinners. Janet Adam Smith mentions in her biography of my father that, according to an article in *Maclean's Magazine* of 15 July 1939, between November 1935 and mid-1939 the following were entertained at Rideau Hall: 2,100 to lunch or dinner, 2,700 to tea, 3,150 to dances, and there were 400 house-guests.

My father's miserable dietary restrictions, although far from amusing to him, did sometimes create comedy at large luncheon or dinner parties. Try as he might, he could never quite manage to spin out a couple of poached eggs, or a piece of steamed fish, for the time needed by his guests to do justice to their own food. Mrs Jackson, the cook, was an acknowledged artist; consequently people looked forward eagerly to their meals at Government House. Unfortunately for some, protocol permitted the domestic staff to remove any plate they could get hold of the minute the Governor-General had finished with his own. Unwary guests, accordingly, pausing to speak or listen politely to their neighbours, would suddenly find themselves plateless and far from satisfied. I remember warning a delightfully greedy Canadian lady of this danger and later, at dinner, being overjoyed to see her put a pair of plump arms round her plate so as to frustrate the footman.

At quiet moments my parents would dine with personal friends among the diplomatists and government servants who largely made up Ottawa society. And they also had many visitors out from England during their time at Government House. Many came on lecture tours, or business of one kind or another, several by special invitation. These last included my sister and her husband, my English grandmother, and the Peebles family. Gran, then in her eightieth year, tiny and frail but indomitable as ever, enjoyed herself greatly. She shocked the ceremonially minded Comptroller severely by refusing to curtsey to her son. She said she was too old to begin curtseying, so she 'just gave him a kindly nod'.

Since this book is intended to be a memoir of my father as I knew him, I can do little more than glance at the work which he did in and for Canada. My stay there lasted only five months. My brothers, on the other hand, both had a larger Canadian experience than I, and both shared in some of the journeys which were such an important feature of JB's years in office.

After one winter spent camping and trapping in the Canadian woods Johnnie's health had improved, but he had not rid himself of the amoeba which had caused his dysentery. Characteristically he decided that the only place where no amoeba could be expected to live would be the Arctic, and so he joined the Hudson's Bay Company and eventually, after training in London and Winnipeg, set off to help run a trading-post at Cape Dorset in Baffin Land, well within the Arctic Circle, in the autumn of 1938.

Alastair was spending his long vacations from Oxford in Canada, and had decided, with JB's agreement, that he should go to the University of Virginia in the autumn of 1939, once he had his Oxford degree.

I left for England, to take up work again after my successful convalescence, in June 1937, shortly after my parents' return from an official visit to Washington as guests of the Roosevelts, another unprecedented occasion. While they were away, I had lived by myself in the Citadel, the great fort designed by Vauban, which is the Governor-General's summer residence, and headquarters of the famous Vingt-Deuxième Regiment. There I was very happy, reading, writing, or gazing out of large windows over the wide blue wash of the St Lawrence; or exploring the Ile d'Orleans in the company of a charming French-Canadian ethnologist and his family.

My time in Canada had been spent mostly in Ottawa or Quebec, with visits to Montreal and weekends ski-ing or sleighing in the Laurentian Hills. My view of the country had been, on the whole, one-sided, taken sometimes from a processional car with motor-cycle outriders, or at charity balls, or state dinners, or squelching up yards of red carpet at a Levee—wearing the same strange outfit as at Holyrood—in pumps a trifle too large, so that I feared to lose one of them before I ever reached the point where I had to bow to my parents. Reading Mordecai Richler's chronicles of life in the back streets of Montreal, or my brother's descriptions of the Arctic in *Hudson's Bay Trader*, or the record of my father's journeyings, I realise that my knowledge of Canada, in addition to being out of date, is rather narrowly specialised.

On that warm summer evening at Quebec, when I said goodbye to my father, I was not to know that I should only ever have three months of his company again.

It is to be noted that my mother, in her 1936 letters from London, had spoken of 'the war' as if it were a fact, almost, rather than a threat. There is no doubt that our elders were as anxious about the future as we were, and particularly those who were in close touch with political affairs.

I have mentioned Franklin D. Roosevelt's visit to Quebec at the end of July 1936, and my parents' return visit to Washington in April 1937. In no official sense, but simply pursuing a friendship begun in 1934, and expressing the deep admiration for the United States which JB had cherished all his life, he had embarked on conversations, both with the President and with Cordell Hull, concerning their country's possible influence on the deteriorating condition of the Western world.

In one of his monthly letters to King George VI JB spoke of his conversations with Roosevelt, and intimated that the latter meant to try to do something towards the pacification of Europe. The idea then began to emerge of a world conference to be called by the President of the United States. In a letter to Baldwin in April 1937 JB wrote:

> He has his country behind him as no President has ever had since Washington—he is quite clear that, in the event of another world war, America could not stay out, and that her participation would probably mean something in the nature of a domestic revolution. He therefore feels that international peace is a bread-and-butter problem for his country, and no mere piece of idealism. His general idea is to make an appeal for a conference to deal with the fundamental economic problems, which are behind all the unrest . . . I see many difficulties in the scheme, most of which I have put before him. But at the same time I feel that it does offer some kind of hope, and that it is very much in our interest to meet any proposals half-way.

On 5 October 1937 President Roosevelt made a now celebrated speech in Chicago, in which he spoke of the Germans, Italians and Japanese, without actually naming them, as contributing to the breakdown of international law, and proposed a boycott of all aggressors, 'a quarantine . . . to protect the health of the community against the spread of the disease'.

During the following month JB wrote to Neville Chamberlain who had succeeded Baldwin as Prime Minister. Cordell Hull had been staying at Government House, and JB gave Chamberlain a résumé of their talks. The answer he received was cool and unenthusiastic.

In January 1938 Roosevelt informed the British government that he was planning to summon the whole Diplomatic Corps in Washington to the White House, where he would speak to them of the horrors of war, the need to reduce armaments and keep treaties. He would, however, only go ahead with this proposition (which he would then follow up with a world conference on the matters discussed) if he could be sure of Britain's wholehearted support.

The British Prime Minister's reply to this proposal was described by the Assistant Secretary of State, Sumner Welles, as 'a douche of cold water'. Chamberlain was dubious of the Americans' ability to turn fine words into positive action. More important, he was vain enough to suppose that he knew best how to deal with the Dictators. And so there was to be no result from the private talks between President Roosevelt and my father.

To anyone who did not live through the thirties it may be hard, now, to imagine how great the effect might have been of an intervention by the United States in 1938. America was very much an unknown quantity in the calculations of the Dictators. She was known to be immensely rich, technically skilful, and firmly on the side of peace. Many of Hitler's actions in Europe had been performed with remarkable audacity, in the name of rectifying the injustices of Versailles, and in the fair certainty of success without interference. If, however, America had decided to take a hand and bring her enormous, almost mythical prestige to bear against what was then known as the Rome–Berlin–Tokyo axis, then something more than bluff would be needed if the Dictators were to plan further expansion.

All this is now ancient history. The Roosevelt my father revered for the aristocratic nature of his mind and the breadth of his vision brought his country into the Second World War, and thus confirmed what some Germans, Italians and Japanese had most feared.

I could be happy for JB in that he did not live to see the final decline of his friend and hero, the neurotic antipathy to all things British, the mesmerism by Stalin, and the final, disastrous capitulation at Yalta. They knew the best of each other, and, had a greater statesman than Chamberlain been in the saddle, and their joint plan tried, they might have earned in peace the gratitude of the whole Western world.

13

THE GAP IN THE CURTAIN

Even after so short a time in Canada, England and Europe had begun to seem far away to me, and I was not sorry to return to London. My father, I could see, was becoming daily more absorbed by what he was doing, was putting down roots, which, he said, would be painful to pull up when his term came to an end. Johnnie had already found in Canada a second homeland, and Alastair who, like JB, had a romantic vision of the United States, would probably, it seemed, find another one there. Europe had always been my magnet, source of all the places and pleasures that I loved. I wanted to hurry back, to see, read and hear as much as I could before the war, which I still obstinately believed to be inevitable, occurred.

After the clear skies, the bright colours of Canada, Liverpool looked particularly dingy. Although it was high summer in England the air somehow seemed darker, the sky lower, the people more drab and unhappy, everything, by comparison, somehow shrunken and small. I settled into a bedsittingroom on Campden Hill, and set about becoming a Londoner again.

Just before Christmas 1937 I visited Peebles. I arrived on 20 December, by bus from Edinburgh, and rang the bell at Bank House, cheerfully sure of my welcome. My Aunt Anna opened the door to me with the news that my grandmother had died early that morning.

I was uncertain of my own feelings, but distressed for my aunt and uncle, they looked so stricken and so lost. It was suggested that I take rooms at the Tontine Hotel, and from there I got into touch with the rest of my family.

On the day of Gran's funeral there was snow on the ground. In Scotland, then, women of the Presbyterian Church did not go to funerals. When the all-male party set off from Bank House I was astonished to see the vast crowd of men, all in black, all in top-hats, waiting quietly in the snowy street to follow the coffin the quarter-mile to the churchyard.

It was the end of a long story. Her eldest son, to whom Gran had perhaps been closer than to anybody in the world, would outlive her by only two years and two months. In a letter to Anna he wrote: 'Thirty years ago we never thought we would have her so long with us, and what a blessing she has been! I begin to realise how much I will miss her, for I always thought about everything, "What will mother think of that?"'

His mother had never been far from his thoughts; punctilious in writing to her, he also made sure she received a copy of his every book—but he probably only guessed at what she thought of them. Anna, in *Unforgettable, Unforgotten*, published five years after his death, tells of their mother's reactions to his books.

> Each one was sent to her with a suitable inscription, and was a treasured possession. The Lives of Scott and Montrose she read with delight, and she gazed with respect at Cromwell and Augustus, but it was a trial to her that she could make so little of his adventure stories. She always kept the new one on her table, announcing that she was going to enjoy it when she could get a really undisturbed time . . . [but] after a few pages she would murmur, 'Tuts, they're beginning to swear already.' . . . Presently, with a discouraged sigh, she would lay down the book, remarking, 'Now he's got them into a cave, and it's so confusing, I think I'll knit for a little.'

When my parents first went to Canada Elsfield was shut up for a year. For my mother's first home visit it was opened once more, and found to have suffered rather badly from lack of occupation. Plaster had fallen; damp from the basement had begun to rise; various cracks and leaks had sprung, particularly in the Victorian side of the house, which was perhaps less soundly built than the older part. It looked, as I have said, as though shutting up the house had not been such a good move.

So my parents decided to let Elsfield for a year, and it was taken by old friends of my family, whose daughter was a friend of Alice's and mine. Those kind people asked me to stay on several occasions, and it was pleasant to see life in the place again, even if odd to find myself a guest, with all a guest's obligations, in my own home.

My mother returned for some months in the spring of 1938, and the house resumed much of its old atmosphere. I went down from London sometimes, to help entertain various guests, and fell easily back into the customs and pleasures of earlier years. Alastair was at Christ Church, and we had a house party for his Commemoration Ball; I suppose that it is only sentimental hindsight which makes me see him and his friends as especially gifted and delightful, since so much brilliance everywhere was so soon to be extinguished.

My father came over from Canada in July of that year, and I went up with him to Edinburgh to see him installed as Chancellor of the University. JB had a habit, sometimes rather trying, of committing his children to enterprises which they would not have chosen for themselves. At one large Edinburgh reception he brought the composer Sir Donald Tovey to meet me, announcing airily that they had been discussing an opera to be based on Thackeray's *The Rose and the Ring*, and that Tovey was to do the music and I the libretto. He was, as sometimes happened, a little ahead of the game. I do not know which of us, Tovey or myself, looked the more horrified.

Directly on his return JB had had a consultation with Lord Dawson of Penn, the King's physician, who had been very firm about the need for him to go to a clinic for a cure, and to try to put on weight, something that he had never succeeded in doing in Canada. So, immediately after the ceremonies in Edinburgh—and much to his regret, since he had wanted to spend some time revisiting old haunts in Scotland—he set off for Ruthin Castle in North Wales, to the clinic run by Sir Edmund Spriggs. I went to keep him company there in early September, and found him much improved in health and already putting on weight. He had a simple regime, and some sort of diet, but what was probably doing him most good were long hours of rest, and a total absence of letters, telephone calls, telegrams or despatch-boxes. He had with him many books that he had wanted to read or re-read and was, for the time being, perfectly happy. If he could have settled to such a quiet and regular existence, I am quite sure that his health would have improved out of measure; but that, of course, by then, was out of the question.

JB left Ruthin in the middle of September. Towards the end of that month the Munich crisis came to a head, and with it all my own, and many other people's, anxieties which had been growing steadily over several years, especially since the annexation of Austria in March. The feeling of tension was everywhere; it infected even those who least understood the situation or its dangers. I had been seeing a lot of refugee friends from Europe, mostly German and mostly Jewish, and had been touched myself by their near-despair.

While we were waiting for Chamberlain to come back from Munich, I was with my father at my grandmother's house. News had come in that children were being evacuated to the country, each with its gas mask in a cardboard box. There was little traffic, and the late September days were warm and sunny. London was looking its best, but we had no eyes for it. My father's mood was grim. He approved of what Chamberlain was trying to do, because he thought that everything humanly possible must be tried, anything at all that might remove the threat of war. Music sounded from outside and my grandmother asked: 'Why is it that at all the worst moments of one's life, there is always a barrel-organ in the street?'

War was indeed averted, that September, at the cost of Czechoslovakia and a pile of broken promises. In the first week of October, JB went back to Canada. In all the anxiety of that time, he had one matter for satisfaction: he had succeeded, after much persistent badgering, in getting agreement from the British Government to a visit to Canada by the King and Queen in May of the following year. This plan had been in his mind ever since the King's accession.

To underline his work in trying to instil a true sense of nationhood, he very much wanted Canadians to have the chance of seeing the man who was as much their own King as he was King of England. The royal visit entailed a vast amount of organisation and, since it was the first of its kind, a number of precedents had be created. JB wrote the four main speeches for the King to deliver at Quebec, Ottawa, Vancouver and, on leaving the country, at Halifax. Shuldham Redfern and his secretariat had also to compose a large number, to be delivered by the mayors of towns which the King and Queen would visit, and the King's replies to these. There was also the organisation of the royal visit to Washington, again an event without precedent. JB thought that he should keep as much in the background as possible since this was to be 'Canada's show': 'I cease to exist as Viceroy, and retain only a shadowy legal existence as Governor-General in council.' Once the ceremonies and social occasions in Ottawa were over, the Royal party, accompanied at every step by Mackenzie King, set off for the West and their American visit. Lord Tweedsmuir went fishing.

We are now familiar with royal 'walkabouts' but I think that this one in Ottawa, after the unveiling by the King of the war memorial, may have been the very first. In a letter to Anna my father wrote:

> The Queen told me that she must go down among the troops, meaning the six or seven thousand veterans. I said it was worth risking it, and sure enough the King and Queen and Susie and I disappeared in that vast mob!—simply swallowed up. The police could not get near us. I was quite happy about it because the veterans kept admirable order.

The King and Queen left Canada on 15 June, sailing back to a distracted Europe and an England deeply shadowed by approaching war; but their visit had been a triumphant success, and had fulfilled my father's highest hopes of a strengthening of national feeling, to the point where even some French-Canadians had begun, for the first time, to speak about 'our King'. JB joined the Royal train in Nova Scotia, on its way to Halifax. The King invested him with the Grand Cross of the Royal Victorian Order (GCVO), after a little trouble with the leather box containing the jewels, which had to be forced open with the point of JB's sword.

> Look not thou on beauty's charming—
> Sit thou still when Kings are arming—
> Taste not when the wine-cup glistens—

During the two years between my return from Canada and the outbreak of war in September 1939 I continued to work in London, and to enjoy the pleasures of the day, pleasures which were perhaps enhanced by the overhanging threat of war. I was far from indifferent to beauty's charming and few wine-cups glistened untasted by me. While kings, or rather dictators, were arming, I sat still because there was precious little else to do.

My father, in his letters, was becoming more remote. That, at least, was my impression. The horrors which he had seen in the First War and, above all, the empty, costly pointlessness of it, had so shocked him that he simply could not accept the possibility of yet another war. In his autobiography he wrote: 'I acquired a bitter detestation of war less for its horrors than for its boredom and futility.' He seemed in Canada to have acquired something of the spirit, common among Americans, which consigns the troubles of

Europe to the realm of the irremediable. The First War had given him a deep distaste for Europe, and his eyes, in any case, all his life had been turned towards the West. He wanted Britain, and of course Canada, kept out of war, partly because he thought that a war with modern weapons would be the ultimate in horror and destruction, partly because he could see neither point nor principle in any cause that might be alleged for starting one. 'What Europe is witnessing at present is not a conflict of genuine principles so much as the wrangling of ambitious mob-leaders. . . . In this wrangling we have no interest except as peace-makers.' When he wrote this sort of thing to me, I thought of our pledges to Czechoslovakia, to Poland, of our mishandled relations with France, and concluded rather sadly that more than three thousand miles of sea were beginning to separate me from my father. Yet I would always defend him against a charge of 'appeasement' in any cowardly or defeatist sense. He had no admiration for Fascism, nor fear of dictators; indeed his mistake seems to me to have been not to take them sufficiently seriously. 'A couple of lunatics' was not really an adequate description of Hitler and Mussolini; and the rule of the Nazis was certainly not, as he called it, 'tomfool'.

In any event, war was on its way. During that last summer of peacetime, that summer which in England seemed the quintessence of all English summers, so smiling was it, and so bountiful, JB made one or two more excursions. Anna and Walter were with him, and together they went up to Hudson's Bay to welcome back Johnnie, released on leave after his long and adventurous Arctic winter. His wireless had broken down, and so he knew nothing of Munich nor that he was returning to a world on the verge of war.

Canada allowed full rein to JB's natural optimism, that optimism which was no shallow preference for 'looking on the bright side' but an expression of his most settled, his deepest beliefs. My brother Alastair wrote in *John Buchan by his Wife and Friends:*

In so far as his writings are more than pure minstrelsy, which is all he claimed for them, he ranged himself with those who respond to Cobbett, Whitman and Chesterton rather than to Bentham, Alexander Hamilton or Marx. It ended in a love of life and a tenderness that was both Greek and Christian. Only twice in Canada did I see the light go out of his eyes: once

237

when endorsing a death warrant; and when signing Canada's declaration of war.

The year that war was declared John Buchan had been working on what was to be his last novel, *Sick Heart River*, thought by many people to be his best. It is certainly the most self-revealing. His faithful secretary, Mrs Killick, who had been closely associated with all his work for thirty years, found it disquieting. 'His Excellency is writing a very odd book . . . so unlike him, so introspective,' she told my mother.

Janet Adam Smith, in *John Buchan*, comments on this 'very odd book':

> In *Sick Heart River* this writer, in general so reticent about himself, lets his guard down. He had always been a rock to so many—to his parents, to his brothers and sister, to his wife and children—and a generator of energy and encouragement. To expose his own doubts, reveal his own disappointments, was a luxury he could not allow himself. But in a novel he could do it at one remove.

The war began, for Great Britain on 3 September 1939. On 9 September the Governor-General signed Canada's declaration of war. Johnnie and Alastair received immediate commissions in the Canadian army, the one in the Governor-General's Footguards, the other in Princess Louise's Dragoons, and both went into training with their regiments. I tried, in London, to join first the Army, then the Navy, but both, at that time, seemed to have no need for unqualified personnel. (In the OTC at school I had been inattentive, and so had no Certificate A which, at that time, the Army seemed to think essential.) Eventually I found my way into the Royal Air Force, signing on as an Aircraftman 2nd Class, to train as a pilot. My father's last letter to me described a visit to an RCAF camp and a flight he had been given in a new bomber. 'If I were a young man,' he wrote, 'nothing should keep me from the air!' My letter telling him of my entry into the RAF crossed his, but never reached him. By the time that it arrived at Ottawa, he was dead.

John Buchan died in the Montreal Neurological Institute on Sunday 11 February 1940. During the past months, as the news from Europe grew worse, and the likelihood of war more evident, his health had been steadily declining. Although Government House, after September 1939, had become a quieter place, with restricted ceremonial and less entertaining, the extra strains and burdens brought by the war and his duties as Commander-in-Chief were clearly beginning to tell. JB slept badly and woke unrefreshed. His internal trouble had come back, and he had to take every opportunity to rest in bed. Mrs Killick has recorded taking down the text of *Sick Heart River*, which JB dictated to her from his manuscript, while he twisted about in bed, unable to find comfort, since he had become so thin. By February 1940 his weight was down to eight stone, twelve pounds.

The Canadian Government had wanted JB to stay on as Governor-General for a second term of five years after the end of the first in September 1940, or at least until the end of the war, but, on the advice of his doctors, and with very real regret, he had declined. The Prime Minister had made a statement to that effect, in Parliament, that winter.

On Tuesday, 6 February, while shaving, my father suffered a fainting fit, fell and struck the back of his head. At first his doctors thought that he had nothing worse than concussion, but he remained unconscious. On Friday, at Government House, he had an emergency trepanning operation to relieve pressure from an embolism on his brain. He was then taken by train to Montreal, where another operation was performed. Even in his reduced state, his physical stamina must have been prodigious to support two cranial operations and a two-and-a-half-hour train journey, all in one day. At the end of the second operation, which lasted for three hours, the doctors were able to speak of a distinct improvement in his condition. He still remained unconscious, however, throughout Saturday, although seeming still to hold his own. On Sunday morning his condition worsened and a further cranial operation was performed, lasting for four hours, and ending at 3.45 in the afternoon, but to no avail. The final bulletin, put out by Shuldham Redfern, said simply: 'The Governor-General died at 7.13 p.m.'

Four doctors had worked devotedly, and with scarcely a break, for three days and two nights to save John Buchan's life. When the news of his death went out there was a spontaneous upsurge of grief all over Canada. Out of a mountain of press references I would choose one to represent them all, a headline in inch-high type: 'Beloved Viceroy Gone'.

There was to be little private grieving for my mother and Alastair over the next few days. Together they bore the burden of the magnificent ceremonial which was the Canadian Government's tribute to the late Governor-General. Johnnie was in England, with the first Canadian contingent, at Aldershot. I was in London and, owing to the delays entailed by decoding telegrams at the Dominions Office, first learned of my father's illness from newspaper posters in the streets. A telegram telling me of JB's accident and urging me not to worry, was followed almost at once by another one announcing his death.

Some time in the last year of his life JB wrote to my sister, asking for some suggestions as to how to make Elsfield a more economical place to run. By that time he knew that he would have to leave Canada at the end of his first term; he was aware that his health would no longer stand the demands that he had been accustomed to make of it, and that consequently his earning capacity would be much reduced. Public servants such as Governors-General are not expected to make money from their offices. Their official salary by no means covers all their expenses—those packing-cases full of presents, for example—and they invariably end out of pocket. The usual custom has been to reward them, on their retirement, with bank or other directorships, or chairmanships of various permanent bodies.

Evidently, when he wrote to my sister, JB must have been considering retrenchment. For all his devotion to Canada, he must have had comfort from the thought of Elsfield, so much a part of an earlier dream, as a place in which to rest and recover. They were all there, waiting for him: the new study which he had built over the drawing-room in 1932, which had all that he needed for peaceful reading and writing, and which had so filled up with books as to be an additional library; the gardens, so faithfully maintained; the village people and the country neighbours still much as they had been five years before.

The first of many memorial services—in Westminster Abbey, St Giles' Cathedral, the University Church in Oxford, and in my grandfather's old church in Glasgow—was held at Elsfield on 17 February, six days after JB's death. The little church was packed with people from the village, all the neighbouring farmers, a number of old friends from the country. Gilbert Murray, not long retired from being Regius Professor of Greek at Oxford, who had known John Buchan since Glasgow days, gave the address:

Death came to him suddenly, painlessly, in the fullness of his powers and at the very height of his great career, in the faithful and successful discharge of a high office which, as he once told me years ago, was the one in all the world which he wished for most.

After the lying-in-state in the Red Chamber of the Canadian Senate; after the gun-carriage, drawn by thirty-five sailors of the Royal Canadian Navy, and escorted by seven hundred Canadian soldiers and airmen, had taken its way from the Parliament buildings to the railway station; after my father had left Ottawa, as he had arrived there, to a salute of nineteen guns, his coffin was taken to Montreal and there cremated. His ashes were to go to England but, since this was wartime, the timing and method of their conveyance had to be kept secret.

Late in February Johnnie and I were told to be ready to go down to Plymouth to collect the ashes, which were coming directly from Canada in a naval vessel. On 25 February we set off for Plymouth with Vincent Massey, the High Commissioner for Canada, and a Canadian officer, and were welcomed as guests at Admiralty House by the C-in-C, Western Approaches. The cruiser HMS *Orion* had just arrived from Canada, bearing the ashes, and we had been sworn to the utmost secrecy, since it was highly important that the enemy should not know the whereabouts of that particular ship.

True to its traditions, the Navy had everything perfectly organised. On the morning of the 26th Johnnie and I mounted the companion ladder of HMS *Orion*, were piped aboard, and shown to the Captain's day-cabin where the bronze casket stood, covered with a Union Jack. Not long afterwards we were piped away, and the Admiral's barge took us to a corner of the harbour where a train of two coaches was drawn up waiting. The casket, still draped with its flag, was put into one empty coach; Johnnie and I and the Canadians were locked into the other.

It was a strange, slow journey. Twice our coaches were un-coupled from one train and attached to another. The Canadians left us at Reading, and we reached Oxford by mid-afternoon. A car we had wired for was waiting, and we set off for Elsfield, over the familiar roads, with Johnnie holding the casket on his knees. We both felt, I think, that we had been away for a long time, as we drove through New Marston, and Old Marston, and over the Wash Brook, and on up the steep little hill, past the Watts's farm, to Elsfield Church.

Mr Aste, the vicar, in surplice and hood, was waiting for us at the churchyard gate. He bowed as Johnnie gave him the casket: Johnnie stepped back and saluted. Not yet being in uniform, and feeling dimly civilian, I took off my hat. A light, sharp wind fluttered the vicar's surplice as he carried his burden into the church. With that small ceremony the final act in a long pageant was complete. Feeling suddenly very tired my brother and I walked on to the house.

We entered the library, looked at the desk, the inkstand, the porcupine-quill penholder, the tall familiar walls of books. We sank into armchairs facing one another. We had talked a lot on the journey from Plymouth, comparing and reinforcing each other's recollections, going back over the twenty years since John Buchan first sat beside his library fire. Now there seemed to be nothing more to say.

14

'A VERY QUEER FISH INDEED'?

It is not given to all people to enjoy their youth. Some, when young, suffer serious ill-health. Some have odious families; many are prevented by poverty from fulfilling crucial ambitions; some simply fall apart psychologically in adolescence and stumble into adulthood loaded with melancholy and torn by doubts.

None of these was the case with John Buchan. After he had recovered—miraculously, as it must seem—from his childhood accident, he grew up strong and sturdy and, in boyhood, pugnacious and daring as well.

I have long speculated on that strange accident to his head, have sometimes even unscientifically wondered whether some beneficent jolt to the mysterious systems of the brain might have produced the effects which I shall not hesitate to describe as attributes of genius.

For the moment, no more need be said than that JB greatly enjoyed being young, even at times when the goals which he had set himself demanded an almost total withdrawal from the society of his contemporaries. Only a boy with an abnormally clear vision of his road in life could have borne to deprive himself of the physical warmth, the vivid affections and antipathies, the inconsequential activity and desultory speculations of people of his own age. Yet this he had to do, between the ages of thirteen and eighteen, to fulfil the tasks he had set himself and to achieve the first of his already envisaged goals.

JB, in his autobiography, has told of his ever-extending horizons when, year by year, he and his sister and brothers grew strong and more adventurous, and so able to explore farther and farther away from the safe surroundings of Broughton Green. He speaks of the two worlds of his Tweedside childhood as 'the desert and the sown', and it was the contrast between the wildness of the moors and glens and the orderliness of the villages and farmlands below that was to have a special appeal for him, when he found it reproduced in his travels abroad. Canada, particularly, must have caught his imagination at once by the contrast between the almost limitless 'desert' and the 'sown' so hardly and courageously achieved.

JB became a fisherman very early in life, toting his short rod and box of worms to try for trout under the heather lips and in the deep pools of tiny burns. He loved water, also, for its own sake.

> From my earliest youth I have been what the Greeks called a 'nympholept', one who was under the spell of running waters. It was in terms of them that I read the countryside. My topography was a scheme of glens and valleys and watersheds. I would walk miles to see the debouchment of some burn with whose head-waters I was familiar, or track to its source some affluent whose lowland career I had followed.

The dream-landscapes of which he writes in his memoirs always contained rivers, and these, he was to find, varied in form but identical in essence, in England, South Africa, Canada and the United States. Rivers and mountains: rivers tumbling between rock cliffs, below high peaks, or placid between quiet fields below mountain-ranges, these were the parts of his ideal landscape. The bald hills of Peeblesshire are not mountains, and Tweed, in some territories, would scarcely be accounted a river, yet to the small boy treading the slippery heather on a summer day they were all that was needed of majesty and movement.

Describing exotic scenes in his writings, it is noteworthy that JB, in whatever country his book is set, continues to speak of burns and waters, of corries and glens. Even the names he gives to people and places—Leithen, Lamancha, Manorwater, Laverlaw—are to be found on the map of Peeblesshire. In all his books landscape is used to assist the story, to convey benignity or menace, to point contrast, or to provoke reflection in his human characters. He never gives his reader description for its own sake. He is never (to use a fashionable critical phrase) 'self-indulgent' in letting himself go on tracts of fine writing. Landscape and weather are there in their eternal manifestations to heighten the happiness or the pain, the hope or the fear of the human creatures struggling among them.

I have suggested that JB's strong sense of place, no doubt innate, was to find its terms in the glens and hills of Tweeddale, at an early age. When, at university, he came to the study of Greek, he had no difficulty in situating the pastoral of Theocritus, of Meleager, in the glens of Drumelzier and Hopecarton and Fruid. Long before he came to the classics, JB, with a head full of Scott and Stevenson and the Border ballads, must have found all that he wanted of romance in the histories and legends belonging to almost every Tweeddale glen.

For instance, the waters of Talla reservoir cover the site of Hay of Talla's peel-tower. The Hays, an unruly brood powerful in the Tweed valley, had no wilder sprig than Talla, who was one of two executed for the murder of Darnley in 1568. A century later Tweedsmuir, in which parish Talla lies, was strong for the Covenant and it was at Talla Linns—the 'Witches' Linn'—that the great conventicle was held in June 1682. This is described by Sir Walter Scott in *The Heart of Midlothian*.

> The place was remarkably well adapted for such an assembly. It was a wild and very sequestered dell in Tweeddale. . . . Here the leaders among the scattered adherents of the Covenant, men who, in their banishment from human society, and in the recollection of the severities to which they had been exposed, had become at once sullen in their tempers and fantastic in their religious opinions, met with arms in their hands, and by the side of the torrent discussed, with a turbulence which the noise of the stream could not drown, points of controversy as empty and unsubstantial as its form.

It was lucky for the Covenanters at their conventicle that the host of the Bield, a small inn on the Edinburgh road, was a man of discretion, for Claverhouse ('Bonnie Dundee' of the ballad) and his troops were lodged there that evening, all unaware that more than a hundred of their quarry were meeting less than four miles away.

The Church of Tweedsmuir was built in 1643. At the height of the covenanting troubles church services were held, if held at all, under great difficulties. Session records of the sixteen-eighties have the following entries:

> No session kept by reason of all the elders being at conventicles.

> No public sermon, soldiers being sent to apprehend the minister, but he, receiving notification of their design, went away and retired.

The collection this day to be given to a man for acting as watch during the time of the sermon.

No meeting this day for fear of the enemy.

There was no sermon, the ministers not daring to stay at their charges.*

It would be a singularly unimaginative boy who would not respond to the contrast between the beauty of that countryside and the violent events of its human past, knowing its clear streams to have been many times coloured with blood, its secret places to have harboured desperate men, robbers and reivers or scholarly fanatics driven into the wild to starve or be murdered for a religious cause.

Those were historical facts. There were also legends. Many years ago the land was largely covered by the great Wood of Caledon, of which only a trace remains. Here wandered for fifty years the seer and poet, Merlin, last of the Druids, who had seen the power and faith of his people fall before Arthur, the Christian king, '*in Silva Caledonis*', at the Battle of Arderydd in 573. This Merlin is known as Merlin Caledonius, or as Merlin the Wild, and should not be confused—although he frequently has been—with the Merlin who was King Arthur's counsellor.

Wild Merlin had lost in battle not only his dear friend and king, Guendollen, but also the last adherents of the old Druidic faith. He held himself responsible for these disasters, crying: 'Death takes all away, why does he not visit me?'

Peeblesshire's own saint, Kentigern, bettern known as St Mungo, was one of the earliest Scottish apostles of Christianity. As Bishop of the Borders, at the end of the sixth century, he fearlessly pursued his mission among the ferocious pagan people of the Tweeddale wilds.

In the course of his wanderings St Mungo found himself in the lonely valley of the Upper Tweed, and one day, as he knelt in prayer . . . the gaunt, wild-eyed half-crazy Merlin stood before him, 'with hair growing so grime, fearful to see'. By the peat and heather, the murmur of running water in their ears, for long the two men talked together. And, at last, the words of the teacher of a Gospel of infinite love and boundless mercy found their way into the broken heart of the old Druid, and St Mungo won him for his fold.

*J. W. Buchan (ed.), *History of Peeblesshire*.

Merlin was baptised by St Mungo with water from a burn and 'when Merlin was driven into Tweed and had stakes driven through his half-drowned body by the rough shepherds of Drumelzier, it was not a fierce worshipper of heather deities whom they martyred, but a believer in the crucified Christ'.

Merlin had found the death which he had sought for so many bitter years and, dying, we might believe that he rejoiced in the hope of reunion with his beloved earthly king. Just below the village of Drumelzier, where the Powsail burn joins the River Tweed, there is a spot marked by an ancient thorn-tree which to this day is known as Merlin's Grave.

It seems trite enough, but I believe that we need to remind ourselves, when considering a Victorian childhood, that the children of those days had largely to make their own pleasures through their own wit and initiative. There was no television, no cinema, no recorded music and, except for especially lucky children in big cities, only the rarest of visits to the theatre. On the other hand, in a household such as my grandfather's, there were plenty of books, and the elders on both sides of the family could repeat ballads and songs and traditional stories, some of which had never been written down. Playing in the glens and firwoods of Tweeddale, the Buchan children made up and acted their own versions of historical events, using the folds of the land, the stones of ruined castles, the tumbling waters of burns, for day-long games of search and concealment, flight and pursuit.

When the first version of *Montrose* came out in 1913, JB's brother Willie had been dead for a year. Nearest to my father in age, Willie had always been John's closest companion, and his death had been a most painful blow. In his poem to Willie, 'Fratri Dilectissimo: W. H. B.', which is the dedication of *Montrose*, JB captured the essence of their summer games:

> When we were little wandering boys,
> And every hill was blue and high,
> On ballad ways and martial joys
> We fed our fancies, you and I.
> With Bruce we crouched in bracken shade,
> With Douglas charged the Paynim foes;
> And oft in moorland noons I played
> Colkitto to your grave Montrose.

Once the days of childish games were over and the children, growing up, began to take independent paths, JB continued, when his work would allow it, to haunt the scenes which had enclosed so much happiness in his childhood. He had early learned to like his own company, something which is essential to both poets and travellers. No boy who was also a poet, a writer, in the making could have failed to respond to facts and legends such as I have recounted, or to absorb them, and their physical setting, into the stuff of his own imagination, his personal view of the world.

Genius is a difficult word, and one of which we are justifiably nervous: it has been much misused. '"Genius" (which means transcendent capacity of taking trouble, first of all),' wrote Thomas Carlyle of Frederick the Great. The remark has been often quoted, but too often without the last three words. Carlyle thought the 'transcendent capacity' a pre-requisite, implying that there should be much else as well. The definitions in the *Shorter Oxford English Dictionary* seems to cover all that I am thinking of in relation to John Buchan: 'Native intellectual power of an exalted type; extraordinary capacity for imaginative creation, original thought, invention or discovery.' Granted that he possessed all these qualifications, and in no mean measure, I am content, as I have said, to ascribe genius to my father. I would add a gloss of my own, by using the word voltage to express a continuous force, a 'head' of energy, physical as well as mental which positively demanded to be used in action. That this force, in JB's case, was governed and directed by benevolent principles—a strong religious sense, a real humanity, great delight in the beauty of the world—made its action beneficial. The same force frustrated, or ill-guided, may produce the effects of genius, but in an evil sense, as we in this century have had ample opportunity to observe.

'The transcendent capacity for taking trouble' was evident throughout the whole of John Buchan's life. In all his public appointments, from the editorial office of the *Spectator* to Government House at Ottawa, he never failed in meticulous thoroughness, was never unpunctual, never scamped the preparations for whatever needed doing and, although faced with schedules of work which would cause most people to despair, had always some extra energy on which to call should the unexpected occur. So much for the 'first of all'. Beyond all considerations of duty, obligation, ambition, the need to make money, his imagination roamed in a dozen different directions. His penetrating curiosity about people and the world, coupled with his great erudition, his knowledge of history and philosophy, his belief in the utter validity of the human struggle, were, I believe, what enabled him to work fruitfully in so many spheres. I have deliberately called the word genius to my aid, for without it I should find it next to impossible not to present JB as someone scarcely human, a success-machine, something altogether too good to be true. It is because I feel that too many people have accepted, enviously perhaps, this view of my father that I have done my best to show him in a different light: in Bunyan's sense as Interpreter, but also with all his humility, his courage, his unshakeable faith in an ultimate good, as Christian.

I realise that I have adopted, once or twice, a somewhat defensive tone in writing about my father. This might, perhaps, be forgiven me by anyone who, like JB's family, has had to read certain idiocies written about him in terms not only of his books, but of his life itself.

It is ironical that JB's 'shockers', of which he had so modest an opinion, should be the only part of his very large *oeuvre* to have attracted the attention of critics since his death. He himself, I am sure, would have preferred to be remembered for his historical works, perhaps especially for *Montrose*, *Cromwell*, *Augustus*, and *Sir Walter Scott*.

Ever since a cold critical wind began to blow from the direction of Cambridge, the simple (or apparently simple) story of action has come under deep suspicion from critics trained in the rigours of the English Literature School. At some point novels became The Novel, and what that should or should not be was very stringently laid down. As a result of these and other influences, straightforward story-telling talents have tended to take themselves off into the realms of science-fiction, espionage and detective stories, the quality of which, at their best, is at present very high. Needless to say, not everyone reads books with the aid of a 'critical apparatus'. Very large numbers of people, for instance, still read John Buchan—most particularly his later, post-1914, novels—for the sake of what, in the slang of his young days, would have been called a 'rattling good yarn'.

Where contemporary critics, or rather those reviewers who use the name of Buchan to pour contempt on what they consider outmoded attitudes, go wrong is in supposing that the speed of action and the smooth flow of a Buchan novel, the dated settings and sometimes old-fashioned slang, were simply the tricks of a popular writer playing up to his public. They deny, actually or implicitly, that there is anything more. I would suggest that there is always a great deal more; that closer study will reveal JB's novels as being more genuinely original, more sophisticated, more truly profound than is readily apparent to the leather-eared groundlings of Eng. Lit.

Much latter-day criticism of JB has been trivial, chip-on-the-shoulder stuff, an expression of fashionable attitudes, ignorance or simple incomprehension. One charge alone requires serious examination.

John Buchan has quite often been accused of anti-Semitism. Such accusations have referred to certain slighting remarks about Jews which are to be found in his novels, and to one brief passage in particular. 'A little, white-faced Jew with an eye like a rattlesnake', working as prime mover of a vile, international conspiracy has been taken by one or two by no means futile or unintelligent critics to imply a rooted racial dislike on my father's part. That there are only about half a dozen disobliging references to Jews in all of JB's many works of fiction goes for nothing against that sharp-edged and fatally memorable phrase. And here, I think, JB has been the victim of his own style, and of a radical change in attitude to racial difference which he was never to live to know. He was guilty, for once, of thoughtlessness, of using a commonplace of his time without considering its implications. For the man who gives, in *The Dancing Floor* a most attractive portrait of a benevolent Jewish financier and who, in *The Prince of the Captivity* gives another Jew an impressive history of courage and integrity, the line quoted above might charitably be thought of as no more than a lapse in taste, as true feeling sacrificed to a brilliant phrase. *Qui s'excuse s'accuse*: I shall not labour this point, beyond remarking that a strong distaste for the Rand financiers—who, as all Milner's young men saw it, hampered their purpose and muddied their good intentions after the South African war—remained with JB for a long time. It is, I would submit, the basis for those disobliging references to which I have referred. That those financiers happened to be Jewish, of a not very exalted variety, was inevitable at the time; and they were as cordially disliked by the more thoughtful and sensitive elements of their own people as by any Anglo-Saxon theorist of Empire. John Buchan was a man of sensibility. One hint from any of his Jewish friends that he was doing them a disservice would have been quite enough to change his mind. Yet no such hint ever came. What is puzzling to me is that John Buchan should have been so persistently tarred with this particular brush, when so many other well-known writers from Henry James to T. S. Eliot could equally well have been indicted. As I have tried to show, my father's character was far from negative. He was never immovably 'anti' anything or anyone, except the forces of evil. Proof that he had no prejudice against Jews, perhaps, was his friendship with Chaim Weizmann, and the work he did inside and outside Parliament to further the Zionist cause. It was scarcely an anti-Semite whose name was inscribed in Israel's Golden Book for his work for the Jewish National Fund. Finally, even John Buchan's prophetic imagination, continually engaged as it was with the dangers threatening civilisation, the permanent presence of evil, simply could not have stretched to encompass the horrors of Auschwitz and Ravensbruck. On a lighter note JB, as a connoisseur of human ambivalences, would have been amused to see a well-known Jewish Canadian writer, Mordecai Richler, one of his most savage accusers, happily accepting the Governor-General's prize for literature, which he himself had instituted.

In 1975, the year of the centenary of John Buchan's birth, Dr David Daniell produced a work of serious criticism, the first to appear in the thirty-five years since my father's death. I shall not spoil that book, *The Interpreter's House*, for the reader by excessive quotation, much as I am tempted to do so. In it Dr Daniell does not only examine the bulk of JB's productions from *Sir Quixote of the Moors* in 1895 to *Sick Heart River*, published posthumously in 1941: he also combats and, I believe, successfully disposes of a number of critical *idées fixes* about JB, including his alleged anti-Semitism which, like his supposed snobbery and worhip of success, has little to do with literature as such.

'It is a personal grief, a heart-wound to me, when I hear a depreciatory or slighting word about Scott.' So wrote George Eliot in 1871. There must be many who enjoy the pleasure of John Buchan's company who feel the same about him. Moreover, he did something important for the English novel that should not be ignored: he wrote novels with a mixture of surface pace of action and a deeper density of content which have a timeless quality, curiously modern still for a writer who was born five years after Dickens died. He worked on the frontier of romance and realism. He peopled his books with ordinary men and women, often in harsh circumstances, and his heroes were conscious of human post-lapsarian frailty. He used narrative skill rather than sex or violence to give an edge to his writing. Over the twenty-seven novels the simple situations of the oldest story-tellers . . . are used with such variety, from so many different narrative points of view, in so many different accomplished styles, and such interlocking complexity, that the whole Buchan *corpus* comes very close to 'interpreting and clarifying a large piece of life', and in the grand manner, too.

When Janet Adam Smith's admirable biography of John Buchan came out in 1965, it received close critical attention on both sides of the Atlantic. One reviewer said, rather querulously, 'It is jealousy, no doubt, which makes one wonder why John Buchan . . . should be thought worthy of a long book all about himself. . . . Altogether he was too good to be true': a familiar phrase, and no one better than I can see why it was used. For what I remember from JB's press cuttings during my childhood, that high respect and admiration which he was almost invariably accorded for the variety of his achievements, has turned, in our time, to a sour depreciation: what once he was admired for has been thought suspect by many, his ambitions have been judged excessive, his achievements trumpery, his ideals stuffy, his literary work almost an irrelevance. For the last, I consider it a dereliction of critical duty—no writer whose work has found and kept a wide public should ever be simply, casually, dismissed. To describe the office of Governor-General merely as 'playing at kingship' is simply to betray a lack of historical knowledge. Historically, constitutionally, that office has much meaning, as is surely proved by the fact that it continues to this day, with Canadian Governors-General, alternately French and English, filling its chair.

I am glad, therefore, to see appearing a new generation of critics with few social or political chips on its shoulders, more dispassionate than its forerunners, and with a better sense of period, penetrating the work of a writer who 'did something for the English novel that should not be ignored'.

In a review of a new biography of Tennyson I read that the biographer, like 'a good, late twentieth-century man', had been much exercised over the nature of his subject's sexuality. In this respect, late twentieth-century man is going to have difficulties with John Buchan.

It has very often been remarked that JB's heroines are unreal as women, often treated perfunctorily or relegated to little more than a decorative role; that he is manifestly happier out of their company, pursuing a life of action in a world of men. This literary judgement is then extended to his own life. I should say, myself, that for one who at such an early age had set himself such formidable tasks, a number of choices must have had to be made. If achievement in several fields was to be so vitally important, then there could be no time for dalliance, dalliance which Calvinist theology might have defined as positively weakening, a shearing of Samson's locks. Women, then, may well have appeared to the young JB as hindrances rather than helpmeets: he would hardly have been the first in history to take this view. 'He travels the fastest who travels alone.' Thus wrote Rudyard Kipling: it was a sentiment which, in his day, would have found plenty of agreement.

A closer consideration of the novels will show that JB, as his art matured, found ever more important functions for his women characters. The parts played by Mary Lamington in *Mr Standfast*, by Mary again (now Hannay's wife) in *The Three Hostages*, when she foils Medina with a most daring trick; by Janet Roylance in her influence over the dictator, Castor in *The Courts of the Morning*, are all of crucial importance to the action of those books: but they are certainly not explicitly sexual.

It has to be remembered, once again, that John Buchan was a Victorian, brought up in a strong Presbyterian tradition. As David Daniell has written:

> There was the complication of the duel between respectability as an artist and Bohemianism. The Scholar Gipsy was a real figure for Buchan. Could the Puritan striving for achievement from hard, even extreme, endeavour, under the eye of God, be at all reconciled with 'Pan playing on his aiten reed', the easy and lawless communion with a pagan nature?

The answer, I feel, was in the negative, when it came to laying down rules for living: and it must be remembered that Victorians were very strong on these. Nevertheless, JB, in many places, pays tribute to older gods, to a defeated, submerged, but in some ways admirable, paganism. Simply, it was not for him. Unlike Stevenson, he had found the Calvinism of his upbringing a gentle and a joyful thing. Here he contrasts strongly with his near-contemporary, André Gide, whose background was not dissimilar, being Protestant French. Each had a very different manner of dealing with his moral and religious inheritance. John Buchan accepted his, modified it with Platonism, and let it be seen to guide him all his days. Gide saw the value of Calvinism chiefly as something against which to rebel.

> It is improper, it is almost paradoxical to claim that we owe to Calvinist puritanism the wonderful English school (I mean the school of novelists), for we cannot easily distinguish in them what belongs to upbringing and what belongs to the race, nor to what a degree the former suits the latter. Furthermore, one must consider that, apart from a few very rare exceptions (Thackeray, for instance), it is by escaping from Calvinism, and only by escaping from it and often by turning against it, that those novelists were able to succeed. So that it could be said that if Calvinism helped them it did so as a sort of restraint that curbs and tightens one's strength and makes Joseph de Maistre utter the remark which has been somewhat misused: 'Whatever constricts man strengthens him'.*

There is no doubt that, for John Buchan, Calvinism, with whatever constraints it put upon him, was a source of strength. 'Calvinism,' he wrote,

> is a strong creed—capable of grievous distortion sometimes, too apt, perhaps, to run wild in dark and vehement emotions, or in the other extreme to dwarf to a harsh formality; but those of us who have been brought up under its shadow know that to happier souls it can be in very truth a tree of life, with leaves for the healing of nations.

Where emotional or sexual relationships are concerned, I have to say that there is no evidence of any such in John Buchan's very well documented early life. He had deep and enduring friendships with men of his own age, all of whom shared his fondness for strenuous exercise, for riding, walking and climbing, for tests of strength and endurance worthy of the tales of Malory. Perhaps, by these means, they 'sublimated' the turbulent instincts of young men as, at that time, it was thought possible to do. Considering family history over a century and a half, I incline to the belief that my father's family, for one reason or another, were not unduly troubled by

* André Gide, *Journal* (1889–1915), translation by Justin O'Brien.

strong sexual drives; their general avoidance of marriage in a society which made no room for any other relationship, seems to confirm this. JB happily gave up an energetic bachelor life to undertake a faithful and successful marriage. It may have been that he did not possess—as Lord David Cecil says so delightfully of Thomas Hardy—'an uncomfortably warm sexual temperament'. That would have been no rarity in some sections of Scottish society (see Robert Burns *passim*), but it would have been an explosive element in my father's.

I set out to write a memoir of John Buchan for reasons already stated, and for one especial reason. JB had always seemed to me a mysterious person. For all his openness, courtesy, kindness, his geniality, his great knowledge which, at any time, he was ready to share, his charity and his questing, eager spirit, together with his pains and disappointments and very human foibles; for all these qualities, which were there for all to see, I believe that he held always a certain part of himself apart, inviolable and inviolate. Perhaps there is nothing remarkable in this; perhaps it is something which, consciously or unconsciously, we all do, are indeed obliged to do by the very mystery of our inevitable end; but it was my sense of its presence in my father which intrigued and pleased and often baffled me during the years when I knew him.

One reviewer, commenting on Janet Adam Smith's *John Buchan*, wrote: 'There is no doubt that the first Lord Tweedsmuir was a very queer fish indeed.' That might, perhaps, have been more elegantly put, but I can see what the writer meant. There is something haunted about JB's imaginative writing. His acute appreciation of evil and its perpetual presence—his intense perception of it, not only in people and politics, but in landscape also and even buildings—and the need to combat it by all means form a salient feature of all his writings. He saw life as something lived on a frontier, a constantly changing frontier, which must be guarded and fought for unremittingly, if evil were not to triumph. Obviously a Calvinist upbringing could easily set a romantic mind in such a mould and thus, for a writer, provide an inexhaustible theme to be worked over, turned about, examined from a hundred different points of view, without ever diminishing its immediacy.

His childhood in the Tweed valley provided all the symbols JB needed to confirm his apprehensions. The kindly landscape which had seen such bloody deeds yet which nurtured such stalwart people; the golden days which, in that least predictable of climates, could turn dramatically to savage storm—*natura maligna* ousting *natura benigna*—held messages for John Buchan which perfectly suited his particular morality. Steeped as he was in *The Pilgrim's Progress*—and one could quickly lose count of the references to Bunyan in all his works—and particularly attracted to seventeenth-century thought, it is clear that he early found a view of the world, and of man's place in it, which would serve him satisfactorily for all his life.

To anyone who cares for JB only as the author of highly acceptable, exciting and amusing adventure stories, my insistence on the fundamental seriousness of his purpose may seem odd. And yet, as I have suggested, even his 'lightest' works contain hints of deep concern, whether about the effects of revolution, as in *Hunting-tower*, or political regimentation, as in *A Prince of the Captivity* and *The House of the Four Winds*, or stale complacency in successful men, as in *John Macnab*. He foresaw much that was later to become a hideous commonplace as, for example, the kidnapping of the children of important people in *The Three Hostages*. The theme of *The Gap in the Curtain*, where a number of men are induced to see their own death-notices in *The Times*, led to a long correspondence with the physicist J. W. Dunne (author of *An Experiment with Time*) and has since caused certain French critics to place JB as one of the fathers of science-fiction. Using his own particular techniques he did find ways to illustrate the anxieties, the fears and tensions of his time, often without seeming to do anything of the kind.

My parents' marriage was as interesting as it was unexpected and was bound, as I have suggested, to make certain difficulties for their children. We were never perhaps quite to know where we belonged. My father's mother, who would certainly have wished all her sons to be ministers, and of the Free Church at that, must have been aghast at the thought of what such an exotic union might do to the set-apart, close, complete circle of her family ('We is the Buchans'), what wild and heady influences might come from an alliance with 'the children of the world'. She must have feared, not without prescience, a centrifugal movement, farther and farther away from the proud and certain centre of her family life, and towards distant and, to her, unhallowed shores. I would submit that JB's upbringing provided the ideal conditions for his development: the safe, trustworthy place from which to set out on high adventurings, the solid grounding in human wisdom and charity, the firm embrace of a truly held religion. I would also submit that it was a place which, if he were to fulfil his aims, must be left behind and that the mother who kept and controlled and limited her little world, and wished for nothing different—she too must be left behind.

Contrary to the widely held belief that John Buchan's life was a story of unbroken successes, he had, in fact, many disappointments. After his failure to win a Fellowship to All Souls at the end of his Oxford career—the first real setback of his life—he was to endure many other blows, to feel sometimes a sense of rejection. There was the job in Egypt on which, after South Africa, he had set his heart, and which did not materialise. There was his failure to make the kind of mark in British politics which, once, he must have been sure of making. There was the noticeable lack of recognition of hard and valuable work for his party. And always, for the last twenty or so years of his life, there was the down-drag of illness, and the sad severance from the youthful pleasures which had meant so much to him.

The world of my father's family was an innocent one, and the quality in him that I see most clearly is a kind of innocence, a real simplicity of heart. The other side of his remarkable ability to get on with people, his passionate interest in them, was that his judgements were often faulty. Giving them all his kindness, perception, even his admiration, he was unaware that they were not always so generous in receiving as he was in giving. He was not always right in supposing that people were as appreciative of him as he was of them; he made no allowance for jealousy in others, or fatuous pride, or simple disagreeableness. His faults were the faults of innocence. If he dropped names, or seemed to rejoice in close acquaintance with important people, this was, I think, only an expression of his pleasure in the richness and variety of the English society in which he, a Scotsman and a historian, had found a place: to call him a snob would imply that he used his grand acquaintance to impress or humiliate others, or to flatter himself with an exclusiveness which his essentially *inclusive* interests would never have led him to seek. Of these things he was incapable. He liked grandees, noble, long-descended, with history behind them, but only if they behaved as such, that is to say, took their position seriously, and gave back to the world as much, in some sense, as it gave to them. To his kindness there could have been many witnesses; some are still with us. It was not until after his death that his family came to have an idea of the extent of his private charities, of which he never spoke.

So there he is, John Buchan, the man, my father. I set out to write this book as a work of exploration. By remembering him and re-telling his story I thought to come nearer to understanding a very complex and, I insist, mysterious man. Yet he eludes me still, as I believe he has eluded everybody. The character of Edward Leithen which he invented comes nearest to giving a complete picture of JB, most particularly in *Sick Heart River*, his last book, perhaps his very best, in which he, the 'worshipper of success', shows where true success might be found.

He was a Victorian by upbringing, who grew up in the last years of the nineteenth century. We have got through a good part of the twentieth without ever quite detaching ourselves from what is called the Victorian age. The great figures of those days continue to speak to us: as time goes on our wonder increases at their astonishing energy, their limitless intellectual striving, their moral fortitude, all that is contained in the melancholy, magnificent courage of Matthew Arnold's *Dover Beach*.

John Buchan—Lord Tweedsmuir, Governor-General of Canada—was never to see Scotland or Oxfordshire again, never to spend the last years as he had planned them: taking up lost threads, revisiting old haunts, returning to the hills and rivers of his earliest inspiration. Of all poems he loved 'The Scholar Gipsy'. Although there was little of the gypsy about him there was much of the scholar and the wanderer, and he knew every wood and field, every lane and hedge and tree of Arnold's own Oxford wanderings: and so that is how I see him, setting off alone on one of his great walks, in comfortable tweeds and stout shoes, cap on head, with, in his hand, the crook which a shepherd in Tweedsmuir had made for him long ago. The day is sunny, the spring woods are green; all nature is stirring around him. But there is nothing in the day brighter than his eye, nor greener than the hope which, untarnished, has sustained him throughout his extraordinary pilgrimage.

February 1982

CHRONOLOGY OF JOHN BUCHAN'S LIFE AND WORKS

(Most of JB's lesser writings are excluded)

1875   26 August—John Buchan born at 20 York Place, Perth.
1877   Family move to Pathhead, Fife; Anna Buchan (O. Douglas) born.
1880   JB's brother William born; 1880/81 JB run over by carriage.
1883   Birth of JB's brother Walter.
1888   Family move to Glasgow when the Rev. John Buchan called to John Knox Free Church in the Gorbals. JB goes to Hutcheson's Grammar School.
1892   JB wins bursary to Glasgow University.
1894   Birth of JB's brother Alastair; JB's first publication: his edition of the *Essays and Apothegms of Francis Lord Bacon*.
1895   Wins scholarship to Brasenose College, Oxford; *Sir Quixote of the Moors*.
1896   *Scholar-Gipsies* (essays): 'Scholar-Gipsies', 'April in the Hills', 'Milestones', 'May-Fly Fishing', 'The Men of the Uplands', 'Gentlemen of Leisure', 'Sentimental Travelling', 'Urban Greenery', 'Nature and the Art of Words', 'Afternoon', 'Night on the Heather', 'On Cademuir Hill', 'An Individualist', 'The Drove Road', 'Nuces Relictae', 'Ad Astra'; *Musa Piscatrix* (fishing poems and songs).
1897   *Sir Walter Raleigh* (The Stanhope Essay 1897)
1898   *John Burnet of Barns*; *The Pilgrim Fathers* (The Newdigate Prize Poem 1898); *Brasenose College*.
1899   January—elected President of the Union; summer—takes first in Greats; *Grey Weather* (stories and poems): 'Ballad for Grey Weather', 'Prester John', 'At the Article of Death', 'Politics and the May-fly', 'A Reputation', 'A Journey of Little Profit', 'At the Rising of the Waters', 'The Earlier Affection', 'The Black Fishers', 'Summer Weather', 'The Oasis in the Snow', 'The Herd of Standlan', 'Streams of Water in the South', 'The Moor Song', 'Comedy in the Full Moon'; *A Lost Lady of Old Years*.

259

1899 Settled in London, reading for the Bar and writing regularly for the
–1900 *Spectator.*
1900 *The Half-Hearted.*
1901 Offered post in Lord Milner's South African Secretariat; 14
      September—sails to South Africa; until 1903 lives in Johannesburg,
      travelling around South Africa, working in refugee camps and
      administration of colonies; (ed. with introduction and notes): Izaak
      Walton, *The Compleat Angler, or the Contemplative Man's Recreation.*
1902 *The Watcher by the Threshold* (stories): 'No-Man's-Land', 'The Far
      Islands', 'The Watcher by the Threshold', 'The Outgoing of the
      Tide', 'Fountainblue'.
1903 August—returns to London and legal and journalistic work; *The
      African Colony.*
1905 *The Law Relating to the Taxation of Foreign Income*
1906 JB's Uncle Willie dies; December—JB joins Nelson's, the pub-
      lishers; becomes engaged to Susan Grosvenor; *A Lodge in the
      Wilderness.*
1907 15 July—marriage; couple take house in Hyde Park Square.
1908 5 June—birth of daughter Alice; *Some Eighteenth Century Byways*
      (essays and articles): 'Prince Charles Edward', 'Lady Louisa
      Stuart', 'Mr Secretary Murray', 'Lord Mansfield', 'Charles II',
      'The Making of Modern Scotland', 'Castlereagh', 'A Comic Ches-
      terfield (the 11th Earl of Buchan)', 'A Scottish Lady of the Old
      School (Lady John Scott)', 'The Victorian Chancellors', 'The First
      Lord Dudley', 'Mr Balfour as a Man of Letters', 'John Bunyan',
      'Count Tolstoi and the Idealism of War', 'The Heroic Age of
      Ireland', 'Rabelais', 'Theodor Mommsen', 'The Apocalyptic
      Style'.
1909 *Brasenose Quatercentenary Monographs* Vol. 2 Pt II
1910 Buchans move to 13 Bryanston Street; JB's parents retire to
      Peebles; *Prester John* (in America *The Great Diamond Pipe*).
1911 Adopted as Conservative candidate for Peebles and Selkirk; 19
      November—death of father; 25 November—birth of son John
      Norman Stuart; first signs of duodenal troubles; *Sir Walter
      Raleigh.*
1912 Move to Portland Place; 11 November—death of JB's brother
      Willie; *The Moon Endureth* (stories and poems): 'From the
      Pentlands, looking North and South', 'The Company of the
      Marjolaine', 'Avignon, 1759', 'A Lucid Interval', 'The Shorter
      Catechism (Revised Version)', 'The Lemnian', 'Atta's Song',
      'Space', 'Stocks and Stones', 'Streams of Water in the South', 'The
      Gipsy's Song to the Lady Cassilis', 'The Grove of Ashtaroth',
      'Wood Magic', 'The Riding of Ninemileburn', 'Plain Folk', 'The
      Kings of Orion', 'Babylon', 'The Green Glen', 'The Wise Years',
      'The Rime of True Thomas'; *What the Home Rule Bill Means.*
1913 *The Marquis of Montrose; Andrew Jameson, Lord Ardwall.*

1914   Outbreak of the First World War; JB ordered to rest.

1915   Works on *Nelson's History of the War* (published in serial parts).
–19

1915   May–September—Correspondent for *The Times* at the Front; becomes a director of Nelson's; *Salute to Adventurers*; *The Thirty-Nine Steps*; *Britain's War by Land*; *The Achievement of France*; *Ordeal by Marriage*.

1916   10 January—birth of son William; June—gazetted Major in Intelligence Corps; August—joins Haig's Staff; October—serious duodenal attack and sent back to England; *The Future of the War; The Power-House; The Battle of Jutland; Greenmantle; The Battle of the Somme, First Phase; The Purpose of War*.

1917   February—'short-circuiting' operation; appointment as Director of Information; March—Tommy Nelson killed; 19 April—brother Alastair dies; *Poems, Scots and English; The Battle of the Somme, Second Phase*.

1918   February—Ministry of Information formed, JB as Director of Intelligence; 9 September—birth of son Alastair.

1919   Purchase of Elsfield Manor; appointed a Director of Reuter's; *Mr Standfast; These for Remembrance*: memoirs of Tommy Nelson, Bron Lucas (Auberon Herbert), Cecil Rawling, Basil Blackwood, Jack Stuart-Wortley, Raymond Asquith; *The Island of Sheep* 'by Cadmus and Harmonia' (with Susan Buchan); *The Battle Honours of Scotland 1914–1918*.

1920   Move to Elsfield; *The History of the South African Forces in France; Francis and Riversdale Grenfell; The Long Road to Victory*.

1921   *The Path of the King*.

1921   *A History of the Great War*.
–2

1922   *Huntingtower; A Book of Escapes and Hurried Journeys*: 'The Flight to Varennes', 'The Railway Raid in Georgia', 'The Escape of King Charles after Worcester', 'From Pretoria to the Sea', 'The Escape of Prince Charles Edward', 'Two African Journeys', 'The Great Montrose', 'The Flight of Lieutenants Parer and M'Intosh across the World', 'Lord Nithsdale's Escape', 'Sir Robert Carey's Ride to Edinburgh', 'The Escape of Princess Clementina', 'On the Roof of the World'.

1923   *The Nations of Today* (ed.); *The Northern Muse* (compiled).
–4

1923   Autumn—meets Mackenzie King at Chatsworth; becomes Deputy Chairman of Reuter's; *The Last Secrets* (essays and articles): 'Lhasa', 'The Gorges of the Brahmaputra', 'The North Pole', 'The Mountains of the Moon', 'The South Pole', 'Mount McKinley', 'The Holy Cities of Islam', 'The Explorations of New Guinea', 'Mount Everest'; *A History of English Literature; Midwinter; Days to Remember*.

1924 Visit to America and Canada; *Some Notes on Sir Walter Scott*; *The Three Hostages*.

1925 *The History of the Royal Scots Fusiliers 1678–1918*; *John Macnab*; *The Man and the Book*; *Sir Walter Scott*; *Two Ordeals of Democracy*.

1926 October—receives visit from Mackenzie King and Vincent Masseys; *The Dancing Floor*; *Homilies and Recreations* (essays and addresses): 'Sir Walter Scott', 'The Old and the New in Literature', 'The Great Captains', 'The Muse of History', 'A Note on Edmund Burke', 'Lord Balfour and English Thought', 'Two Ordeals of Democracy', 'Literature and Topography', 'The Judicial Temperament', 'Style and Journalism', 'Scots Vernacular Poetry', 'Morris and Rossetti', 'Robert Burns', 'Catullus', 'The Literature of Tweeddale', 'Thoughts on a Distant Prospect of Oxford'.

1927 May—takes seat in Parliament as Member for the Scottish Universities; *Witch Wood*.

1928 *The Runagates Club* (stories 1913–28); 'The Green Wildebeeste', 'The Frying-Pan and the Fire', 'Dr Lartius', 'The Wind in the Portico', '"Divus" Johnston', 'The Loathly Opposite', 'Sing a Song of Sixpence', 'Ship to Tarshish', 'Skule Skerry', 'Tendebant Manus', 'The Last Crusade', 'Fullcircle'; *Montrose*.

1929 Ramsay MacDonald heads new Labour Government; JB unopposed as Member for the Scottish Universities; contract with Nelson's expires; *The Courts of the Morning*; *The Causal and the Casual in History* (Rede Lecture).

1930 *The Kirk in Scotland* (with George Adam Smith); *Montrose and Leadership*; *Castle Gay*; *Lord Rosebery, 1847–1930*.

1931 General election: National Government under Ramsay MacDonald; JB unopposed as Member for Scottish Universities; *The Blanket of the Dark*; *The Novel and the Fairy Tale*.

1932 Created Companion of Honour; *Sir Walter Scott*; *Sir Walter Scott: 1832–1932*; *The Gap in the Curtain*; *Julius Caesar*; *The Magic Walking Stick* (for children); *Andrew Lang and the Borders*.

1933 Appointed High Commissioner to the General Assembly to the Church of Scotland; *The Massacre of Glencoe*; *A Prince of the Captivity*; *The Margins of Life*.

1934 Awarded Hon. DCL from Oxford, Hon. Fellowship of Brasenose College; Visit to New York, meets Roosevelt; *The Free Fishers*; *Gordon at Khartoum*; *Oliver Cromwell*.

1935 March—JB's appointment as Governor-General of Canada announced; created Baron Tweedsmuir, GCMG; 10 June—awarded Freedom of the City of Edinburgh; 2 November—Tweedsmuirs arrive Quebec. Settle in Rideau Hall, official residence in Ottawa; *The King's Grace*; *The House of the Four Winds*.

1936 20 January—death of George V; March—Johnnie arrives in Canada; 31 July—official visit to Quebec from President Roosevelt; visit from Mrs Buchan and Anna; October—Susan visits England; 11 December—Edward VIII abdicates; Susan returns to Canada with William; *The Island of Sheep* (in America *The Man from the Norlands*)

1937 April—visits Roosevelt in Washington; June—William returns to England; JB elected Chancellor of Edinburgh University; made Privy Councillor; 20 December—Mrs Buchan dies; *Augustus.*

1938 Spring—Susan visits England, joined by JB in June; 20 July—JB installed as Chancellor of Edinburgh University; spends August and September in clinic at Ruthin; October—returns to Canada; *The Interpreter's House; Presbyterianism Yesterday, Today and Tomorrow.*

1939 May—King George VI and Queen Elizabeth visit Canada; JB invested with GCVO; outbreak of Second World War; 9 September—JB signs Canada's declaration of war; November—goes to New York for medical treatment.

1940 6 February—suffers cerebral thrombosis; 11 February—dies in Montreal; funeral in Ottawa; 26 February—Johnnie and William collect ashes to take to Elsfield; *Memory Hold-the-Door* (in America *Pilgrim's Way*); *Comments and Characters* (from contributions to the *Scottish Review*); *Canadian Occasions* (addresses).

1941 *Sick Heart River* (in America *Mountain Gold*); *The Long Traverse* (in America *Lake of Gold*).

Two planned works: *The Island Called Lone*, a novel, and *Pilgrim's Rest*, a book about fishing, the two completed chapters of which are printed at the end of *Memory Hold-the-Door.*

SELECT BIBLIOGRAPHY

Adam, Frank, *Clans, Septs and Regiments of the Scottish Highlands*, Edinburgh, 1908, last edn, 1977

Adam Smith, Janet, *John Buchan: A Biography*, London, 1965

——— *John Buchan and his World*, London, 1979

Buchan, Alice, *A Scrap Screen*, London, 1979

Buchan, Anna (O. Douglas), *Unforgettable, Unforgotten*, London, 1945

Buchan, James Walter (ed.), *A History of Peeblesshire*, Glasgow, 1925–7

Daniell, David, *The Interpreter's House*, London, 1975

Elliot, Rt Hon. Walter, *Long Distance* (collection of broadcasts)

Gillon, S. A., article in the *Dictionary of National Biography* 1931–40

Monet, Professor Fr. Jacques, *The Canadian Crown*, Toronto, 1979

Trevelyan, G. M., *English Social History*, London, 1944

Tweedsmuir, Lord (J. N. S. Buchan), *Always a Countryman*, London, 1953

——— *Hudson's Bay Trader*, London, 1951

Tweedsmuir, Susan, *The Edwardian Lady*, London, 1966

——— *John Buchan by his Wife and Friends*, London, 1947. Includes contributions from Charles Dick, Roger Merriman, Violet Markham, Sir Roderick Jones, Lord Macmillan, Lord Baldwin, Walter Elliot, Catherine Carswell, A. L. Rowse, Janet Adam Smith, Leonard Brockington, Sir Shuldham Redfern, Alastair Buchan.

Many of the papers used in this book are from private sources; others are from the National Library of Scotland in Edinburgh. The bulk of JB's notebooks, manuscripts, letters and volumes of press-cuttings is now the property of Queen's University, Kingston, Ontario.

INDEX